## Get the eBook FREE!

(PDF, ePub, Kindle, and liveBook all included)

We believe that once you buy a book from us, you should be able to read it in any format we have available. To get electronic versions of this book at no additional cost to you, purchase and then register this book at the Manning website.

Go to https://www.manning.com/freebook and follow the instructions to complete your pBook registration.

That's it!
Thanks from Manning!

## Praise for the First Edition

*A very clear and concise depiction of the best parts of PowerShell.*

—Justin Coulston, Intellectual Technology

*A great resource for those who want to create scripts for task automation.*

—Bruno Sonnino, Revolution Software

*Real-world examples, best practices, and tips from two of the most respected PowerShell MVPs.*

—Roman Levchenko, Microsoft MVP

*It makes you stop and think, not just "read and nod."*

—Reka Horvath, Wirecard CEE

*The book to read, if you want to become an informed expert in PowerShell Scripting.*

—Shankar Swamy, Stealth Mode IoT Device Startup

# Learn PowerShell Scripting in a Month of Lunches, Second Edition

## WRITE AND ORGANIZE SCRIPTS AND TOOLS

JAMES PETTY, DON JONES, AND JEFFERY HICKS

MANNING

SHELTER ISLAND

Manning Publications Co.
20 Baldwin Road
PO Box 761
Shelter Island, NY 11964

Development editor: Frances Lefkowitz
Technical editor: Wes Stahler
Review editor: Kishor Rit
Production editor: Kathy Rossland
Copy editor: Julie McNamee
Proofreader: Mike Beady
Technical proofreader: Krzysztof Kamyczek
Typesetter: Dennis Dalinnik
Cover designer: Marija Tudor

ISBN: 9781633438989
Printed in the United States of America

*To Kacielynn, my unwavering source of support and encouragement, thank you for your boundless patience and understanding. Your love has been my anchor, providing the stability and inspiration to undertake ambitious projects like this one. This book stands as a testament to the strength of our partnership.*

*To our two daughters, whose laughter and curiosity fill our home with joy, you are my constant reminder of the importance of simplicity and the beauty of learning. May this book inspire you to pursue your passions with the same enthusiasm that you approach the world.*

*—James Petty*

# contents

# *preface*

As someone who has experienced the transformative power of PowerShell firsthand, I am excited to guide you through a monthlong exploration of its scripting capabilities. Whether you're a seasoned IT professional or a newcomer to the scripting world, this book is designed to make your learning journey informative and enjoyable.

In the spirit of the *Month of Lunches* series, each chapter is crafted to be consumed during your lunch break, making it convenient for even the busiest schedules. The goal is to empower you to become proficient in PowerShell scripting, one step at a time and one lunch break at a time.

Throughout these pages, you'll find practical examples, hands-on exercises, and real-world scenarios that will enhance your PowerShell skills and equip you with the confidence to apply them in your daily tasks. This book covers various topics, from the fundamentals to advanced scripting techniques, to ensure a comprehensive understanding of PowerShell.

As you delve into the world of PowerShell scripting, keep in mind the dedication to my family. They have been my inspiration and motivation to create a resource that is informative but also accessible and enjoyable.

Wishing you a fulfilling and rewarding journey as you *Learn PowerShell Scripting in a Month of Lunches.*

—James Petty

# *acknowledgments*

I extend my heartfelt gratitude to those who supported and contributed to the creation of this book. Special thanks to my daughters and my wife for their unwavering encouragement.

I am also grateful to Manning Publications for the opportunity to share my knowledge and for all the support they have shown me during the course of writing this book.

In particular, I'd like to thank my development editor Frances Lefkowitz, technical proofreader Krzysztof Kamyczek, and all members of the production team for their support with *Learn PowerShell Scripting in a Month of Lunches, Second Edition.*

Special thanks go to technical editor Wes Stahler, CISSP, GCWN, GCIH, GSTRT, MCSD, who is an associate director at The Ohio State University Wexner Medical Center. He enjoys evangelizing PowerShell's merits and has presented nationally at the Microsoft Health Users Group, as well as locally for the Central Ohio PowerShell Users Group and Central Ohio ISSA chapter.

Thank you to all the reviewers: Al Pezewski, Dave Corun, Glen Thompson, Jeffrey Yao, Keith Kim, Kent Spillner, Maria Ana, Oliver Korten, Peter A. Schott, Piti Champeethong, Ranjit Sahai, Roman Levchenko, and Satej Kumar Sahu—your suggestions helped make this a better book.

—James Petty

# *about this book*

*Learn PowerShell Scripting in a Month of Lunches* is a comprehensive guide that navigates readers through a transformative journey in the intricate world of scripting. Divided into four parts, the book systematically builds and enhances PowerShell scripting skills. Part 1 serves as a foundational gateway, laying prerequisites and considerations for script creation. Transitioning to Part 2, readers move from foundational concepts to practical implementation, crafting robust PowerShell scripts focusing on design principles and strategic thinking. Part 3, the sophisticated phase, explores advanced techniques and professional-grade practices, challenging conventional thinking and emphasizing security. The concluding Part 4 delves into advanced scripting intricacies, defining mastery in the scripting domain.

Catering to IT professionals, system administrators, developers, and enthusiasts, the book's companion website offers code examples and resources, fostering a comprehensive learning experience. Engage in dynamic discussions in the liveBook forum and benefit from real-world insights from James Petty. The acknowledgments express gratitude to supporters and recognize reviewers' valuable contributions. *Learn PowerShell Scripting in a Month of Lunches* is more than a book; it's a transformative journey, empowering readers to overcome challenges, present scripts with finesse, and embrace perpetual growth in the scripting realm. Let the pursuit of mastery begin!

## Who should read this book

Designed for IT professionals, system administrators, and those aiming to gain practical skills in PowerShell scripting, *Learn PowerShell Scripting in a Month of Lunches* is also accessible to beginners. However, we recommend beginners initiate their learning journey with *Learn PowerShell in a Month of Lunches, Fourth Edition* (Manning, 2022), for a comprehensive foundation. Tailored for individuals with limited scripting experience, the content employs a structured, hands-on approach to mastering PowerShell. Whether you're a newcomer to scripting or pursuing practical automation and system administration skills, this book provides valuable insights. Building on the foundational knowledge in *Learn PowerShell in a Month of Lunches* enhances the learning experience, facilitating a smoother transition to more advanced scripting concepts within these pages.

This book, *Learn PowerShell Scripting in a Month of Lunches*, is geared toward a structured and hands-on learning approach, especially for day-to-day tasks, automation, and system administration. You'll find this book is an invaluable resource. The *Month of Lunches* format ensures a manageable and structured learning path, catering to busy professionals aiming to integrate PowerShell into their workflow efficiently. Whether operating in a Windows environment or managing Microsoft technologies, *Learn PowerShell Scripting in a Month of Lunches* equips you with the essential knowledge and practical skills required to harness PowerShell's power for scripting and automation tasks.

## About the code

The code provided in this book follows clear conventions to enhance readability and understanding. The code examples, scripts, and additional resources are found in our GitHub repository. Detailed explanations accompany each piece of code, ensuring that readers grasp the syntax and understand the underlying principles of practical scripting.

This book contains many examples of source code both in numbered listings and in line with normal text. In both cases, source code is formatted in a `fixed-width font like this` to separate it from ordinary text. Sometimes code is also **in bold** to highlight code that has changed from previous steps in the chapter, such as when a new feature adds to an existing line of code.

In many cases, the original source code has been reformatted; we've added line breaks and reworked indentation to accommodate the available page space in the book. In rare cases, even this was not enough, and listings include line-continuation markers (➥). Additionally, comments in the source code have often been removed from the listings when the code is described in the text. Code annotations accompany many of the listings, highlighting important concepts.

You can get executable snippets of code from the liveBook (online) version of this book at https://livebook.manning.com/book/learn-powershell-scripting-in-a-month-of-lunches-second-edition. The complete code for the examples in the book is available for download from the Manning website at www.manning.com/books/learn-powershell-scripting-in-a-month-of-lunches-second-edition and from GitHub at https://github.com/psjamesp/MOL-Scripting.

## *liveBook discussion forum*

Purchase of *Learn PowerShell Scripting in a Month of Lunches, Second Edition*, includes free access to liveBook, Manning's online reading platform. Using liveBook's exclusive discussion features, you can attach comments to the book globally or to specific sections or paragraphs. It's a snap to make notes for yourself, ask and answer technical questions, and receive help from the author and other users. To access the forum, go to https://livebook.manning.com/book/learn-powershell-scripting-in-a-month-of-lunches-second-edition/discussion. You can also learn more about Manning's forums and the rules of conduct at https://livebook.manning.com/discussion.

Manning's commitment to our readers is to provide a venue where a meaningful dialogue between individual readers and between readers and the author can take place. It's not a commitment to any specific amount of participation on the part of the author, whose contribution to the forum remains voluntary (and unpaid). We suggest you try asking the authors some challenging questions lest their interest stray! The forum and the archives of previous discussions will be accessible from the publisher's website as long as the book is in print.

# about the authors

**JAMES PETTY** is currently the Director of Information Technology at TextRequest. He is a four-time awardee of the Microsoft MVP award. In a dedicated capacity, he also assumes the role of volunteer CEO at DevOps Collective Inc., a nonprofit organization operating within technology education. The organization's primary focus revolves around PowerShell, automation, and DevOps. It has garnered recognition for providing an array of free online resources, notably PowerShell.org.

In the literary domain, James is the lead author of two published works: *Learn PowerShell in a Month of Lunches*, now in its fourth edition, and *Learn PowerShell Scripting in a Month of Lunches*, in its second edition. Manning proudly publishes both of these insightful publications.

At the core of James's passion lies automation, where he adeptly wields tools such as PowerShell, Azure, and all facets of Windows Server environments. His prowess in this domain has been honed over more than a decade of service as an infrastructure administrator, catering to businesses spanning a diverse range of sizes.

James has woven his life in the tranquil environs outside Chattanooga, Tennessee, where he resides with his cherished wife, daughters, two dogs, and two cats.

**DON JONES** is a 16-year recipient of Microsoft's MVP Award, a co-founder of Power-Shell.org and The DevOps Collective, and the author of more than 60 technology books—including market-defining works like the *In a Month of Lunches* series and the career-focused *Own Your Tech Career* (Manning). Don is also the author of over a dozen fantasy and sci-fi novels and can be contacted at DonJones.com/.

**JEFFERY HICKS** is an IT veteran with over 30 years of experience, much of it spent as an IT infrastructure consultant specializing in Microsoft server technologies with an emphasis on automation and efficiency. He is a multi-year recipient of the Microsoft MVP Award. Jeff is a respected and well-known author, teacher, and consultant. Jeff has taught and presented PowerShell content and the benefits of automation to IT Pros worldwide for the last 20 years. He has authored, co-authored, and edited several books, writes for numerous online sites and print publications, is a Pluralsight author, and is a frequent speaker at technology conferences and user groups. Learn more about Jeff at https://github.com/jdhitsolutions/jdhitsolutions.github.io.

# Part 1

Welcome to the foundational segment of our scripting journey—Introduction to Scripting. This part serves as your gateway into the intricate yet fascinating world of scripting, designed to empower you with the knowledge and skills needed to navigate the scripting landscape confidently. As you embark on chapter 1, we'll lay the groundwork for your scripting adventure, discovering essential prerequisites, considerations, and the mindset required before delving into the intricacies of script creation. Chapter 2 guides you through the critical steps of establishing an environment conducive to effective scripting, emphasizing the importance of a well-configured setup for a seamless and efficient scripting experience. We'll dig into the philosophy of PowerShell scripting in chapter 3, which uncovers the principles and decision-making processes that guide PowerShell and provides valuable insights into crafting scripts aligned with this powerful scripting language. As we progress, chapters 4 to 7 revisit and reinforce fundamental concepts, from parameter binding and the PowerShell pipeline to a crash course in scripting languages and an exploration of diverse scripting forms, all while prioritizing the crucial aspect of script security. Through these chapters, you'll acquire the fundamental knowledge and skills to embark on the scripting journey. Now, let's dive in and unravel the art and science of scripting!

# *Before you begin* 1

PowerShell has been around for more than 15 years, but it's been a fantastic journey. If you missed the memo, PowerShell is now cross-platform, meaning it's available on more than just Microsoft Windows. I'm still blown away that Microsoft has open sourced PowerShell. It was initially created to solve the specific problem of automating Windows administrative tasks, but a much simpler "batch file" language would have sufficed. PowerShell's inventor, Jeffrey Snover, and its entire product team had a grander vision. They wanted something that could appeal to a broad, diverse audience. In their vision, administrators might start very simply by running commands to accomplish administrative tasks quickly—that's what our previous book, *Learn PowerShell in a Month of Lunches, Fourth Edition* (Manning, 2022), focused on. The team also imagined more complex tasks and processes being automated through varying complex scripts, which is what *this* book is all about.

The PowerShell team also envisioned developers using PowerShell to create all-new units of functionality, which we'll hint at throughout this book. Just as your microwave probably has buttons you've never pushed, PowerShell likely has functionalities you may never touch because they don't apply to you. But with this book, you're taking a step into PowerShell's deepest functionality: scripting or—if you buy into our worldview—*toolmaking*.

## 1.1 What is toolmaking?

We see many people jump into PowerShell scripting much the same way they'd jump into batch files, VBScript, Python, and so on, and there's nothing wrong with that. PowerShell can accommodate a lot of different styles and approaches. But you end up working harder than you need to unless you take a minute to understand

3

how PowerShell *wants* to work. We believe that toolmaking is the intended way to use PowerShell.

PowerShell can be used to create highly reusable, context-independent *tools*, which it refers to as *commands*. Commands typically do one small thing and do it very well. A command might not be helpful, but PowerShell is designed to make it easy to "snap" commands together. A single LEGO brick might not be much fun (if you've ever stepped on one in bare feet, you know what we mean), but a box of those bricks, when snapped together, can be amazing (hello, Death Star!). That's the approach we take to scripting in this book, and it's why we use the word *toolmaking* to describe that approach. Your effort is best spent making small, self-contained tools that can "snap on" to other tools. This approach makes your code usable across more situations, which saves you work, and it reduces debugging and maintenance overhead, which saves your sanity.

Scripting with PowerShell involves creating sequences of PowerShell commands and instructions in a text file, usually with the .ps1 file extension. These scripts are essentially programs written in the PowerShell scripting language, which is designed for task automation and configuration management in Windows systems. PowerShell scripts can be used to perform a wide range of tasks, from simple administrative tasks to complex automation workflows.

Here are some key aspects that differentiate scriptmaking with PowerShell from working with commands in the PowerShell console:

- *Reusability*—In a PowerShell script, you can define a set of instructions or functions that can be reused across different tasks. This allows for modular and maintainable code. In contrast, when working in the command line at the PowerShell console, you often type commands interactively, and reusability is limited to the history of commands or manually copying and pasting.

- *Script structure*—PowerShell scripts have a structured format with elements such as variables, loops, conditions, and functions, making them suitable for more complex and organized tasks. Command-line usage in the PowerShell console typically involves entering one-off commands, which can be less organized and harder to manage for complex operations.

- *Automation*—PowerShell scripts excel at automation. By scripting sequences of commands, you can automate repetitive tasks, perform bulk operations, and schedule scripts to run at specific times. This level of automation isn't easily achievable through the interactive use of commands in the console.

- *Interactivity versus noninteractivity*—When working in the PowerShell console, you can interactively enter commands and see immediate results. In contrast, scripts are typically noninteractive, running a series of commands without user input. However, scripts can also be designed to prompt for user input or accept parameters to make them more flexible.

- *Script execution policy*—PowerShell scripts may be subject to execution policies that control their ability to run. These policies help prevent the inadvertent execution of malicious scripts. When working with commands in the console, there's no analogous execution policy by default, as each command is executed individually.

- *Error handling*—PowerShell scripts can include error-handling mechanisms, allowing you to gracefully manage errors and exceptions. When entering commands in the console, error handling is more limited, and you often must rely on manual intervention or debugging after an error occurs.

Scriptmaking with PowerShell involves creating reusable, structured sequences of commands to automate tasks, whereas working with commands in the PowerShell console is more interactive and typically used for immediate, one-off tasks. PowerShell scripts provide a powerful tool for system administrators and IT professionals to streamline and automate Windows management tasks.

## 1.2  Is this book for you?

Before you go any further, you should ensure this is the right place for you. This is the second book in the *Month of Lunches* series, and it's designed for those who are already comfortable with using PowerShell at the command line and creating reusable scripts. Because this book focuses as much on process and approach as on syntax, it's okay if you've been scripting for a while and are just looking to improve your technique or validate your skill set. That said, this is *not* an entry-level book on PowerShell itself. To continue successfully with this book, you should be able to answer the following questions right off the top of your head:

- What command would you use to query all instances of `Win32_LogicalDisk` from a remote computer? (**Hint:** if you answered `Get-WmiObject`, you're behind the times and need to catch up for this book to be useful to you.)
- What are the two ways PowerShell can pass data from one command to another in the pipeline?
- Well-written PowerShell commands don't output text. What do they output? What commands can you use to make that output prettier on the screen?
- How would you figure out how to use the `Get-WinEvent` command if you had never used it before?
- What are the different shell execution policies, and what does each one mean?

We're not providing answers to these questions—if you're unsure of any of them, this isn't the right book for you. Instead, we'd recommend *Learn PowerShell in a Month of Lunches, Fourth Edition* (Manning, 2022; http://mng.bz/ddVz). Once you've worked through that book and its many hands-on exercises, this book will be a logical next step in your PowerShell education. We also assume you're fairly experienced with the Windows operating system because our examples will pertain to that.

## 1.3    *What you need for this book*

Let's quickly run down some of what you'll need to follow along with this book.

### 1.3.1    *PowerShell version*

We wrote this book using PowerShell 7.2, but 99% of the book applies to earlier versions of Windows PowerShell. Download PowerShell from https://docs.microsoft.com/en-us/PowerShell/. Now, look—don't install new versions of PowerShell on your server computers without doing some research. Many server applications (we're looking at you, Exchange Server) are picky about which version of PowerShell they'll work with, and installing the wrong one can break things. In addition, be aware that each version of PowerShell supports only specific versions of Windows—for this book, we're using Windows 11 and macOS.

We're using PowerShell 7.2 (or higher as the newer version comes out), but most of the content will work on Windows PowerShell (5.1), although we haven't tested everything against that version. The content we're covering is so core to PowerShell, so stable, and so mature that it's essentially *evergreen*, meaning it doesn't change from season to season. We use free e-books on https://PowerShell.org to help teach the of-the-moment, new-and-shiny stuff related to a specific version of PowerShell; this book is all about the solid core that remains stable.

### 1.3.2    *Administrative privileges*

You need to be able to run the PowerShell console and your editor As Administrator (as shown on the Start menu) on your computer, mainly so that the administrative examples we're sharing with you will work. If you don't know how to run PowerShell as an administrator of your computer, this probably isn't the right book for you.

### 1.3.3    *Script editor*

Finally, you'll need a script editor. Windows PowerShell's Integrated Script Editor (ISE) is included on client versions of Windows and only works with Windows PowerShell. We recommend you remove this from your machine, as the PowerShell team hasn't performed any maintenance or support since Windows 7 was released. These days, Microsoft recommends Visual Studio Code (VS Code), which is free and cross-platform. Download that, and in chapter 2, we'll show you how to set it up for use with PowerShell. Start the download at https://code.visualstudio.com/.

> **NOTE**  VS Code and PowerShell are both cross-platform. Every concept and practice in this book applies to PowerShell running on systems other than Windows. But the *examples* we use will only run on Windows as of this writing. We recommend sticking with Windows unless you're willing to be very patient and perhaps translate our running examples into ones running on other operating systems.

## 1.4    *How to use this book*

You're meant to read one chapter of this book daily, and it should take you under an hour to do so—except in one case, where we have a Special Bonus Double Chapter, which we'll call to your attention when we get there. Spend additional time, even a day or two, completing any hands-on exercises at the chapter's end. *Do not* feel the need to press ahead and binge-read several chapters at once, even if you have an exceptionally long lunch "hour." Here's why: we're going to be throwing a lot of new facts at you. The human brain needs time—and sleep!—to sort through those facts, connect them to things you already know, and start turning them into *knowledge*. Cognitive science has identified some consistent limits to how much your brain can successfully digest in a day, and we've been careful to construct each chapter with those limits in mind. So, seriously—just read one chapter per day. Try to get in at least three or four chapters per week to keep the narrative in mind, and make sure you're doing the hands-on exercises we've provided.

> **TIP**   We'd rather you repeat a chapter and its hands-on exercises for two or three days to ensure it's cemented in your mind than try to binge-read many chapters in just a day or two. Doing the former will get this stuff into your brain more reliably.

Speaking of those exercises—*do not* just skip ahead and read the sample solutions we've provided. Again, cognitive science clearly states that the human brain works best when it learns new facts and immediately uses them. Even if you find a particular exercise a struggle, the struggle itself forces your brain to focus and bring facts together. Before you consult the sample solution for an easy answer, it's better to go back and skim through previous chapters. Constructing the response in that fashion will make the information stick for you. It's a bit more work for you, but it'll pay off. If you take the lazy approach, you're just cheating yourself, and we don't want that for you.

## 1.5    *Expectations*

Before you get too far into the book, we want to ensure you know what to expect. As you might imagine, the book's topic is pretty big, and we could cover a lot of material. But this book is designed for you to complete in a month of lunches, so we had to draw the line somewhere. We aim to provide you with fundamental information that everyone should have to start scripting and creating basic PowerShell tools. This book was never intended as an all-inclusive tutorial.

## 1.6    *How to ask for help*

You're welcome to ask us for help in Manning's online author forum, which you can access at http://mng.bz/rjgE, but we encourage you to consider an online forum such as https://PowerShell.org. We monitor the Q&A forums there, but, more importantly, you'll find hundreds of other like-minded individuals asking and answering questions. The critical thing with PowerShell is for you to engage and become part of its community, meet your peers and colleagues, and become a contributor yourself in time. PowerShell.org offers tips-and-tricks videos, free e-books, an annual in-person conference, and a ton more, and it's a great way to start making PowerShell a formal part of your career path.

## Summary

Hopefully, at this point, you're eager to dive in and start scripting—or, better yet, to start *toolmaking*. You should have your prerequisite software lined up and ready to go, and you should have a good idea of how much time you'll need to devote to this book each week. Let's get started.

# Setting up your scripting environment

We know you're ready to jump feetfirst into the deep end of the scripting pool. But first, we need to take some time to make sure you have an adequate environment set up to use throughout this book. This chapter may be a lunch and a half, but you must follow along with each step to ensure you have an environment where you can safely complete the hands-on labs that will appear at the end of most chapters.

## 2.1 The operating system

While PowerShell is cross-platform for this book's duration, we'll primarily focus on the Windows operating system because PowerShell is still prominently used on Windows devices. You'll first need a computer running Windows 10 or 11. You could use a Windows 7 computer, but that's out of support by now, so you should probably upgrade if you can. While PowerShell is cross-platform, some of the examples we use are Windows specific, which is why we recommend following along on a Windows machine. If you don't own a Windows computer (maybe you're a Mac or Linux person), you can spin up a Windows 11 virtual machine (VM) in your favorite cloud provider. Power it on when you need it, and turn it off when you're done with lunch for the day. You can also follow along with a Windows Server (2019 or higher) if that's what you have available.

## 2.2 *PowerShell*

It shouldn't be surprising that you need PowerShell installed for the remainder of this book. However, note that we'll be using PowerShell 7, not the Windows PowerShell (5.1) installed by default on your system. PowerShell 7 (which, from this point forward, will be referred to as simply PowerShell) needs to be installed. If you followed along with *Learn PowerShell in a Month of Lunches, Fourth Edition* (Manning, 2022), you should have this installed already. Instructions on how to install PowerShell can be found all over the internet, but here is a link to the official GitHub repository with the latest installation instructions: https://github.com/PowerShell/PowerShell. You can also use your favorite package manager such as Chocolatey or Winget. We don't recommend installing a prelease, preview, or beta version. We'll stick with PowerShell 7.2.x for this book as that is the long-term support version of PowerShell. You can follow along with 7.3 or higher if you wish, and there shouldn't be any problems.

## 2.3 *Administrative privileges and execution policy*

You need to ensure that you can run PowerShell As Administrator on your computer. That might not be possible on a company-owned computer, so it's worth checking. First, start the PowerShell console (press Windows-R, type `PowerShell`, and press Enter). If Administrator doesn't appear in the window's title bar, right-click the PowerShell icon in the taskbar, and select Run as Administrator. That should open a new window that *does* display Administrator in the title bar (you may get a User Access Control prompt beforehand, which you'll need to allow). If that doesn't work, *stop*. You'll have difficulty following along with the examples in this book, and you need to resolve your administrator access before proceeding.

With the shell open as Administrator, run `Get-ExecutionPolicy`. This must return something other than `AllSigned`, such as `RemoteSigned`, `Unrestricted`, or `Bypass`. If it doesn't, you can try running `Set-ExecutionPolicy RemoteSigned`. If that works, you're good to go. But if you get any errors or warnings, then your execution policy probably won't change, and you need to resolve that with your company's IT team before you can follow along with this book. Pop over to the forums on PowerShell.org (https://forums.PowerShell.org/) if you need help figuring this out!

## 2.4 *Script editors*

You're going to need a scripting editor to follow along with the examples and labs. In 2017, Microsoft announced it would deprecate the Integrated Script Editor (ISE), and PowerShell 7 doesn't run in the ISE. We recommend (and will be using) Microsoft's free, cross-platform Visual Studio Code (VS Code). Head over to https://code.visualstudio.com to download and install it. As always, we recommend you download and install the latest stable release and not the preview or insider build. You can use any editor you prefer, but for this book, we'll be using VS Code, and we'll assume you are as well.

Once you have VS Code installed, it will look similar to figure 2.1. We've changed to the Light+ theme so you can see it when it's printed.

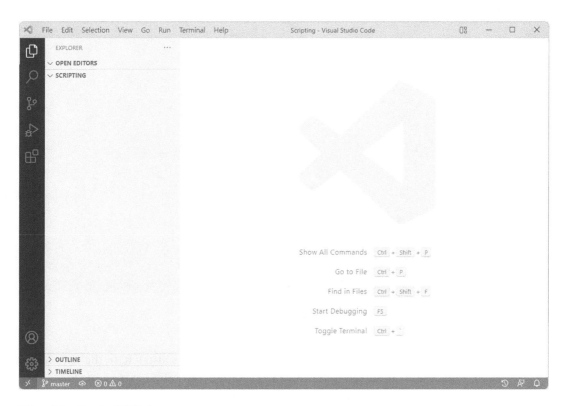

**Figure 2.1  Opening VS Code**

Occasionally, you'll find that VS Code has updated itself and wants to restart. Let it— the update takes only a second, and it's a good way to make sure you have the most stable release.

Right away, you'll want to install the extension that lets VS Code understand Power-Shell. In the vertical ribbon on the left, the bottom icon provides access to VS Code's *extensions*. Selecting that should bring up a screen somewhat like the one in figure 2.2; you'll notice that we have several extensions already installed.

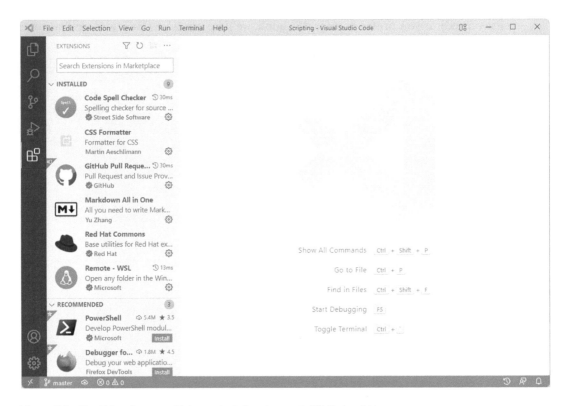

**Figure 2.2  The Extensions panel lets you install and manage VS Code add-ins.**

The PowerShell extension hasn't been installed yet, so let's install it. In the search bar, enter PowerShell, as shown in figure 2.3. Click the PowerShell extension (make sure it's not the preview version), and then click Install.

The PowerShell extension for VS Code is updated frequently, and you'll get a notification in the bottom-right corner of the VS Code window. We always encourage you to update the extension whenever a new release is available. Here are a few more useful settings:

1. To easily find the settings.json file, open the Command Palate by clicking View a Command Palette. For you keyboard junkies, you also can press Ctrl-Shift-P.

2. You can set the default file extension to PS1 by adding this to your settings.json file: "files.defaultLanguage": "powershell" (the value powershell *must* be in all lowercase).

3. We highly encourage you to add colors to your brackets. Add the following to your settings.json file (this may already be enabled by default):

```
"editor.bracketPairColorization.enabled": true
```

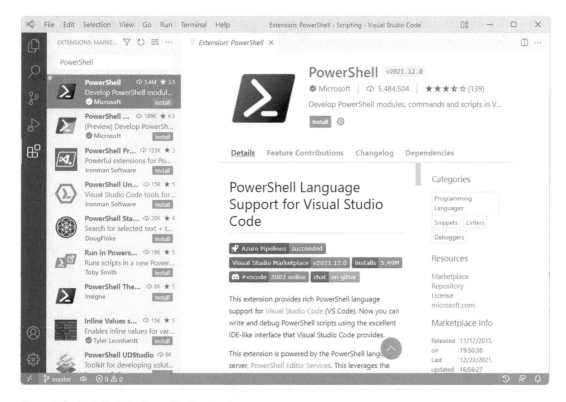

**Figure 2.3  Installing the PowerShell extension**

This book isn't intended to be a tutorial on VS Code, of course, but as we go, we'll point out useful tips and tricks for working more efficiently with PowerShell in this editor.

> **NOTE**  We know a lot of you are still stuck with Windows PowerShell. Go ahead if you're bound and determined to use the PowerShell ISE and Windows PowerShell (5.1). You'll have a lot less functionality (even with stellar add-ons such as ISESteroids), especially when it comes to debugging. At this point, VS Code is the official editor for PowerShell, and we don't know why you wouldn't want to use it, but it's your computer!

## 2.5  Our lab environment

For this book, we have a lab setup of four machines with the following names and operating systems:

- Srv01—Windows Server 2022
- Srv02—Windows Server 2022
- DC01—Windows Server 2022
- Client1—Windows 11

We suggest that you set up an environment similar to this if possible to make it easier for you because your screen will look like the one used to run the examples and write this book. There are a few options for creating your lab. Of course, if you can deploy four VMs in a lab or dedicated space at work, that's the best scenario. If you're running Windows 10 or 11 Pro or Enterprise, you can enable Hyper-V and create a virtual lab on your local machine. There are other free, open source, and paid versions to create VMs on your local machine; pick one that is right for you.

AutomatedLab was used to create the lab for this book. AutomatedLab is a free and open source project that works great for our needs. The lab definition file is included in the Resources folder of this book for your reference.

## 2.6 Example code

Finally, we strongly recommend that you download this book's sample code. Manning hosts it in a zip file on this book's page: https://github.com/psjamesp/MOL-Scripting. The file is organized by chapter; there's a text file for everything formatted as a code listing in the chapter. Later in the book, we'll introduce some modules, which are also organized under each chapter.

You can download the Zip file from GitHub, or you can clone the repository to your local computer. We suggest the clone so that you can always make sure you have the updated files if we make any changes. As you look through the code samples, you'll see that the module names are repeated. That's because subsequent chapters build on what came before. We don't necessarily expect you to import and use the modules, although we'll provide instructions to do so.

Finally, so there are no misunderstandings, let's be crystal clear that all the code samples in the book are for *educational* purposes only. Nothing should be considered ready for use in a production environment, even though you may be tempted.

## 2.7 Your turn

Take some time to make sure you've downloaded the sample code and successfully installed VS Code and its PowerShell extension. If VS Code is *working*, you should be able to save an empty file with a .ps1 filename extension and then, in the editor, type something like Get-P. VS Code's IntelliSense should kick in and offer to autocomplete command names such as Get-Process for you. If that's working, then you're clear to proceed. If not, stop here, and get it working. Again, we'll keep an eye on the forums at https://forums.PowerShell.org for questions; you're welcome to drop by there if you need help. Manning also has a great liveBook forum for this book (and many others) that can also be a great resource.

### Summary

As we wrap up this chapter on setting up your scripting environment, we must emphasize key takeaways. Firstly, ensure an environment conducive to completing the hands-on labs presented throughout this book. This includes having access to a Windows 10 or 11 computer, preferably with administrative privileges, and PowerShell 7 installed. Additionally, setting up Visual Studio Code (VS Code) as your scripting editor, along with installing the PowerShell extension, will greatly enhance your scripting experience.

Furthermore, we've provided insights into creating a lab environment similar to ours, facilitating smoother navigation through the examples and exercises. Whether deploying virtual machines locally or utilizing tools like AutomatedLab, having a lab setup like ours will optimize your learning journey.

Lastly, we stressed the importance of downloading the sample code provided with this book and familiarizing yourself with VS Code's features, such as IntelliSense. Remember, the code samples are for educational purposes only, and caution should be exercised before implementing them in a production environment. By ensuring you have the necessary tools and resources, you're now well-equipped to delve into the exciting world of scripting with PowerShell. If you encounter any difficulties along the way, don't hesitate to contact the supportive communities available online for assistance. Happy scripting!

# WWPD: What would PowerShell do?

Before we dive in, let's have a quick conversation about the "right way" to do things in PowerShell. One of PowerShell's advantages—and one of its biggest disadvantages—is that it's pretty happy to let you take a variety of approaches when you code. If you come from a VBScript background, PowerShell will let you write scripts that look a lot like VBScript. If you're a C# person, PowerShell will happily run scripts that strongly resemble C#. But PowerShell is neither VBScript nor C#; if you want to take advantage of PowerShell and let it do as much heavy lifting for you as possible, you must understand the PowerShell way of doing things. We'll harp on this *a lot* in this book, starting here. But it's also important to keep in mind that just because we do things a certain way, that doesn't mean it's the only way—it's just the way we prefer to do things. We generally follow the community's best practices when it comes to scripting.

Think of it this way: a car is useful for getting from point A to point B, but there are many different ways in which you could do so. You could, for example, put the car in neutral, get out, and push it to point B. You could walk, ride a bike, or take the bus. Or, you could hitch a horse to the car and let the horse pull it. Horses have been a great approach to transportation for centuries, so why change? But the most efficient way is to use the car as it was meant to be used: fill it with gas, get in, and step on the accelerator. You'll go faster than the horse could, you'll expend less effort than you would by pushing, and you'll be a happier, healthier traveler overall.

That's what we want to do with PowerShell. Unhitch the horse, get in the car, and *go*.

## 3.1 One tool, one task

Be sure to pay attention to what you see in figure 3.1 because it's the most critical rule you need to learn in the book.

Rule number

A script should accomplish a single task

**Figure 3.1 The single, most important rule you need to remember**

PowerShell is predicated on using small, single-purpose tools (you know them as cmdlets and functions) that you can string together in a pipelined expression to achieve amazing results with minimal effort. If you come from another programming or scripting background, you know how long the code can be for some commands. The Sort-Object command alone can be tens of lines long in some languages. For instance, here's how you'd write that command:

```
Get-ciminstance win32_logicaldisk -filter 'drivetype=3' `
    -computername SRV1| Select PSComputername,DeviceID,`
    Size,FreeSpace | Select-Object FreeSpace
```

It would be best to embrace this golden rule in your toolmaking endeavors. This is so critical that you'll see this more than once, we can promise. Please don't try to create one gigantic script that does a dozen different things. Write small, single-purpose tools that do one thing and do it very well. The tools you create should act and behave no differently than any other PowerShell command you get out of the box.

**The single-task tool rant**

A lot of folks have a hard time with the "single-task tool" principle. We get it—it's a new concept to many people, and it's hard to adjust to it. Chapter 17 will focus on some before-and-after examples to help make the point even clearer, but we want to say something specific about it now.

It's easy to think, for example, that provisioning a new user is a single task, but, no, it isn't. It's a *process*, and if you think about how you'd perform it manually, you'd instantly realize that it consists of multiple tasks. You have to create the user, set up a home folder, assign a Microsoft 365 (M365) license, create a mailbox, create a user library in SharePoint, and so on. Were you to start coding the process, you'd create a tool for each task: new user, new home folder, M365 tasks, SharePoint account, and so forth (many of those tasks can be accomplished using tools Microsoft

**(continued)**

has already written). You'd then "connect" those tools into a process by writing a *controller script*. We'll cover those later in the book.

Even something as simple as writing information to a CSV file is a single task (and PowerShell has a tool that does that). If you have a script that produces new information and takes the time to format it as a CSV and write it to a file, you're not only doing it wrong, you're also working too hard.

From this point on, start thinking about *making things smaller*. For any given process that you need to automate, ask yourself these questions: What are the smallest units of work you can create to accomplish each task? Can anything be made smaller or broken into multiple discrete pieces? This is the essence of toolmaking. We do this for two reasons. The first is to make our code reusable so that we're not reinventing the wheel repeatedly, and the second is for speed.

## 3.2 Naming your tools

We'll cover quite a few hot topics in this book. If you browse the PowerShell forums (https://forums.PowerShell.org) or talk to anyone in any of the PowerShell Slack or Discord channels, you'll find people who will stand their ground and argue with you on the "correct" way to write code. That's usually fine; their way isn't wrong, and everyone has a valid opinion. That's one of the beauties of PowerShell being open source and community driven. There are multiple ways to do things. Just because we show one way to do something in this book doesn't mean it's the *only* way. It's just how we feel is the best way to do things.

When it comes to naming your tools, what naming convention should you use? A tool named `ListAllIISWebServersInTheIISWebFarm` is self-explanatory but doesn't fit into the PowerShell model. As discussed in the previous book *Learn PowerShell in a Month of Lunches, Fourth Edition*, PowerShell follows a `Verb-Noun` naming syntax.

> **TRY IT NOW**  Run the command `Get-Verb`, and look at the output.

- For the noun, always use a singular noun, for example, *User* as opposed to *Users*.
- Prefix the noun with something meaningful to your company (never us "PS"). If your company name is Globalmantics, then your tool could be called `Get-GlobalUser`.
- Start with a verb—but not just any verb as PowerShell has a list of approved verbs. (These "approved" verbs are more like suggestions because you can actually use any verb, but let's stick with the approved ones.) The PowerShell team does occasionally add new verbs to the list.

We are so picky here because PowerShell has a lot of code built around this naming convention and the specifically approved verbs. `Get-Command`, for example, understands the difference between a verb and a noun and can help locate commands based on either. As another example, `Import-Module` knows the approved verb list and issues warnings when you attempt to load unapproved verbs. Perhaps most importantly, all the cool kids in the PowerShell community will chuckle at you for using improperly constructed command names.

You can easily find the full list of approved verbs by running the `Get-Verb` command, or you can go to http://mng.bz/VRzr.

## 3.3    Naming parameters

Believe it or not, parameter naming is just as important (some may say even more important) than command naming. As you'll learn, parameter naming is key to enabling commands to connect to each other in the pipeline. Parameter naming is also crucial for command discovery by using `Get-Command`.

---

**Quiz Time**

1  If you write a command that can connect to remote computers, what parameter name will accept those remote computer names or addresses?
2  If you write a command that can output a data file, what parameter name will accept the file location and name?
3  What parameter name might accept the session object to use if you write a command that can work over an existing PowerShell remoting session?

You may need to research a bit to answer these quiz questions—and that's the point.

---

When deciding on a parameter name, focus on the core, native PowerShell commands (rather than add-in modules such as Active Directory). What would *they* use in the same situation? Core commands invariably use `-ComputerName` rather than an alternative such as `-Host`, `-MachineName`, or something else. Here are a couple more examples:

1  Core commands are a bit inconsistent here, but *most* use either `-FilePath` or `-Path`. We'd use a command like `Out-File`, which uses `-FilePath`, as our exemplar.
2  The core remoting commands, such as `Invoke-Command`, perform this task, and they do so using a `-PSSession` parameter.

Wondering if a parameter name is a good choice? Use PowerShell to see if other commands are using it:

```
get-command -CommandType Cmdlet -ParameterName ComputerName
```

If you don't find a match, that doesn't mean you *shouldn't* use it, but there might be a better alternative.

The idea is to *be consistent*. Again, you'll see how this becomes crucial when wiring up commands so that they can connect in the pipeline. A lot of under-the-hood stuff relies on consistent parameter naming, so don't think you've got a great reason to diverge from the norm.

**Quiz Time**

1 Why do you think using the parameter `-Host` is a bad idea?

a When using `Invoke-Command` or `Enter-PSSession`, we can use `-Computer-Name` or `-hostname`. `ComputerName` uses Windows Remote Management (WinRM) and `Hostname` uses SSH to connect to the remote machine.

## 3.4 Producing output

Output is an area where observing PowerShell's native approach can be misleading because a lot goes on under the hood with PowerShell output. If you've read our book *Learn PowerShell in a Month of Lunches, Fourth Edition* (Manning, 2022), then you know some of this; if you haven't, we heartily recommend you do so. But in brief, here's what you need to know about PowerShell output:

1 PowerShell commands produce objects as output as you'll learn in this book. Objects are a form of structured data, not unlike an Excel spreadsheet. An object represents a row in the sheet, and each column is essentially a *property* of the object. By referring to the property names, you can access their contents. Structured data output—objects—are at the deep core of what PowerShell is. If you ignore this maxim, your PowerShell experience will be miserable.

2 Objects are output and placed into the PowerShell *pipeline*, which ferries the objects to the next command in the pipeline. Therefore, commands need to, in many cases, accept input from the pipeline so that they can work in this execution model. You can continue this process for as long as you need. But realize that objects may change in the pipeline depending on what cmdlets you're using.

3 When the last command has output its objects to the pipeline, the pipeline carries the objects to the formatting system. At this point, the objects are still just structured data. Their properties don't appear in any particular order and aren't explicitly destined to be displayed in any particular way.

4 The formatting system, through a fairly complex set of rules we covered in *Learn PowerShell in a Month of Lunches, Fourth Edition* (Manning, 2022), decides how to draw an onscreen display for the objects. This involves deciding to display a list or a table, coming up with column headers, and so on.

5 The result of the formatting system is a bunch of specialized formatting directives, meaning the original structured data is gone. These directives are useful only for drawing an onscreen display or sending an equivalent to a text file, a printer, or an output device.

Your tools shouldn't be doing any work in steps 4 or 5. That is, you should focus on outputting useful, structured data in the form of objects—and explicitly *not* worry about the *onscreen* results. We can't tell you how many people we've seen bang their heads against their desks trying to create "attractive" output. We'll show you how to do that *the PowerShell way*, which essentially involves educating the formatting system that fires off in step 4. But for your tools, focus on getting the right data into the output, and don't worry about what that will look like on the screen.

## 3.5   Don't assume

We've spent years teaching, writing, and speaking about PowerShell to IT professionals all over the world. If there's one constant challenge we see people encounter, it's making assumptions about what PowerShell is and how it should behave. As the ancient Greek philosopher Epictetus said, "It is impossible for a man to begin learning what he thinks he knows."

You'll recognize many patterns as you work with PowerShell, especially if you have other programming or scripting experience. That is to be expected. When PowerShell was being developed, the product team looked at many languages to adopt ideas and principles that fit the paradigm they were building. (Check out Don Jones's book, *Shell of an Idea* (2020), if you want to know more about the history of how PowerShell was developed.) But just because you recognize something that looks like Python, don't assume it will behave like Python. We find that those who approach PowerShell thinking they can treat it like some other language they know are the most frustrated. Here are some things to keep in mind:

- Although PowerShell has a rich and robust pipeline, it isn't Bash. PowerShell's pipeline works completely differently.
- Although running a command may produce a certain kind of onscreen output, that doesn't mean that's all the command produced. PowerShell's "visuals" don't always correspond exactly with its "internals."
- Although PowerShell has scripting constructs such as `If` and `ForEach`, it isn't a full programming language. If you approach it as one, you'll likely work at cross-purpose with the shell.
- Although PowerShell uses .NET Framework for much of its functionality, PowerShell isn't C#. PowerShell has become more programming language-ish over the years, but there are still times when the right answer is "Just do it in C#." You could be at that point if you find yourself writing almost entirely in .NET classes and not in PowerShell commands.

Perhaps the most important tip is to try not to drag your past experiences into PowerShell too much. PowerShell isn't VBScript, Perl, Python, KiXtart, or batch; the more you try to treat it like those things, the more you're going to struggle and be frustrated. Don't try to force PowerShell to meet some preconceptions you might have. PowerShell is its own thing. *Learn PowerShell in a Month of Lunches, Fourth Edition* should have prepared you for how PowerShell wants to be *used*. Similarly, this book will prepare you to extend the shell the way it wants to be *extended*.

## 3.6    *Avoid innovation*

We'll end this chapter with this related piece of advice: *don't try to invent new ways of doing things.* I'm sure you're thinking, "Isn't the whole point of this book to make your own scripts?" Yes, it is, but you're not the first person in the world to ever have your problem, we promise. The whole strength of PowerShell—quite literally the entire reason for its existence—is to create a consistent administrative surface from a sea of chaos. Don't contribute to the chaos by coming up with a novel approach. Even if you think Microsoft missed the boat on this one and you've got a much better way of doing something, stop thinking that way. The goal of creating tools in PowerShell isn't to do it *better* than Microsoft—it's to remain *consistent* with what has come before.

> **But contribute**
>
> We don't want to stifle you. Make your voice heard if you have a great idea or suggestion about how Microsoft can do something better.
>
> PowerShell is now an open source project on GitHub (https://github.com/PowerShell/PowerShell). Have an idea? Post an issue. Even better, fork the GitHub repository, develop the improvement, and submit a pull request. You can have a say in what future versions of PowerShell look like!

### *Summary*

All we're trying to stress in this chapter is that you need to take the time to observe how PowerShell approaches problems and try to emulate its approaches, rather than invent your own. Your results will become more comprehensible to others, require less effort on your part, and form a much more consistent solution within the shell.

Unlike a car, which you've observed in everyday life—presumably noticing the lack of an attached horse—PowerShell's approach isn't always obvious. Worse, it isn't always consistent because many different people, even inside Microsoft, have declined to follow our advice from this chapter. It's worth the time to research a bit, especially the core commands provided by the PowerShell team, to discover PowerShell's approach and emulate it as best you can.

# Review: Parameter binding and the PowerShell pipeline

Take traditional pipeline behavior from shells like Bash and Cmd.exe, mix in Power-Shell's unique object-oriented nature, and add a dash of Linux-style command parsing. The result is PowerShell's pipeline, a fairly complex and deeply powerful tool for composing tools into administrative solutions. Our goal is to turn you from a scripter into a toolmaker; to do so, you must understand the pipeline at its most basic level and create tools that take full advantage of the pipeline. Although we covered these concepts in *Learn PowerShell in a Month of Lunches, Fourth Edition* (Manning, 2022), we'll go deeper in this chapter and focus on the pipeline as something to *write for*, rather than just *use*.

## 4.1 The operating system

Let's start with a little practice exercise. Grab a sheet of paper (or a tablet you can write on), and draw something similar to what you see in figure 4.1. Now, write some command names in those boxes: maybe `Get-Process` in the first box, `ConvertTo-HTML` in the second box, and `Out-File` in the third box.

**Figure 4.1 Visualizing the pipeline**

**TRY IT NOW** Go on—*draw* the boxes. We could have just repeated the finished figure here in the book, and believe us, our editor wanted us to, but there's value in you doing this physical thing for yourself.

This exercise may have seemed a bit silly, but this is an excellent visual depiction of how PowerShell runs commands in the pipeline: as one command produces objects, they go into the pipeline *one at a time* and get passed on to the next command. At the end of the pipeline, when there are no further commands, any objects in the pipeline are passed to PowerShell's formatting system to be formatted for onscreen display.

The pipe symbols (|) in our diagram are concealing a great deal of under-the-hood functionality, which is important to understand. It's easy enough to say that Power-Shell passes the objects from one command into the next, but *how* does that happen?

## 4.2    *It's all in the parameters*

PowerShell uses two methods to figure out how to get data—objects—dynamically out of the pipeline and "into" a command on the other side of the pipe. Both of these methods rely on the accepting command's parameters. In other words—and this is important—the *only* way a command can accept data is via its parameters. This implies that when you design a command and when you design its parameters, you're deciding how that command will accept information, including how it will accept information from the pipeline. This process is, therefore, not magic; it's a science that is determined in advance by whoever designed the command.

It can look like magic, though. Consider this:

```
Get-Service | Where Status -eq "Running" | ConvertTo-HTML |
Out-File stats.html
```

We don't want you to go further than this chapter until you understand why that command works. Start by embracing that all commands only get their input by using parameters. Period. No exceptions. Full stop. The problem is that a lot of the time, you're not *typing* parameter names. Instead, PowerShell lets you use *positional* parameters, where the order of the values you provide implies the parameters those values get fed to. To dispel the magic, it's helpful to rewrite the command with every parameter spelled out in full:

```
Get-Service | Where-Object -Property Status -eq -Value "Running" |
ConvertTo-HTML
```

That `Where-Object` command is particularly interesting. We've used three parameters: `-Property`, the `eq` operator (which needs no value because it's an operator), and `-Value`. You'll *never* see this written out this way in the real world, but writing it out is a helpful way to understand that everything the command is doing is coming from parameters.

The last piece of the magic is how the pipeline carries objects of data from one command to another. For that, PowerShell has two techniques it can use: `ByValue` and `ByPropertyName`.

## 4.3   Pipeline: ByValue

PowerShell has a hardcoded preference to pass *entire objects* from the pipeline into a command. Because of that hardcoded preference, it will always attempt to pass entire objects before it tries to do anything else. To do so, the following must be true:

- The accepting command must define a parameter that supports accepting pipeline input ByValue.
- That parameter must be capable of accepting whatever type of object happens to be in the pipeline.

For example, refer to your diagram with Get-Process in the first block. What kind of object does that command produce? In PowerShell, try running Get-Process | Get-Member—the first line of output will contain the TypeName, which identifies the kind of object that the command produced. Turns out, it's a System.Diagnostics .Process object.

Now, peruse the help for the second command we suggested. You'll want to first make sure you've run Update-Help to have help files, and then run Help ConvertTo-HTML –ShowWindow to explore the complete help. Do you see any parameters of the command that are capable of accepting a [Process] object? Don't worry, you didn't miss one because one doesn't exist.

You probably *do* see a parameter capable of accepting an [Object] (or [Object[]]), right? In the Microsoft .NET Framework, System.Object is like the mother type for everything else. That is, everything *inherits* from the Object type. PSObject (i.e., Power-Shell Object) is more or less equivalent to Object in PowerShell. So, whenever you see that a parameter accepts PSObject, you know that it can accept basically anything. In the help for ConvertTo-HTML, you'll find an –InputObject parameter, which fulfills our two criteria:

- It can accept pipeline input using the ByValue technique.
- It can accept objects of the type System.Diagnostics.Process because it can accept the more generic PSObject.

Therefore, PowerShell will take the output of Get-Process and attach it to the –Input-Object parameter of ConvertTo-HTML. Reading the help for the second command, that parameter "specifies the objects to be represented in HTML." So, anything you pipe into ConvertTo-HTML will be captured, ByValue, through the –InputObject parameter, and will be presented in HTML format.

### 4.3.1   Introducing Trace-Command

The pipeline can still be a bit tricky and hard to understand at first as it's a tough concept. Lucky for us, PowerShell has a built-in way for you to see this passing-of-the-objects process happening called Trace-Command. It's a really useful way to debug pipeline parameter binding and will show you, in detail, the decisions PowerShell is making and the actions it's attempting to take. To run the command, you'll run something like

`Trace-Command -Name Parameterbinding -Expression { Your command goes here }` -PSHost. Keep in mind that your command *will actually run,* so you need to be careful not to run anything that could be damaging, such as deleting a bunch of user accounts or deleting everyone's home folder, just to see what happens! This isn't a replacement of -Whatif.

> **TRY IT NOW** Open up PowerShell, run the following command, and look at the output:
>
> ```
> Trace-Command -Name ParameterBinding -Expression {get-process |
> select -first 1} -PSHost
> ```

### 4.3.2 *Tracing the ByValue parameter binding*

Let's apply Trace-Command to the current example. Here's the command we ran, which you should run too:

```
PS C:\> trace-command -Expression { get-process | convertto-html |
out-null } -Name ParameterBinding -PSHost
```

You'll notice that we ended our command with Out-Null; we did that to suppress the normal output of ConvertTo-HTML to keep the output a little cleaner. You will, however, see PowerShell dealing with getting objects from ConvertTo-HTML into Out-Null, so it's a useful illustration.

You'll first see PowerShell attempt to *bind*—that is, attach—any NAMED arguments for Get-Process. There weren't any—that is, we didn't specify any—parameters manually in our command:

```
DEBUG: ParameterBinding Information: 0 : BIND NAMED cmd line args
[Get-Process]
```

PowerShell next looks for POSITIONAL parameters, which we also didn't have. PowerShell then checks to make sure that all the command's MANDATORY parameters have been provided, and we pass that check. Here's what you'll see:

```
DEBUG: ParameterBinding Information: 0 : BIND POSITIONAL cmd line args
[Get-Process]
DEBUG: ParameterBinding Information: 0 : MANDATORY PARAMETER CHECK on
cmdlet [Get-Process]
```

This entire process—named, positional, and then a mandatory check—repeats for the ConvertTo-HTML and Out-Null commands. This is an essential lesson: regardless of how a command is wired up to accept pipeline input, specifying named or positional parameters *always* takes precedence because PowerShell binds those first. If we'd manually specified -InputObject, for example, then we'd have prevented the ByValue parameter binding from working because we'd have "bound up" the parameter ourselves before ByValue was even considered. Here's what you'll see:

```
DEBUG: ParameterBinding Information: 0 : BIND NAMED cmd line args
[ConvertTo-Html]
DEBUG: ParameterBinding Information: 0 : BIND POSITIONAL cmd line args
[ConvertTo-Html]
DEBUG: ParameterBinding Information: 0 : MANDATORY PARAMETER CHECK on
cmdlet [ConvertTo-Html]
DEBUG: ParameterBinding Information: 0 : BIND NAMED cmd line args
[Out-Null]
DEBUG: ParameterBinding Information: 0 : BIND POSITIONAL cmd line args
[Out-Null]
DEBUG: ParameterBinding Information: 0 : MANDATORY PARAMETER CHECK on
cmdlet [Out-Null]
```

Next, PowerShell calls the BEGIN code for each of the three commands. This is code that is executed once before any pipeline objects are processed. Not all commands specify any BEGIN code, but PowerShell gives them all the opportunity. Here's what you'll see:

```
DEBUG: ParameterBinding Information: 0 : CALLING BeginProcessing
DEBUG: ParameterBinding Information: 0 : CALLING BeginProcessing
```

The next bit is a little surprising because PowerShell is attempting to bind a pipeline object to a parameter of Out-Null. Here's what you'll see:

```
DEBUG: ParameterBinding Information: 0 :      BIND PIPELINE object to
parameters: [Out-Null]
```

How the heck did anything even get into the pipeline at this point? Well, the previous command, ConvertTo-HTML, has clearly taken the opportunity to produce some output from its BEGIN code—sneaky. PowerShell now has to deal with that, even though the first command, Get-Process, hasn't even run yet!

Then, comes something interesting. Here's what you'll see:

```
DEBUG: ParameterBinding Information: 0 : PIPELINE object TYPE =
[System.String]
DEBUG: ParameterBinding Information: 0 : RESTORING pipeline
parameter's original values
```

PowerShell identifies the type of object in the pipeline as a System.String. Take a minute and read the full help for Out-Null. Do you see any parameters capable of accepting a String from the pipeline using the ByValue method?

PowerShell is about to discover that the -InputObject parameter of Out-Null accepts either Object or PSObject, so it's going to bind the output of ConvertTo-HTML to that -InputObject parameter:

```
DEBUG: ParameterBinding Information: 0 : Parameter
[InputObject] PIPELINE INPUT ValueFromPipeline NO COERCION
DEBUG: ParameterBinding Information: 0 : BIND arg [<!DOCTYPE
html PUBLIC "-//W3C//DTD XHTML 1.0 Strict//EN"
```

```
"http://www.w3.org/TR/xhtml1/DTD/xhtml1-strict.dtd">] to parameter
[InputObject]
DEBUG: ParameterBinding Information: 0 : BIND arg
[<!DOCTYPE html PUBLIC "-//W3C//DTD XHTML 1.0 Strict//EN"
"http://www.w3.org/TR/xhtml1/DTD/xhtml1-strict.dtd">] to param
[InputObject] SUCCESSFUL
```

In fact, it appears to have accepted a couple of String objects from the pipeline. These look like header lines for an HTML file, which makes sense—ConvertTo-HTML probably gets these out of the way as boilerplate before it settles down to its real job.

Next, we see that the MANDATORY check on Out-Null succeeds, and we continue to deal with initial boilerplate issued by ConvertTo-HTML:

```
DEBUG: ParameterBinding Information: 0 : MANDATORY PARAMETER CHECK
on cmdlet [Out-Null]
DEBUG: ParameterBinding Information: 0 : BIND PIPELINE object to
parameters: [Out-Null]
DEBUG: ParameterBinding Information: 0 : PIPELINE object TYPE =
[System.String]
DEBUG: ParameterBinding Information: 0 : RESTORING pipeline
parameter's original values
DEBUG: ParameterBinding Information: 0 : Parameter
[InputObject] PIPELINE INPUT ValueFromPipeline NO COERCION
DEBUG: ParameterBinding Information: 0 : BIND arg [<html
xmlns="http://www.w3.org/1999/xhtml">] to parameter [InputObject]
DEBUG: ParameterBinding Information: 0 :  BIND arg [<html
xmlns="http://www.w3.org/1999/xhtml">] to param [InputObject]
SUCCESSFUL
```

Let's skip ahead a bit, past all the boilerplate "header" HTML. We'll go down to the point where Get-Process runs and where PowerShell recognizes the type of object it has produced:

```
DEBUG: ParameterBinding Information: 0 : BIND PIPELINE object to
parameters: [ConvertTo-Html]
DEBUG: ParameterBinding Information: 0 : PIPELINE object TYPE =
[System.Diagnostics.Process#HandleCount]
```

Next, we'll see those Process objects being bound to the -InputObject parameter of ConvertTo-HTML:

```
DEBUG: ParameterBinding Information: 0 : Parameter [InputObject]
PIPELINE INPUT ValueFromPipeline NO COERCION
DEBUG: ParameterBinding Information: 0 : BIND arg
[System.Diagnostics.Process] to parameter [InputObject]
DEBUG: ParameterBinding Information: 0 : BIND arg
[System.Diagnostics.Process] to param [InputObject] SUCCESSFUL
```

The trace output goes on, of course, but this is what we were looking for: proof that PowerShell is doing what we expected. You'll notice the phrase NO COERCION quite a bit in the preceding; that's an indication that PowerShell was able to bind the output as is, without trying to convert it to something else. Coercion is one of the things that can make pipeline parameter binding more confusing, and it's what this trace output can help you see and understand. For example, PowerShell is capable of *coercing*, or converting, a number into a string so that the resulting string can bind to a parameter that accepts `String`.

### 4.3.3   *When ByValue fails*

That was pretty in-depth for `ByValue`, but what do we do when that fails? Go back to your paper diagram. Erase or cross out `ConvertTo-HTML` and `Out-Null`, and, in the second box, write `Stop-Service`. Don't run the resulting command yet—we need to talk about what happens.

You know that the first command produces `Process` objects. Examining its full help file, do you see any parameters of `Stop-Service` that will do both of the following?

- Accept pipeline input `ByValue`
- Accept an input type of `Process`, `Object`, or `PSObject`

We don't see any parameters that fit the criteria, so the `ByValue` method fails. What do we do now?

## 4.4   *ByPropertyName*

You may notice one parameter of `Stop-Service` that accepts pipeline input `ByProperty-Name`: specifically, the `-Name` parameter. That parameter does accept `ByValue`, but we've moved past that—it's the `ByPropertyName` part that interests us now. Here's what it means: because the *parameter* is spelled *N A M E*, PowerShell will look at the objects in the pipeline to see if they have a *property* spelled *N A M E*. If they do, PowerShell will take the values from the property and feed them to the parameter—just because they're spelled the same.

Try using `Trace-Command` to run `Get-Process | Stop-Service -whatif` (we included `-whatif` just to prevent any possibility of something going wrong). Can you see how PowerShell attempts to bind the object's `Name` property to the command's `-Name` parameter?

PowerShell will try to "pair" as many properties and parameters as it can. If the object in the pipeline has properties named `Name`, `ID`, `Description`, and `Status`, and the next command in the pipeline has parameters named `-Name` and `-Status`, then two of the object's properties will bind to parameters (assuming that `-Name` and `-Status` were both programmed to accept pipeline input `ByPropertyName`). This can be a really useful technique. For example, suppose you have a CSV file named Users.csv that contains columns named samAccountName, Name, Title, Department, and City. Looking at the help file for `New-ADUser` (`Get-Help New-Aduser -Online` if you don't have the Active Directory module installed), what do you think would happen if you ran this?

```
Import-CSV Users.csv | New-ADUser
```

Give it some thought. If you have a test domain that you can play with, go ahead and create a CSV like that, and fill in a few rows' worth of user information for made-up users that don't exist. Run the command, and see if it does what you expect.

### 4.4.1   *Let's trace ByPropertyName*

Consider another example of ByPropertyName binding, and look at the portions of a trace where the binding happens. Here's our command (we're limiting Get-Process to retrieving processes whose names begin with the letter *O* because we know we only have one such process, and it will make the output shorter):

```
PS C:\> trace-command -Expression { Get-Process -Name o* |
Stop-Job } -PSHost -Name ParameterBinding
```

Let's see what happens. First, we run through the parameter binding for Get-Process. This time, we do have a NAMED parameter, -Name, to which we've provided the value o*. There's a problem, though, in that the parameter wants an *array* of strings—shown as [string[]] in its help file—and we've provided only one. PowerShell therefore creates an array, adds our o* to it, and attaches that one-item array to the parameter:

```
DEBUG: ParameterBinding Information: 0 : BIND NAMED cmd line args
[Get-Process]
DEBUG: ParameterBinding Information: 0 : BIND arg [o*] to parameter
[Name]
DEBUG: ParameterBinding Information: 0 : COERCE arg to [System.String[]]
DEBUG: ParameterBinding Information: 0 : Trying to convert
argument value from System.String to System.String[]
DEBUG: ParameterBinding Information: 0 : ENCODING arg into collection
DEBUG: ParameterBinding Information: 0 : Binding collection parameter Name:
argument type [String], parameter type
[System.String[]], collection type Array, element type [System.String],
coerceElementType
DEBUG: ParameterBinding Information: 0 : Creating array with element type
[System.String] and 1 elements
DEBUG: ParameterBinding Information: 0 : Argument type String is not IList,
treating this as scalar
DEBUG: ParameterBinding Information: 0 : COERCE arg to System.String]
DEBUG: ParameterBinding Information: 0 : Parameter and arg types the same,
no coercion is needed.
DEBUG: ParameterBinding Information: 0 : Adding scalar element of type
String to array position 0
DEBUG: ParameterBinding Information: 0 : Executing VALIDATION metadata:
[System.Management.Automation.ValidateNotNullOrEmptyAttribute]
DEBUG: ParameterBinding Information: 0 : BIND arg [System.String[]] to
param [Name] SUCCESSFUL
```

Next is the usual check for POSITIONAL parameters, followed by a MANDATORY check:

```
DEBUG: ParameterBinding Information: 0 : BIND POSITIONAL cmd line args
[Get-Process]
DEBUG: ParameterBinding Information: 0 : MANDATORY PARAMETER CHECK on
cmdlet [Get-Process]
```

Now we start in on the `Stop-Job` command, handling NAMED, POSITIONAL, and MANDATORY again:

```
DEBUG: ParameterBinding Information: 0 : BIND NAMED cmd line args
[Stop-Job]
DEBUG: ParameterBinding Information: 0 : BIND POSITIONAL cmd line args
[Stop-Job]
DEBUG: ParameterBinding Information: 0 : MANDATORY PARAMETER CHECK on
cmdlet [Stop-Job]
```

PowerShell then gives each of the two commands a chance to run any BEGIN code that they may contain:

```
DEBUG: ParameterBinding Information: 0 : CALLING BeginProcessing
DEBUG: ParameterBinding Information: 0 : CALLING BeginProcessing
```

The only process returned, in our case, is one named OSDUIHelper, and it appears next in the trace output:

```
DEBUG: ParameterBinding Information: 0 : BIND arg
[System.Diagnostics.Process (OSDUIHelper)] to parameter [Job]
```

Let's see what PowerShell does with that because we're pretty sure ByValue won't work:

```
DEBUG: ParameterBinding Information: 0 : Binding collection parameter Job:
argument type [Process], parameter type
[System.Management.Automation.Job[]], collection type Array, element
type [System.Management.Automation.Job], no coerceElementType
DEBUG: ParameterBinding Information: 0 : Creating array with element type
[System.Management.Automation.Job] and 1 elements
DEBUG: ParameterBinding Information: 0 : Argument type Process is not
IList, treating this as scalar
DEBUG: ParameterBinding Information: 0 : BIND arg
[System.Diagnostics.Process (OSDUIHelper)] to param [Job] **SKIPPED**
```

That SKIPPED portion at the end (bolded in the output) is what tells us ByValue ultimately didn't work out. PowerShell tried! The -Job parameter of Stop-Job accepts input ByValue, so PowerShell gave it a shot. The parameter expects one or more objects of the type Job, so PowerShell created an array and added to it our OSDUI-Helper object, which is of the type Process. But it couldn't do anything to make a Process into a Job, so it gave up. Time for plan B:

```
DEBUG: ParameterBinding Information: 0 : Parameter [Id] PIPELINE
INPUT ValueFromPipelineByPropertyName NO COERCION
DEBUG: ParameterBinding Information: 0 : BIND arg [5248] to parameter [Id]
DEBUG: ParameterBinding Information: 0 : Binding collection parameter Id:
argument type [Int32], parameter type [System.Int32[]],
collection type Array, element type [System.Int32], no coerceElementType
DEBUG: ParameterBinding Information: 0 : Creating array with element type
[System.Int32] and 1 elements
DEBUG: ParameterBinding Information: 0 : Argument type Int32 is not IList,
```

```
treating this as scalar
DEBUG: ParameterBinding Information: 0 : Adding scalar element of type
Int32 to array position 0
DEBUG: ParameterBinding Information: 0 : Executing VALIDATION metadata:
[System.Management.Automation.ValidateNotNullOrEmptyAttribute]
DEBUG: ParameterBinding Information: 0 : BIND arg [System.Int32[]] to param
[Id] SUCCESSFUL
DEBUG: ParameterBinding Information: 0 : MANDATORY PARAMETER CHECK on
cmdlet [Stop-Job]
```

The `Process` object has an ID property, and the `-Id` parameter of `Stop-Job` accepts pipeline input `ByPropertyName`. The property contains, and the parameter accepts, an integer, although the parameter wants an array of them. So, PowerShell creates a single-item array, adds our ID of 5248 to it, and attaches it to `-Id`. It works! Well, it sort of works. We know, and you've probably guessed, that `Stop-Job` is expecting the ID number of a *job*, whereas we're providing the ID number of a *process*—not quite the same thing. It's like trying to use your house number as a phone number: they're both numbers, but they refer to different kinds of entities. That's why we eventually get an error:

```
Stop-Job : The command cannot find a job with the job ID 5248. Verify
the value of the Id parameter and then try the command again.
At line:1 char:52
+ trace-command -Expression { Get-Process -Name o* | Stop-Job } -PSHost ...
+ CategoryInfo : ObjectNotFound: (5248:Int32) [Stop-Job],
PSArgumentException
+ FullyQualifiedErrorId : JobWithSpecifiedSessionNotFound,Microsoft.
PowerShell.Commands.StopJobCommand
```

The trace output, should you care to try this on your own (and you should!), shows PowerShell attempting to construct the error message record that eventually appears onscreen, which is a fairly arduous process that involves a few dozen more lines of trace output. `Trace-Command` can be a handy cmdlet for troubleshooting, so take the time to read the full help and examples.

### 4.4.2   *When ByPropertyName fails*

What if you get into a situation where you have an object in the pipeline and a command ready to receive it, but neither `ByValue` nor `ByPropertyName` works? It's entirely possible—the command may not be able to do anything with the type of object in the pipeline, for example, or may not accept pipeline input at all. This should be rare, and we created a simple PowerShell command to demonstrate:

```
PS C:\> "frances" | set-foo
set-foo : The input object cannot be bound to any parameters for the
command either because the command does not take
pipeline input or the input and its properties do not match any of the
parameters that take pipeline input.
At line:1 char:13
```

```
+ "frances" | set-foo
+            ~~~~~~~
    + CategoryInfo          : InvalidArgument: (frances:String) [Set-Foo],
ParameterBindingException
    + FullyQualifiedErrorId : InputObjectNotBound,Set-Foo
```

As you can see, the entire pipeline will fail. Because the objects *can't* be passed into the command and PowerShell doesn't want to just discard the pipeline objects, it will throw an error message and quit running.

### 4.4.3 *Planning ahead*

Let's consider a key principle when developing your tools, especially those leveraging parameter binding. Ideally, you should designate only one parameter to accept pipeline input by value. Imagine having two parameters, Foo and Bar, designed for input by value. If you execute the command as Get-content data.txt | get-magic, it becomes unclear whether incoming values should go to -Foo or -Bar. PowerShell lacks the means to determine this, emphasizing the importance of having only one parameter for value input. Although having multiple such parameters using parameter sets is technically possible, it's a more advanced concept.

On the other hand, you can have numerous parameters designed for input by property name. It's even possible to have one parameter accept input both by value and property name, but this requires a thoughtful approach. Consider the likely usage patterns for your tools: Will users commonly pipe results to your command or run it as the initial command in a pipeline expression? Testing various usage scenarios is crucial to ensure proper parameter binding. If problems arise, use Trace-Command to gain insights into the pipeline's internal processes.

### *Summary*

Our goal with this chapter—and we hope we've achieved it—was twofold. First, we wanted you to get a fresh understanding of how pipeline objects move from command to command. We also wanted you to understand how useful command tracing can be in visualizing that process and in diagnosing unexpected pipeline behavior. Before long, you're going to be designing your own commands that will accept pipeline input, and we want you to continually think about this process and how it works as you do so.

# Scripting language: A crash course

In this book, you'll notice that you're only given general information immediately after using it. In this case, though, I'm going to make an exception. You'll be writing scripts throughout this book, and that means including a certain amount of code. PowerShell's scripting language is super simple, containing a few dozen actual keywords, and I'm only going to use about a dozen in this book. But we need to get the most important of those into our heads to use them when the time comes. The goal of this chapter isn't to provide complete coverage of these items but to give you a quick introduction. They'll begin to make more sense when you see them in use throughout the rest of the book.

> **TIP** To learn even more about the material in this chapter, the first place to look is PowerShell's help system. Much of this is documented in About topics. For example, you can look at information regarding `about_if` and `about_comparison_operators`. You also can grab a copy of *PowerShell in Depth*, 2nd ed. (Manning, 2014; http://mng.bz/xjzq).

## 5.1 Comparisons

Almost all the scripting bits we introduce in this chapter rely on *comparisons*. That is, you give them some statement that must be evaluated to be either `True` or `False`, and the scripting constructs base their behavior on that result. To make a comparison in PowerShell, you use a *comparison operator*. Unlike traditional scripting or programming languages, PowerShell doesn't use the traditional operator characters (<, >, +, =, −), but instead uses an English abbreviation. Here are the core operators that you'll likely use throughout this book:

- -eq—Equal to
- -ne—Not equal to
- -gt—Greater than
- -ge—Greater than or equal to
- -lt—Less than
- -le—Less than or equal to

For string comparisons, these are case-insensitive by default, which means "Hello" and "HELLO" are the same. If you explicitly need a case-sensitive comparison, add a c to the front of the operator name, as in -ceq or -cne.

When you use these operators, PowerShell will return a True/False value:

```
PS C:\> 1 -eq 1
True
PS C:\> 5 -gt 10
False
PS C:\> 'James' -eq 'Jim'
False
PS C:\> 'James' -eq 'james'
True
PS C:\> 'james' -ceq 'James'
False
```

PowerShell has a different extensive range of operators than some languages. For example, no "exactly equal to" comparison forbids the shell's parser from coercing a data type into another type.

**TRY IT NOW** Is 5 -eq "Five" true or false?

## 5.1.1 *Wildcards*

There's a wildcard comparison, -like and –not like, along with the case-sensitive versions –like and –not like. These let you use common wildcard characters such as * (zero or more characters) and ? (a single character) in making string comparisons:

```
PS C:\> 'james' -eq 'Jim'
False
PS C:\> 'james' -eq 'James'
True
PS C:\> 'james' -ceq 'James'
False
PS C:\> 'PowerShell'-like '*shell'
True
PS C:\> 'james' -notlike 'james*'
False
PS C:\> 'james' -like 'jam?s'
True
PS C:\> 'james' -like 'Jim'
False
```

These wildcards aren't as rich as the full regular-expression language; PowerShell does support regular expressions through its `-match` operator, although we won't be diving into that one in this book. Check out the chapter on PowerShell and regular expressions in *PowerShell in Depth*, 2nd ed. (Manning, 2014; http://mng.bz/xjzq).

### 5.1.2 Collections

PowerShell's `-contains` and `-in` operators operate against collections of objects. They get tricky, and people almost always confuse them with wildcard operators. For example, we see this a lot:

```
If ("DC" -in $ServerList) {
  $IsDomainController = $True
}
```

This doesn't work the way you might think. It reads just fine in English, but it's not what the operator does. If you start with an array, you can use these operators to determine whether the array (or collection) contains a particular object:

```
$array = @("one", "two", "three")
$array -contains "one"
$array -contains "five"
"two" -in $array
"bob" -in $array
```

> **TRY IT NOW**  Run those five lines of code in PowerShell, typing the lines in one at a time and pressing Enter after each.

### 5.1.3 Troubleshooting comparisons

About 50% of the script bugs are due to a comparison that doesn't work as expected. Our best advice for troubleshooting these is to stop working on your script, jump into the PowerShell console, and try the comparison.

> **TRY IT NOW**  What will `"55" -eq 55` result in? We won't give you the answer— try it and see if you can explain to yourself why it did what it did.

## 5.2 The If construct

You'll often need an `If` construct, which allows your code to make logical decisions. In its full form, the `If` construct looks like this:

```
If (<expression>) {
    # code
} ElseIf (<expression>) {
    # code
} ElseIf (<expression>) {
    # code
} Else {
    # code
}
```

Here's what you need to know:

- An `<expression>` is any PowerShell expression resulting in either `$True` or `$False`. For example, `$something -eq 5` will be `$True` if the variable `$something` equals 5. Read PowerShell's "about_comparison_operators" article for a list of valid comparison operators, including `-eq`, `-ne`, `-gt`, `-like`, and so on.

- The expressions in your `If` statement can be as complicated as they need to be. Just remember that the entire expression has to result in `True` for the script block code to execute:

```
$now = Get-Date
if ($now.DayOfWeek -eq 'Monday' -AND $now.hour -gt 18) {
  #do something
}
```

- The `If` portion of the construct is mandatory and must be followed by a `{script block}` that will execute if the expression is `True`.

- You may have zero or more `ElseIf` sections. These sections supply their own expression and script block, executing if the expression is `True`. But you must remember an important point: only the script block of the first expression that is `True` will run. So, in the previous skeleton example, if the first expression is `True`, then only the first script block will run; none of the `ElseIf` expressions will even be evaluated. If you have multiple `ElseIf` statements, PowerShell will continue to evaluate them until it finds one `True`. When it does, PowerShell will jump to the command after the `If` structure.

- You may have an optional `Else` section at the end. This defines a script block that will execute if no preceding expression is evaluated to `True`.

- There is no `End If` statement like you might find in other languages.

- In the previous skeleton example, you'll notice lines that start with a # symbol. Those are comments. PowerShell will ignore everything after a # at the end of that line.

PowerShell is forgiving about formatting. For example, we think this is a nice way to format the construct:

```
If (<expression>) {
    # code
} ElseIf (<expression>) {
    # code
} ElseIf (<expression>) {
    # code
} Else {
    # code
}
```

Some people like to put the opening { on a separate line. One way is not more correct than another, but we wanted you to be aware that some people may do it this way:

```
If (<expression>)
{
    # code
}
```

However, PowerShell will let you do stuff like this as well:

```
If (<expression>) { # code }
ElseIf (<expression>) { # code }
ElseIf (<expression>) { # code }
Else { # code }
```

That's harder to read, especially if any of the script blocks need to contain multiple lines of code. We certainly don't recommend you use this method, but you'll see other people do so sometimes. The bottom line is that although PowerShell doesn't care, you should. Pick a formatting style that makes your code easy to read, and stick with it.

> **Quick Tip**
>
> Code formatting is important. It may seem like an irrelevant aesthetic detail, but it makes your code easier to follow, which means fewer bugs. Trust us on this. Take a travesty like this:
>
> ```
> If ($user) { ForEach ($u in $user) {
> Set-ADUser -Identity $user -Pass $True }
> ```
>
> It's hard to tell if that's valid code or not (it isn't), given how the curly braces are mangled and the way the ForEach starts on the same line as the If.
>
> If you're using a good editor, such as Visual Studio (VS Code), it's pretty easy to keep your code neat: just let the editor do its thing. When you open a construct with { and press Enter, VS Code will automatically add the closing } and place your cursor—indented a perfect four spaces—inside the construct. Focus on letting VS Code do the work—use the Tab key when you need to indent a line, for example, rather than pressing the spacebar. In addition, if you haven't already, turn on bracket colorization in VS Code.
>
> If things aren't lining up vertically, here's a trick: highlight the affected region (or your entire script document), right-click, and select Format Selection. VS Code will clean up, properly indenting within each construct. You can also open the command palate and choose Format Document to format the entire document.

Let's look at a practical example of this construct. Suppose you have a Process object in the variable $proc, and you want to take some action if the process's virtual memory (VM) property exceeds a specific predetermined value:

```
If ($proc.vm -gt 4) {
  # take some action
}
```

Notice that we've used a comment—remember, anything after a # symbol is ignored until the end of that line—to indicate where the action-taking code would go. What if, instead, you wanted to take an action for VM values less than 2 but greater than 4?

```
If ($proc.vm -gt 4 -or $proc.vm -lt 2) {
  # take some action
}
```

The -or Boolean operator lets you "connect" two conditions. Note that the comparison on either side of an -or an- must be *complete*. This, for example, wouldn't work:

```
If ($proc.vm -gt 4 -or -lt 2) {
  # take some action
}
```

In this "wrong" example, the "less than" comparison isn't complete. It has nothing on the left side; PowerShell will ask, "What, exactly, is supposed to be less than 2?" and toss an error. If it helps, you can use parentheses to set off each comparison visually:

```
If ( ($proc.vm -gt 4) -or ($proc.vm -lt 2) ) {
  # take some action
}
```

Next, let's look at an example that has additional options:

```
If ($proc.vm -gt 4) {
  # take some action
} ElseIf ($proc.vm -lt 2) {
  # take some other action
} Else {
  # nothing was true; do this instead
}
```

As we explained earlier, PowerShell will perform the first of these actions whose condition evaluates to `True` and then stop evaluating anything after that.

## 5.3 The ForEach construct

You'll often use a ForEach construct, which is sometimes referred to as an *enumerator*. ForEach is used in most programming languages, so it will likely look familiar. It works a bit like PowerShell's ForEach-Object command, but it has a different syntax:

```
ForEach ($item in $collection) {
    # code to run for each object referenced at $item
}
```

The idea here is to take a collection or an array of objects and go through them one at a time. Each object, in its turn, is placed into a separate variable so that you can refer to it easily. After you've enumerated all the objects in the collection or array, the loop exits automatically, and the rest of your script executes.

The second variable in the construct, `$collection`, is expected to contain zero or more items. The ForEach *loop* will execute its {script block} once *for each* item contained in the second variable. That is, if you provide three computer names in `$collection`, the ForEach loop will run three times. Each time the loop runs, one item is taken from the second variable and placed into the first. So, within the previous script block, the `$item` will contain one thing at a time from the `$collection`.

**TIP** We made up the variable names `$item` and `$collection`. You'd ordinarily use different variable names that correspond to what those variables are expected to contain.

You'll often see people use singular and plural words in their ForEach loops:

```
$names = Get-Content names.txt
ForEach ($name in $names) {
    # code for each $name
}
```

This approach makes it easier to remember that `$name` contains one thing from `$names`, but that's purely for human readability. PowerShell doesn't magically know or care that *name* is the singular of *names*. The previous example could easily be rewritten as follows:

```
$names = Get-Content names.txt
ForEach ($purple in $unicorns) {
    # code
}
```

PowerShell would be perfectly happy with this. That code would be a lot harder to read and keep track of, but if you like unicorns, go for it. In some cases, though, you'll notice that the second variable isn't plural, although it feels like it should be:

```
foreach ($computer in $computername) {
```

It's often because `$ComputerName` is one of a function's input parameters. PowerShell's convention is to use singular words for command and parameter names. You won't see -ComputerNames; you'll only see -ComputerName as a parameter. You want to stick with the convention, so, in that case, your ForEach loop wouldn't follow a singular/plural pattern. Again, PowerShell doesn't care, and we feel it's more important that your outward-facing elements—command and parameter names—follow PowerShell naming conventions.

**BEST PRACTICE** In a script, we greatly prefer using ForEach over the ForEach-Object command. There are some advantages: you get to name your single-item variable rather than using `$_` or `$PSItem`, making your code more readable; and the construct often executes more quickly than the command over large collections too. With large collections of arrays, the construct can force you to use more memory because the entire array or collection must be in a single variable. When you use the command, objects can be piped in one at a time and dealt with, consuming less memory in some scenarios.

There's one *gotcha* with the `ForEach` construct: it doesn't write to the pipeline after the closing curly brace. We've seen people try to create something like this, only to have it fail:

```
$numbers=1..10
foreach ($n in $numbers) {
 $n*3
} | out-file data.txt
```

If you try this in VS Code or other code editors, you'll most likely see an error about an empty pipe. Everything *inside* the script block is written to the pipeline. You can't pipe anything *after*. But you can write the code like this:

```
$numbers=1..10
$data = foreach ($n in $numbers) {
 $n*3
}
$data | out-file data.txt
```

This will work as expected. In this second example, `$n*3` is implicitly writing its output to the pipeline (`Write-Output` is PowerShell's default command), and the end result of the `ForEach` construct is captured to the `$data` variable. That, in turn, is then piped to `Out-File`. Much of this confusion happens because the alias for the `ForEach` *object* is `ForEach`, although it works differently from the `ForEach` *construct*. The construct that we're teaching here always has the `($x in $y)` syntax right after it, whereas the `ForEach-Object` command doesn't use that syntax.

With all this in mind, we urge you to think carefully about when to use the `ForEach` enumerator because it's easy to fall into a non-PowerShell habit. I've seen code like this from people just getting started or who haven't grasped the PowerShell model:

```
$services = Get-Service -name bits,lanmanserver,spooler
Foreach ($service in $services) {
  Restart-service $service -passthru
}
```

This will obviously work if you care to try, and it's what we did in the days of VBScript, but this isn't the PowerShell way. There's no need for such contorted code when this works just as well:

```
$services | restart-service -passthru
```

## 5.4    *The Switch construct*

The `switch` construct is great as a replacement for a huge `If` block that contains multiple `ElseIf` sections. Here's a prototype:

```
switch (<expression>) {
  <condition> { <script block> }
  <condition > { <script block> }
  <condition > { <script block> }
  default { <script block }
}
```

Here's how it works:

1   The expression is usually a variable containing *a single value or object*. This is important because the `switch` alone won't enumerate collections or arrays.

2   Each condition is a value that you think the expression might contain. Each condition is followed by a script block (which can be broken into multiple lines), and if the expression contains the condition, then the associated script block will execute.

3   The `default` block executes if no conditions match; you can omit the `default` if you don't need it.

Each matching condition will execute. It's possible to have multiple matches; if so, each matching script block will execute. This may seem nonsensical until you dive into some of the construct's advanced options:

```
$x = "d1234"
switch -wildcard ($x)
    {
        "*1*" {"Contains 1"}
        "*5*" {"Contains 5"}
       "d*" {"Starts with 'd'"}
        default {"No matches"}
    }
```

The `-wildcard` switch makes it possible for multiple conditions to match. In this example, if `$x` contained "1 of 5 dying worms", then you'd get two lines of output: `"Contains 1"` and `"Contains 5"`. The third pattern doesn't match, and because at least one pattern did match, the `default` block won't execute. Be sure to read the "about_switch" article on PowerShell's help system.

## 5.5    *The Do/While construct*

You'll be using this guy later on. `While` lets you specify a script block of statements, which will execute *while* some condition is true. You get two basic variations:

```
While (<condition>) {
 # code
}
```

```
Do {
 # code
} While (<condition>)
```

These both do essentially the same thing: they repeat the code inside the construct until the specified <condition> is no longer true. Here's the difference:

- With the first version, the construct's code *might never run*. It will only run if the <condition> is true.
- With the second version, the code inside the construct *will always run at least once*. It doesn't check the <condition> until after the first execution.

You need to be a bit careful about writing these loops because there's no automatic exit the way there is with a Switch, If, or ForEach construct. Unless you're sure that your <condition> will eventually change and evaluate to false, then a Do/While construct can basically loop forever—called an *infinite loop*. In most PowerShell hosts, like the console, you can press Ctrl-C to break out of the loop if you realize you've created an infinite loop.

## 5.6 *The For construct*

The last of the scripting constructs, For, is so rarely used that we debated even putting it in the book (you can even skip this one if your head is swimming at this point). But just in case someone would be upset that we left it out, For typically looks like this:

```
For (<start>; <condition>; <action>) {
  # code
}
```

This loop is meant to repeat the code inside the construct *several times*. It can be a bit easier to explain with a more concrete example:

```
For ($i = 0; $i -lt 3; $i++) {
  Write $i
}
```

The idea is that the <start> item gets executed before the construct runs, setting $i to a value of 0. The <condition> keeps the construct running as long as it evaluates to True. Finally, *after* the construct's script block executes, the <action> is performed each time. So, in this example, the script will execute four times:

1  $i is initially set to 0, and then the script block executes.
2  Because $i is less than 3, $i is incremented by 1, and the script block executes.
3  Because $i is less than 3, $i is incremented by 1 (now 2), and the script block executes.
4  Because $i is less than 3, $i is incremented by 1 (it's now 3), and the script block executes.
5  Now, $i is 3, which isn't less than 3, so the script block doesn't execute, and the construct exits.

This isn't different from using PowerShell's range operator and a `ForEach-Object` command:

```
0..3 | ForEach-Object { Write $_ }
```

The `For` construct is easier to read and feels more declarative to us, and if we ever needed to perform that kind of task, we'd opt for the construct over the range operator trick. But we rarely use `For` because we only run into a few situations where we must do something a set number of times. Instead, we tend to use `ForEach` more often because we have a collection of objects and want to perform some operation against each one. You can do that with `For`, but it's a bit ugly. Assuming `$objects` contains a collection of things, here are two ways you could enumerate them:

```
For ($i = 0; $i -lt $objects.Count; $i++) {
  Write $objects[$i]
}
ForEach ($thing in $objects) {
  Write $thing
}
```

The second example is easier to read. We suspect that people using the first technique are coming to PowerShell from a language that doesn't have an enumeration construct like `ForEach`, and they default to `For` because it's what they know.

## 5.7   *Break*

There's one more scripting critter you should know about: the `Break` keyword. It exits whatever it's in—with some caveats:

- In a `For`, `ForEach`, `While`, or `Switch` construct, `Break` will immediately exit that construct.
- In a script, but outside of a construct, `Break` will exit the script.
- In an `If` construct, `Break` won't exit the construct. Instead, `Break` will exit whatever *contains* the `If` construct—an outer `For`, `ForEach`, `While`, `Switch`, or the script itself. The `If` is invisible to `Break`, so whatever the `If` is within is what `Break` sees.

The break is useful for aborting an operation. For example, suppose you have a list of computers in the variable `$computers`. You want to review each one and ping them to see if they respond. But should one computer not respond to its ping, for whatever reason, you want to stop everything and quit immediately. You might write this:

```
ForEach ($comp in $computers) {
  If (-not (Test-Ping $comp -quiet)) {
    Break
  }
}
```

You need to be aware of a bit of an antipattern. Some folks will write a loop that's intentionally infinite. Instead of specifying a natural condition to end the loop, they'll use Break to abort. Here's a short example:

```
While ($true) {
  $choice = Read-Host "Enter a number."
  If ($choice -eq 0) { break }
}
```

Often, we wonder if those folks weren't aware of the loop's other options. In this case, for example, it seems they wanted to ensure that the loop's contents were executed at least once, but they didn't know how to go into the loop the first time. I'd rewrite this as follows:

```
Do {
  $choice = Read-Host "Enter a number."
} While ($choice -ne 0)
```

This is a little cleaner in terms of code execution. A problem with Break is that it provides an alternative way out of a construct, creating a secondary flow of logic that's harder to follow. Because Break is often used inside an If construct—as shown here—it becomes difficult to predict the behavior of the script without running it. That, in turn, creates all kinds of debugging and troubleshooting problems that we feel are best avoided. In short, we try to write constructs with a meaningful natural endpoint, and we try to avoid Break when possible.

> **TIP** Try to avoid using Break when you can. Break creates what we call a *non-natural* exit to a loop; that is, the loop isn't coming to its natural conclusion. Especially in a loop that contains a lot of code, it's easy to skim through it and miss the Break keyword, making it harder to understand why the loop is bailing out prematurely. When we *do* have to use Break, surround its use with blank lines and worded comments indicating what's happening.

## Summary

The constructs we covered in this chapter form the core of what we consider to be PowerShell's scripting language. Unlike commands, these constructs exist to provide logic and structure to your scripts. If you can keep these four core constructs in mind, you'll probably find that they're all the scripting code you need to know for most of the scripts you'll write.

# The many
## forms of scripting
## (and which to choose)

You probably think you're the victim of bait-and-switch tactics by Manning. We use words such as *tool* and *toolmaking* but haven't talked much about scripting. After all, the title of this book is *Learn PowerShell Scripting in a Month of Lunches*. But what if I told you that scripting equals toolmaking in this instance? Scripting is a pretty generic word, and in the PowerShell universe, we feel that it can refer to a couple of specific and valuable things that we'll go over in this chapter.

## 6.1 Tools vs. controllers

Think about a hammer. A hammer is a tool, and it's probably one you've at least seen before, even if you've never wielded one. A hammer is self-contained; it's main purpose is to strike other things. A hammer has no context about its life and no clue about its destiny. A hammer may be used one day to help build a house, another day to break a window, and another day to smash your thumb. Sitting alone in a toolbox, a hammer is useless unless someone is swinging it.

You're the one that is going to swing the hammer to strike the nail (or your thumb). Think of the hammer for a second again. You must think about how hard you'll swing it and what you'll hit (be it a nail, window, or thumb). The desired output is to hit the nail and drive it into the wood, producing an audible ping as the nail head is struck. But what happens if you hit the nail at an angle? It will bend or break, having unintended consequences.

What if I told you PowerShell is just like a hammer? It takes input from you and produces output. Sometimes, it works the way you want it to and, sometimes, it doesn't, but PowerShell will always do *exactly* what you tell it to do—nothing more and nothing less. This is the beauty of PowerShell. What PowerShell calls a *command*—a catchall word referring to cmdlets, functions, and other executable artifacts—we call a *tool*. A tool should do one thing and one thing only. That's why we have tools named `Get-Process`, `Start-Process`, `Stop-Process`, and so on—each of them does one thing and one thing only. We don't have a tool called "Manage-Processes," capable of starting, stopping, or listing processes depending on your parameters. Such a super-tool goes against the PowerShell ethos of one tool per single task.

Think about `Stop-Process`. It's no good at all on its own. Like a hammer, it needs to be given context and purpose. It needs to be controlled. The tool gains meaning and purpose when used as part of a controller script.

This chapter is about learning to draw the line between these two equally important kinds of script. There are specific techniques suitable for tools and different ones ideal for controllers. Each set of techniques is designed to reduce your workload, reduce debugging, reduce maintenance, and increase readability and reusability. Knowing which kind of script you're writing will help direct you to the right set of techniques, and that's the key to being a successful scripter and, ultimately, toolmaker!

## 6.2   Thinking about tools

Tools have some important characteristics in the PowerShell world:

- *Tools do one thing, which the verb portion of their name should describe.* It's better to make five small tools that do one thing than one big tool that does five things. Smaller, more tightly scoped tools are easier to write, easier to test, and easier to debug and maintain.

- *Tools don't know where their input data is generated, any more than a hammer knows in advance whether it will be held in hand or duct-taped to some robotic contraption.* Tools accept all input only from their parameters, just as a hammer accepts input only from what's holding its handle. (Yeah, we're playing pretty loose with the metaphor, but you get the idea.) Other tools may be used to create the input and then fed to a tool's parameters.

- *Tools don't know how their output will be used, and they don't care, any more than a hammer cares if it will be hitting a nail or a thumb.* Tools don't worry about making their output pretty—other tools can handle that. Tools don't worry about where their output will go—again, other tools can handle that.

We tend to think about several different types of tools informally. This isn't a strict taxonomy, but it does give you an idea of how they can relate to one another:

- *Input tools*—These tools are designed to create data primarily consumed by other tools. You might write a tool that gets a bunch of computer names from Microsoft Entra ID, for example. `Get` is a common verb for input tool names, but you'll also see `Import` and `ConvertFrom`.

- *Action tools*—These tools usually require additional input before they do something, and that "something" can be anything you imagine. Plenty of commands have verbs like `Set` and `Remove`.

- *Output tools*—These tools are usually designed to take the output of an input tool or an action tool and render it for some specific purpose. They might create a specially formatted data file, render a particular kind of onscreen display, and so on. Verbs such as `Out`, `Format`, `ConvertTo`, and `Export` are common for output tools.

Imagine that you need to write a script that will report the password age of all the service accounts in your environment and format that into a CSV so the Security Information and Event Management (SIEM) tool used by your cybersecurity department can parse logs to see where these accounts are being used. Upper management wants a nice HTML report to display on their video board during the daily operations brief. How many tools do you need to write? You have to start by thinking of the discrete tasks involved, and see what tasks are already solved by a PowerShell tool:

- First, we need to find the command that will get the account password age; in this case, `Get-AdUser` is what we want to use. We'll grab some of the attributes, save that as an array, export it to a CSV, and then do some fun HTML manipulation as well. If you're missing this command, use this one to install it:

```
Install-WindowsFeature -Name "RSAT-AD-PowerShell" `
-IncludeAllSubFeature
```

- We must figure out how to filter based on password age. Fortunately, the native `Where-Object` command can do that, so you have to write a fancy widget to filter this.
- You'll need to convert those results to CSV and save them to a file, and the native `Export-CSV` command can do that for you—no work for you here!
- You'll also need a way to make an HTML report. If the native `ConvertTo-HTML` command isn't sufficient, then the `EnhancedHTML2` module from the Power-Shell Gallery includes `ConvertTo-EnhancedHTML`, which should do the trick. You'll need to learn to use it, but you won't have to code anything.

So, you only need to write one tool for all of that. That's the beauty of the tool-based approach: So many great, generic tools already exist in PowerShell and out in the broader world that you often only need to focus on the stuff that's entirely specific to your environment. Do that correctly, and your custom tools will connect seamlessly to everything that already exists.

But your prospective `Get-ServiceAccountPassword` tool is useless by itself. It needs to be given purpose and context, which means it needs a controller.

> **NOTE** We should point out that you may not find the terms *tool* and *controller* in Microsoft documentation or the greater PowerShell community. For many people, it's just *scripting*. But to truly understand the PowerShell way of automating things, you should keep the concepts of *tool* and *controller* in mind. Many beginning students struggle to write reusable PowerShell code because they're trying to do everything simultaneously. Defining the tool separately from how it will be used is very important.

## 6.3  *Thinking about controllers*

Whereas tools are generic and lack context, controllers are all about context. The purpose of a controller is to put a tool to a specific use in a specific situation. This is a good thing for you because a tool you create can be used in many different scenarios, which is what the controller is about. We don't use command-style, verb-noun names for controllers; we give them friendlier, more English-like names. For example, Password-HistoryReport.ps1 is the script we might create to generate that HTML report of customers who've been inactive for a year or more. That script might be really simple, containing only a single pipeline:

```
Get-ServiceAccountPassword |
Where-Object { $_.passwordlength -lt (Get-Date).AddDays(-365) } |
ConvertTo-HTML |
Out-File \\intranet\www\reports\inactive-customers.html
```

It's not a complex script, and that's the idea. Controllers often *are* simple because they're just stringing together some tools. None of these tools knew beforehand that they'd be involved in creating HTML customer reports, but this controller gave them purpose. We'd probably have another one, PasswordHistoryReportCSVDataFile.ps1, that would take care of generating the required CSV data file. For fun, we might also create DisplayPasswordHistoryReport.ps1, which would query inactive customers and format the output for an attractive onscreen display. It never hurts to go above and beyond!

Like tools, controllers have some specific characteristics:

- *A controller is tied to a context.* It automates a business process, interacts with a human being, or does some other situation-specific thing.
- *A controller often has hardcoded data.* Examples of hardcoded data include a filename that will be read as input or a database connection string that will give the output a place to go.
- *A controller is responsible for putting its output into a particular form, which may not be structured data.* For example, a controller may display information onscreen or send it to a printer. The tool writes objects to the pipeline.
- *Whereas a tool performs a task, a controller solves a problem.* That "problem" is often a business need or management directive.

People often ask about writing "graphical scripts" in PowerShell using either .NET Framework's Windows Forms library or its newer Windows Presentation Foundation (WPF) library. You can do it, and we consider such scripts to be *controllers.* They should contain minimal code and mainly rely on running tools. The PowerShell paradigm is that the commands executed from a graphical controller are the same commands you could run from an interactive console prompt. The graphical scripts merely put those tools to a specific purpose, tied to the eyes and fingers of human beings.

> **Controllers from commands**
>
> If you look at the previous sample controller script that uses our fictitious `Get-ServiceAccountPassword` tool, it's just a PowerShell command. Your "controller" can be you typing a command interactively in the console. This is a great way to ensure your tool does what you intend.
>
> Putting the commands in a controller script saves a ton of typing and makes running your command consistent. A controller script can also be a bit more complex if you need it to be. By using a script file, anyone can run it, and the results will be consistent and predictable.

## 6.4 Comparing tools and controllers

Think about an automotive assembly line. These days, they're largely staffed by specialized robots. One robot paints the car; another one welds two pieces together. Those robots are tools: in a warehouse all by themselves, they're useless. It's when you add a controller—the production line, which places the robots in sequence and coordinates their activities—that you have something useful. Table 6.1 outlines some of the key differences.

**Table 6.1   Tools vs. controllers**

| Tools | Controllers |
|---|---|
| Do one thing and one thing only | Connect multiple tools |
| Accept input on parameters | May have hardcoded input, and may use tools to retrieve data that will be fed to other tools |
| Produce data as objects | May produce any kind of output, including formatted data, special files, and so on |
| Complete a task | Solve a problem or meet a need |
| Often useless or minimally useful on their own | Self-contained |
| Useable across a variety of situations | Used only for a specific situation |

In this book, we'll focus a great deal on creating tools. How they're used is no different from using any other PowerShell command such as `Get-Eventlog`. Anyone who has access to your tools can create their own controller.

## 6.5 Some concrete examples

Let's walk through real-world examples of this tools versus controllers design concept. You'll see little code in these examples, but we'll walk through the thought process behind them.

### 6.5.1  *Emailing users whose passwords are about to expire*

This is a great example, which we'll put some code to later in this book. Say you wanted to send a quick email reminder to users whose passwords were about to expire in a day or two. What's involved there?

Start by getting a list of users with expiring passwords—those whose accounts aren't disabled and don't have a "password doesn't expire" setting. You probably need to calculate exactly when their password expires and filter out anyone whose password wasn't within whatever range you cared about. You then email them all and perhaps log that information to a file for diagnostic purposes.

You have five distinct tools to build, each one performing a single *task* from that overall *process*:

- Get expiring user accounts
- Get password expiration date
- Filter accounts based on the number of days
- Send email
- Create an audit trail

If you did it right, your "controller" script might look like this:

```
Get-EnabledExpiringUser |
Add-ExpiryDataToUser |
Where-Object { $_.DaysToExpire –lt 2 } |
Send-PasswordExpiryMessageToUser |
Export-CSV report.csv
```

Three of those are new tools you need to build, and two are native to PowerShell. You're maybe looking at writing a hundred or so lines of code to build those three tools—and some of them would have been used in other business processes. For example, getting enabled and expiring user accounts could be useful elsewhere. Getting a list of all users and adding their password expiration data could also be useful in other scenarios. Modularizing these tasks as *tools* and then calling them from a controller makes a lot of sense. Remember, the controller doesn't necessarily have to be a script. It could be you running the commands in a PowerShell session. Using a script saves typing and ensures consistency.

### 6.5.2  *Provisioning new users*

This is our classic tools-vs.-controllers example. Think about what goes into provisioning a new user in your organization. You probably have to set up an account, mailbox-enable it, set up a home folder somewhere, maybe add the user to something in Share-Point, and so on. Each of those is a discrete task within the process, and each should be a tool. Many of those tools—such as `New-ADUser`—are provided by Microsoft.

There's an opportunity to be clever here too. For example, *where* do you set up the new home folder? What's your standard business logic? The answer might be the following: "Well, we look at the existing file servers, and we usually don't put more than 1,000 users per home folder file server. So, we find a server with fewer than 1,000 home folders already and use that one. But if the server we pick has less than 75 GB free, then we leave it alone and pick another one." That's a *task*, and it's one you could automate. Perhaps you'd create a Select-UserHomeFolderFileServer tool that does all the analysis and returns a list of eligible servers, and then a New-UserHomeFolder tool that uses the first eligible server to create the new user's home folder on. Those are two discrete tasks and should be two discrete tools.

---

### Let the verb be your guide

One time, we needed to grab a bunch of users from Active Directory. Get-ADUser does that just fine, but we wanted to enrich the user objects with additional data. Specifically, we wanted to add a property that indicated how long it had been since the user account had been used. In some older domains, that requires pinging every domain controller. We also wanted to filter out user accounts that had *never* been used to log on. So, we started thinking about the name such a tool would have.

We always start with the PowerShell documentation on Microsoft Learn (http://mng .bz/XqQG), which lists the official, allowed verbs for command names. In this case, the Add verb seemed like it could work. After all, we were *adding* information to the user objects, and the description for that verb says it means to "[attach] an item to another item." But *adding* doesn't communicate the *filtering* process we also wanted to do. We struggled with it for a while. What about Process as a verb because we're really processing these user objects? Nope, that's not a valid verb. Evaluate, maybe? Nope.

That's when it dawned on us. We were having trouble because our tool was doing *two things*: it enriched an object by adding information and filtered objects out of the processing queue. The existing Where-Object command already does that filtering—we didn't need to duplicate that within another tool.

Once we stopped trying to force the verbs to work, everything made sense. We needed to create one tool to enrich the user objects, and we also needed to use an existing tool to filter out the ones we wanted. Instead of doing two things in one tool, we did one thing—and we were better off for it. Listening to PowerShell's verbs and honoring their intent can help you make better toolmaking decisions.

---

### 6.5.3  *Setting file permissions*

Here's a task that may be a bit trickier: "I want to set a file permission on an entire hierarchy of files, but I need to exclude certain file types." What are the tasks there? This is where it's sometimes helpful to think about how you'd do this manually. And we mean manually, not using the GUI. Like, if you were Windows *itself*, how would you do this?

You start by getting a list of the files. For this, PowerShell has a tool that can recurse through subfolders and even exclude files based on a specification you provide. Then, you need to get their existing permission object or access control list (ACL). Again, PowerShell has a native command to do that. Next, you need to add permission to each ACL. There's a command for that too. So, your "script" might be a complex one-liner in this case. It would be a controller because all the tools you need to use already exist.

> **NOTE** This example raises a good point that's sometimes a hard truth to face: if you don't know much about how Windows (or whatever you're managing) works under the hood, you'll have a hard time automating it in PowerShell. The GUI hides a lot of how Windows works, and PowerShell doesn't; start using PowerShell a lot, and you'll quickly realize how much of an expert you are!

### 6.5.4 Helping the help desk

Suppose your help desk consists mainly of entry-level folks with less experience than you. To help them solve common problems and complete common tasks, you create a set of tools for them. They're not comfortable with command-line tools yet, so you decide to create a GUI for them using WPF or a commercial tool such as PowerShell Studio.

As we've mentioned, a GUI is a form of controller. That means it should have minimal code, that is, zero code beyond what is *needed* to make the GUI work. Clicking a button in the GUI might run a separate *controller script* designed to automate a given process; that script might call on multiple *tools* to accomplish the tasks within that process. This may seem like a lot of layers, but consider these arguments in favor of the approach:

- *GUIs are hard to write and harder to debug.* The less code you have in them, the happier you'll be.
- *GUIs are never the only place where a given task is accomplished.* They should be a way of *triggering* the task, but not the place where the task actually "lives." A GUI that runs a controller script is great because that same script could be run from elsewhere too.
- *A standalone controller script that calls standalone tools is easier to develop and debug.* You can focus on solving one task at a time in your tools, bring them together in the controller script, and then call that from whatever GUI you've built.
- *By separating things into layers, you'll help your help desk get better at their jobs.* As stated by the *I* in GUI, this is an *interface*—a means of accessing functionality. A PowerShell console is another such interface—a command-line interface (CLI). Suppose your help desk can summon functionality from either interface. In that case, you'll be able to slowly move them over to the CLI, which will ultimately offer them more flexibility and control as their experience grows. Building your functionality to be interface-independent is a great idea.

## 6.6 Control more

One last thought on this whole tools-vs.-controllers idea is that you shouldn't forget all the other tools you have at your disposal. Sure, this is a PowerShell book, so we've been looking at PowerShell commands and concepts. But if there's a non-PowerShell tool—perhaps a Microsoft Windows Resource Kit Tool or a vendor-supplied command-line tool—and it makes sense to use, then use it. There's no requirement that your controller script can only use PowerShell.

Imagine that, for compliance purposes, you must create a report for each server in your domain from the `MSInfo32.exe` command-line tool. What tools might you need to use? Perhaps `Get-ADComputer` from the Active Directory module can be used to get the computer accounts. You might want to ping the computer first with `Test-Connection`, and then, if the computer is online, run the `MSInfo32` command. Your boss could even ask that you record the server names that aren't online in a separate text file. In the end, you might not need to create any new tools, but rather a controller script to pull together this collection of PowerShell and non-PowerShell tools. It might look something like this:

```
#GetComplianceInfo.ps1
Get-ADComputer -filter * | foreach {
  if (Test-Connection $_.name -quiet) {
     msinfo32 /computer "\\$($_.name)" /report "c:\work\
å $($_.name)-msinfo.txt"
  }
  else {
     $_.name | out-file c:\logs\offline.txt -Append
  }
}
```

## 6.7   *Lab*

This chapter should have you thinking about the most important top-level element of scripting: what kind of script to make. Although we haven't explicitly stated it, often, the first step in scripting doesn't involve writing any code but rather writing down what you need to accomplish in a very granular fashion. If we did our job in this chapter, you're starting to think about *tools* and *controllers* in the right way—the PowerShell way—and you're beginning to see how they work together to accomplish business tasks. If you can completely embrace the distinction between the two and respect their individual purposes, then you'll be set to succeed in PowerShell scripting.

With that in mind, let's see how much you understand about what we've been trying to explain and demonstrate in this chapter. Break out a pencil and paper, and figure out what tools you'd need to accomplish these business problems. Identify those you might have to create and those that already exist. Finally, draft at least an outline of how you might use them. This doesn't have to be actual code:

1  You need to review departmental shares and identify files that haven't been modified in over a year. Your boss wants an Excel spreadsheet that shows the file path, the size of the file, when it was created and last modified, and the file owner. Here's a tip: don't worry about automating Excel. All you need is a CSV file that can be opened and saved in Excel.

**2** You get a list of user accounts to be terminated every week. Your manual process is to disable the user account in Active Directory. Add a comment to the user account indicating the date terminated, add the user account to the Terminated-Users group, and email the removed user's manager.

We aren't supplying any answers or solutions here because your process is more important than the end result.

## Summary

This chapter covered the core concepts of tools and controllers in PowerShell scripting. By distinguishing between these two elements, you should now grasp the importance of leveraging tools for specific actions and controllers for orchestrating these tools within a broader context to address business needs effectively. We used various illustrative scenarios, such as user provisioning and file permission settings, to emphasize the modular nature of PowerShell scripting and the value of utilizing existing tools. Furthermore, we discussed using graphical interfaces as controllers to underscore the versatility of PowerShell automation. Ultimately, your takeaway should be the significance of thoughtful planning and granularity in script development to achieve success in PowerShell scripting endeavors, along with the essential understanding of PowerShell's underlying mechanisms for effective automation.

# Scripts and security

Let's take a few minutes and talk about security. We covered this in the predecessor book (*Learn PowerShell in a Month of Lunches, Fourth Edition,* Manning, 2022), but we want to discuss this in depth. From our experiences in the field, the instant knee-jerk reaction is that PowerShell should be disabled on every desktop and server on the face of the planet because of how powerful and straightforward it is. Major corporations have a company-wide ban on using PowerShell for this very reason.

Viruses and malware are becoming increasingly sophisticated and harder and harder to detect. The security engineers for the top companies are good at identifying new attack vectors and helping fix the problems. Still, there are more bad guys out there with so much free time that they are finding vulnerabilities and attack vectors faster than they can be patched or fixed (this is why it's essential to patch your systems!). The good news is that many bad actors use PowerShell as the attack vector. You're probably wondering how in the world this is good news. Microsoft and a few trusted community members helped strengthen the security features built into PowerShell. Think of it as an in-depth defense program with multiple layers of security in place. PowerShell isn't antimalware and isn't intended to protect you should malware become present in your environment. Understanding PowerShell's security goals is essential so that you don't overestimate them.

## 7.1 Security is number one

First things first, PowerShell will do what you tell it to do. I write a script to `Get-Process | Stop-Process`, it will do just that. No warnings, no confirmation, and no "Are you sure you want to do this?" prompts—it will simply go off and execute the command. That said, there isn't a way to stop a user from purposely running code they copied and pasted from the internet. That is an HR problem, not a technology problem. But we can put safeguards in place to stop a code's unintentional/unattended execution, which may or may not be malicious. Microsoft's primary concern is the *accidental* or *unintentional* execution of a PowerShell script.

But you'll be creating tools and scripts for yourself and others with the intent of executing (safely) in your organization. To do that, you must know the script security concepts discussed here.

---

### PowerShell as a malware vector

There's little doubt that some bad actors consider PowerShell a convenient way to introduce malware into your environment. But there's something massively important you need to remember: anything attackers can do in PowerShell, they can do without PowerShell just as quickly.

PowerShell is a wrapper around the .NET Framework at its deepest level. If PowerShell didn't exist, those underlying things would still exist, and attackers would use them instead. Even if your organization completely locks down PowerShell so it can't be used, that's just a false sense of security because all the underlying functionality is still available to an attacker.

PowerShell's original goal was to provide an easier way to use things such as the component object model (COM), .NET Framework, and Windows Management Instrumentation (WMI); PowerShell doesn't add any new functionality to your environment. It just adds new *ways of using* the same functionality that's been there all along. Therefore, locking down PowerShell doesn't lock down anything except a way to use something—the "something" is still there.

It's like telling someone your house can't be accessed because you've buried all the door keys. The keys were never the only means of accessing your home. They're just the most convenient way. Picking a lock, kicking in a door, and breaking a window are still on the table—only, with the keys buried, *you'll* have to use those less convenient means too.

As product team member Lee Holmes famously repeats, "If you're pwned, you're pwned." If you've got a bad actor in the environment, you're already in a bad spot—PowerShell is the least of your concerns. Keeping the bad actors *out* should be your goal, and limiting what they can *get to*, should they break in, should be your second goal. From a security perspective, simply locking down the tools they might use is a red herring.

---

## 7.2 Execution policy

By default, on client OSs, PowerShell won't run any PowerShell script files, no matter who you are or what permissions you have. These files have a .ps1, .psm1, .pssc, or .ps1xml extension. A machine-wide execution policy controls this behavior. Technically, there are some fine-grained exceptions, but those don't matter for our purposes. Policies only need to be set once, and the effect is immediate. To discover your current setting, run `Get-ExecutionPolicy`. You should see one of the values listed in table 7.1.

**Table 7.1  Execution policies**

| Policy | Description |
|---|---|
| Restricted | This is the default setting for Windows clients. It means no PowerShell script files will be executed, including profile scripts. |
| AllSigned | This requires any PowerShell script file containing a valid digital signature from a code-signing certificate issued by a trusted certificate authority. We'll cover script signing in chapter 21. |
| RemoteSigned | PowerShell will run any script created locally, signed or not, but will require any other script to be digitally signed. This is the default server setting starting with Windows Server 2012 R2. |
| Unrestricted | PowerShell will run any script with very few questions asked. You might get a prompt when running a script that PowerShell detects as something downloaded from outside your machine. This is the default setting for UNIX and Linux. |
| Bypass | PowerShell will run anything with no questions asked. This policy implies that you've taken your steps to ensure script safety and integrity. |
| Undefined | No execution policy can be found. PowerShell will move down the scope list and use the first effective policy it finds. We'll discuss this further in a moment. |

Remember, you only need to allow script execution where you intend to run scripts, which should be your desktop or a centralized management server. You should be able to leave servers at their default settings and only modify your local client settings. You might also consider leaving the policy as Restricted on end-user desktops unless you need them running scripts.

**TRY IT NOW**  What is your execution policy set to? Run the command Get-ExecutionPolicy to find out.

It's recommended that you set the execution policy via Group Policy. This will ensure that each machine in your environment gets the correct execution policy you and your company have decided to use. Read the about_execution_policies help topic for more details on these policies.

**What about servers?**
By default, PowerShell disallows script execution on client computers. Those are the ones most typically operated by less technically sophisticated users surfing the web and accessing email.

Servers, however, are different animals. Users shouldn't have interactive access to them (except Remote Desktop servers, which are more of a multiclient computer than a server in this sense). Even administrators shouldn't be interactively logging on to servers (that's right, we said what we said). Stop deploying servers with the Servers with Desktop Experience option, and please start using the Server Core option! Therefore, on a server OS, modern versions of PowerShell default to allow script execution often because of the server's configuration tools, such as Server Manager or Windows Admin Center—PowerShell is required for them to do their job.

This gets back to PowerShell's security goal: to *slow down* an *unintentional* script execution by an *uninformed* user. *Uninformed* and *unintentional* shouldn't be happening on a server; if they are, you have what we refer to as a "human resources problem."

So, what do *we* use? For obvious reasons, Microsoft won't tell you exactly which setting to use in your environment. But you and the rest of your team must sit down and discuss the best route to go. Microsoft made specific default settings for a reason, so maybe that is where you should start.

### 7.2.1  Execution scope

PowerShell's execution policy can be set at one of three scope levels, in this order of precedence:

- *LocalMachine*—Applies to the entire machine and is stored in the configuration JSON file at C:\Program Files\PowerShell\7\PowerShell.config.json.
- *CurrentUser*—Applies only to the current user and is stored in the current user configuration JSON file in your Documents folder (\Documents\PowerShell), assuming it isn't undefined.
- *Process*—Controls the current session and is stored in the system variable `$env:PSExecutionPolicyPreference`. This setting will go away once the PowerShell session is closed.

The setting remains effective for as long as your PowerShell session is open. You can set this by specifying an execution policy switch when you run PWSH.exe. This demonstrates how easy it is for an informed, intentional user to get around the execution policy—no matter what you do elsewhere, someone can run the shell with `Bypass` if they want to.

These policies are applied in the order we listed them, even if a more restrictive policy is set lower. For example, scripts will still be executed if you've set the current user policy as `RemoteSigned`, but the machine policy is `Restricted`. From a practical point of view, setting a machine policy should be sufficient for most organizations. We feel the other settings are for special-use cases and exceptions.

> **NOTE** Before you get yourself worked up, if someone or something can make an unauthorized execution policy change, you're already in trouble. If it's some breach, the intruder can already run other arbitrary code outside of PowerShell, and changing your execution policy is the least of your concerns.

If nothing else, this order of application demonstrates that PowerShell's execution policy was never intended to be a security boundary. We think of the execution policy more like the little hinged plastic shield covering the Big Red Button that launches the nuclear missiles. The execution policy, like that shield, is meant to get in the way of some idiot who leans their elbow in the wrong place at the wrong time. It's not intended to stop someone from taking deliberate action, nor is it designed to stop an intruder who breaks into the missile silo with bad intentions. The intruder can flip back the cover as quickly as an authorized user, meaning the cover isn't a security mechanism. The security mechanisms would be card-keyed doors and armed guards, not the little button cover.

### 7.2.2   Getting your policies

To see your current execution policy settings, use `Get-ExecutionPolicy`:

```
PS C:\> Get-ExecutionPolicy
Restricted
```

The cmdlet will return the effective policy based on your scope settings. In other words, it will return the policy that the current shell instance will obey, regardless of where that setting came from. You can also get the settings for all scopes like this:

```
PS C:\> Get-ExecutionPolicy -List
        Scope ExecutionPolicy
        ----- ---------------
MachinePolicy      Undefined
   UserPolicy      Undefined
      Process      Undefined
  CurrentUser      Undefined
 LocalMachine      Restricted
```

The *policy* scopes would be set via Group Policy, which we're not using. In addition, it's worth noting that this list *isn't in order of application*—the order of this list isn't meaningful. In this situation, the `Restricted` policy will apply, which we can verify:

```
PS C:\> C:\work\test.ps1
C:\work\test.ps1 : File C:\work\test.ps1 cannot be loaded because running
scripts is disabled on this system. For more information, see
about_Execution_Policies at https:/go.microsoft.com/fwlink/?LinkID=135170.
```

Naturally, we need to make a change if we want our scripts to run.

### 7.2.3   Setting an execution policy

The cmdlet to modify the policy is `Set-ExecutionPolicy`. You need to specify a policy setting and, optionally, a scope. The default is the local machine. To run this command, you must have permission to modify the relevant scope. In other words, if you're trying to alter the local machine setting, you need to run the shell with the As Administrator option because the local machine setting is stored in the machine configuration JSON file located in Program Files, which only administrators can write to. Note that you can't change either of the Group Policy–managed settings this way; you need to—obviously—use Group Policy for that. You also can't change the process scope's execution policy; that must be established when you run PowerShell, not once it's already running and you're inside it:

```
PS C:\> Set-ExecutionPolicy -ExecutionPolicy RemoteSigned
Execution Policy Change
The Execution Policy helps protect you from scripts that you do not trust.
Changing the Execution Policy might expose you to the security risks
described in the about_Execution_Policies help topic at
https:/go.microsoft.com/fwlink/?LinkID=135170. Do you want to change the
Execution Policy?
[Y] Yes  [A] Yes to All  [N] No  [L] No to All  [S] Suspend  [?] Help
(default is "N"):
```

Answer Y at the prompt to make the change. The change is immediate. Note that a normal user can change the execution policy for themselves or the process; that's why none of this is considered a security boundary.

## 7.3 PowerShell isn't the default application

Remember, these settings prevent PowerShell scripts from accidental or unintentional execution. So, what happens when Missy clicks the attachment in her email to check the shipping status of her Amazon order? If it's a PowerShell script, it won't execute automatically. By default, the associated application for a .ps1 file is in Notepad, not PowerShell. When Missy clicks because she can't help herself, the script will be displayed in Notepad. Sure, you can change this association, and some scripting editors will associate themselves with .ps1 and the other filename extensions for script editing. This also applies to any PowerShell file in Windows Explorer: double-clicking will open the file in Notepad.

It's possible to create an Execute association with these filename extensions (as opposed to an Edit association). Doing so would make the files execute when double-clicked. We think this is an awful idea, by the way.

## 7.4 Running scripts

Finally, assuming you're configured to run scripts, you must provide the path to the script file, even if you're in the same directory. For example, suppose we have a test script in the current directory that we try to run:

```
PS C:\work> test
test: The term 'test' is not recognized as the name of a cmdlet, function,
script file, or operable program. Check the spelling of the name, or if a
the path was included; verify that the path is correct and try again.
```

Nope. This is intended to prevent *command hijacking*, where someone or something puts a malicious script in the folder that uses a common command name such as dir. You need to tell PowerShell you intend to run a script:

```
PS C:\work> .\test
Handles  NPM(K)     PM(K)      WS(K)     CPU(s)     Id  SI ProcessName
-------  ------    -----      -----     ------     --  -- -----------
   2517     276  1146832    1082780   2,365.03   1328   1 dwm
      0       0     1884     748852     115.84   5408   0 Memory Compress…
   1538     208   992756     353264   4,789.05   8284   1 firefox
    483      62   215324     218868     169.59  12232   1 slack
   1999     111   202616     199176     945.55   4284   1 WINWORD
```

You aren't required to include the file extension, but it never hurts. That way, there's no mistaking what script you intend to run. If you use tab completion, PowerShell will add the filename extension anyway.

> **You are part of the security system**
>
> Keep in mind that you are a part of the overall system when it comes to security. "But we have administrators who can't be trusted to know when a script is safe to run!" Well, that's again what we call an HR problem—those people shouldn't be DevOps engineers.
>
> That's where command hijacking comes into play. It was a real problem in MS-DOS back in the day due to how it prioritized things. If you ran `Dir`, it would first look for batch files with that name, then executables, and then internal commands—or something like that. It was possible, in other words, to drop in an executable or batch with the *same name* as an internal command and trick people into running the executable or batch instead of the command.
>
> With PowerShell, the trick is more obvious. `Dir` is almost always[a] going to run `Get-ChildItem`, whereas `./Dir` would run `Dir.ps1` from the current directory. But *you* have to know the difference. The security "protection" doesn't work if you don't know the difference or if you ignore it. You can still be tricked if you're not vigilant because *you* are integral to what makes the security work.
>
> ---
> [a] It's possible to make `Dir` run something other than `Get-ChildItem`. It's even easy. Just redefine the alias to run another command, or load an alternate command named `Get-ChildItem`. It'd be incredibly easy, for example, for a piece of malware to inject this into your PowerShell profile script, which is, after all, a plain-text document located in your personal Documents folder that you obviously have full rights to. It runs every time you open the shell, and you'd never know anything had gone wrong. That's one argument for using the `AllSigned` execution policy—injecting stuff into your profile would break the signature on it, causing an error when you opened the shell. Provided your code-signing certificate wasn't installed locally (which would be deeply inconvenient), or you password-protected it (better idea), the injection couldn't re-sign the script.

## 7.5    Recommendations

What do we typically recommend when it comes to execution policy? You may be surprised:

- We suggest using `AllSigned` in cases where certificates will be used to control script releases. This isn't a security thing so much as a procedural thing; your company decides that the signature in the script will certify the script as being ready for production. This also helps clamp down on profile-script injection, which we described in the sidebar in the previous section. `AllSigned` can also be helpful on client computers where you need scripts to run (otherwise, stick with `Restricted`) and where you want to impose limitations on which scripts your users can run. Remember that a user running a script still *can't* do anything they don't have permission to do and that a script isn't the only way malware can take advantage of your users. This isn't a security thing—it's a minor hurdle to stop someone from accidentally doing something they might regret.

- We tend to use `RemoteSigned` in most cases. It's a good balance between inconvenience and protection against accidental stupidity. Scripts downloaded through a Microsoft application such as Internet Explorer, Edge, or Outlook will be marked as remote by the application, meaning PowerShell won't run them without prompting the user. Of course, this isn't a *security* feature—it's just an extra hurdle. We all know that when confronted with an "Are you sure?" prompt, almost all users reflexively answer Yes, so this isn't intended to *stop* anyone or make them think twice. At most, it makes them think 1.1 times.

- We don't see that much practical difference between `RemoteSigned` and `Unrestricted`, except that *most* scripts accessed via a universal naming convention (UNC) will prompt under `RemoteSigned` and not under `Unrestricted`.

- We suggest `Bypass` when you're not using `AllSigned` for one of the reasons we've stated here and when you don't want the sometimes false sense of security that `RemoteSigned` and `Unrestricted` can present. Using `Bypass` says, "Hey, I know this execution policy isn't a security layer per se; I'm confident enough in my other security measures, such as strict access control, that I don't even want to use this because I'm afraid *some* people might *perceive* it to be a security layer, and I want to remove that option from their minds."

Here's why that last bullet is important: many so-called information security "professionals" won't take the time to understand PowerShell's execution policy. Here's their thought process:

1 In college, we learned that scripts were terrible for security.
2 The execution policy lets me shut down scripting.
3 Malware might not need scripting, but "defense in depth" means I shut down as much as possible.
4 Therefore, we'll use `Restricted` for our execution policy.

This thought process misses the idea that any malware author can bypass the `Restricted` execution policy with two brain cells rubbed together. We challenge these "professionals" by asking, "Okay, how would you protect the environment if we forced you to set the execution policy to `Bypass`?" Their answers range from outright proper—"Make sure our firewalls are multilayered and that our antimalware defenses are updated and multilayered"—to the outrageous—"Unplug all the power cords and run for the hills!"

Take the execution policy off the table, so to speak, as a security layer (because it isn't one), and start thinking about actual security policies.

## Summary

The settings surrounding script execution in PowerShell are intended to be as restrictive as possible out of the box. Any changes you make will only relax these settings. You should consider other typical Windows best practices such as least-use privilege, email filtering, and good file security. You'll want to use PowerShell scripts—that's why you're reading this book. Your job is to make doing so as safe and secure as possible. Hopefully, we've now given you some guidance in that direction. Your action plan for this chapter is to figure out how you'll apply these ideas in your organization.

# Part 2

Welcome to our scripting journey's dynamic and hands-on segment—Building a PowerShell Script. In this part, we seamlessly transition from foundational concepts to practical implementation, guiding you through the step-by-step process of crafting robust PowerShell scripts. From immersing yourself in the importance of design in chapter 8 to starting your scripting journey by minimizing bugs and errors in chapter 9, subsequent chapters 10 to 16 propel you to new heights in script development. You'll progress to constructing basic functions and script modules, dive deeper into advanced functions, and explore the power of objects as script output. Then, you'll achieve proficiency in using various streams for input and output, master the art of documentation through comments, and navigate the challenges of errors while gaining insights into dealing with them effectively. Concluding this part is chapter 16, where you fill out a manifest, understanding its significance in ensuring your scripts are well-defined and ready for deployment. As you progress through these chapters, you'll build practical scripting skills and gain a deeper understanding of the strategic thinking behind effective PowerShell script development. So, roll up your sleeves and dive into the code, and let's build powerful PowerShell scripts together!

# Always design first 8

Most of our scripts start as a simple one-line command to do a thing, such as creating a new user. The script will read from a CSV, make the new users, and fill in all the information you received from HR. You save the script in your C: drive somewhere and move on to the next fire.

Does this sound familiar? There are two types of scripters and toolmakers in the world: those who plan and those who shoot from the hip. Our goal by the end of the book (hopefully even this chapter) is to make a tool designer. Look at it from the process in reverse. What is the desired outcome, and how do I get there? Then, fill in the blanks from there.

In this chapter, we'll lay out some of the core PowerShell tool design principles to help you stay on the path of "Toolmaking Righteousness." To be clear, we're building on what we laid out in part 1 of this book. Now, we're ready to provide some more concrete examples.

## 8.1 Tools do one thing

If you've ever heard James, Don, or Jeff talk about toolmaking or scripting, you've heard each of us get on our soapbox and yell from the top of the rafters that a script should perform a single task. It doesn't create the Active Directory user (AD user) and an M365 mailbox—that is two tasks and should thus be separated. This has been the design of PowerShell since the beginning. Look at all the commands that ship with PowerShell natively; they do one thing. Let's look at `Get-Service`, it doesn't stop or start them. It retrieves information about the service(s) and returns the data to you. If you want to stop the service, use a different `Stop-Service` command.

This concept is one we see newcomers violate the most. For example, we'll see folks build a command with a `-ComputerName` parameter for accepting a remote machine name and a `-FilePath` parameter so they can alternately read computer names from a file. From PowerShell's perspective and ours, that's dead wrong because it means the tool is doing two things instead of just one. A correct design to follow the paradigm would be to stick with the `-ComputerName` parameter and let it accept strings (computer names) from the pipeline. You could also feed it names from a file using a `-ComputerName (Get-Content servers.txt)` parenthetical construct, or you could define the `-ComputerName` parameter to accept input by value:

```
Get-Content servers.txt | Get-ServerInfo
```

The `Get-Content` command exists for the sole purpose of getting data from a file, so why should you create something that does that? Spend time on the important things, and stop reinventing the wheel. The good folks at Microsoft spent a lot of time producing meaningful PowerShell commands.

Let's explore that antipattern for a moment. Here's an example of using a completely fake command (meaning, don't try this at home) in two different ways:

```
# Specify three computer names
Get-CompanyStuff -ComputerName ONE,TWO,THREE
# Specify a file containing computer names
Get-CompanyStuff -FilePath ./names.txt
```

That approach overcomplicates the tool, making it harder to write, harder to debug, harder to test, and harder to maintain. We'd go with this approach to provide the same effect in a simpler tool:

```
# Specify three computer names
Get-CompanyStuff -ComputerName ONE,TWO,THREE
# Specify a file containing computer names
Get-CompanyStuff -ComputerName (Get-Content ./names.txt)
# Or if you were smart in making the tool...
Get-Content ./names.txt | Get-CompanyStuff
```

Those patterns do a much better job of mimicking how PowerShell's core commands work. But let's explore one more antipattern: "But I have the computer names in a specially formatted file that only I know how to read." Folks will convince themselves that this is okay:

```
# Specify three computer names
Get-CompanyStuff -ComputerName ONE,TWO,THREE
# Specify a file containing computer names
Get-CompanyStuff -FilePath ./names.dat
```

> **TIP** Did you know that PowerShell can't read a .DAT file natively? This was introduced in PowerShell 6.

## 8.2 Tools are testable

Another thing to bear in mind is that—if you're trying to make tools like a real pro—you'll want to create automated unit tests for your tools. We'll get into how that's done in chapter 20. There is a huge debate in the PowerShell community regarding testing. Some community members say you should write your test first and then write the code after the fact. This ensures that you're working toward your result. The other half says that you should get your code working correctly first, and then write your tests to ensure it keeps working correctly once you add new functionality.

We can't tell you which method is correct because it's a personal preference you must decide on. But from a design perspective, you want to make sure you're designing tools are, in fact, testable. Again, one way to do that is to focus on tightly scoped tools that do just one thing. The fewer pieces of functionality a tool introduces, the fewer things and permutations you'll have to test. The fewer logic branches within your code, the easier it will be to thoroughly test your code using automated unit tests.

For example, let's say you're tasked with creating a new process for onboarding new employees. You could create a monolithic 100+ line script that will read the CSV from HR, create a login name that fits your company standards, check AD to see if that name already exists, create the user in AD with all the information you received from HR, create the user's mailbox in Microsoft 365, add the user to SharePoint online groups, and so on. You can see where this is going. Now, here's the bad news: this is the exact thing we're talking about. This script does way too many things and needs to be broken out into four different scripts, as shown in figure 8.1.

**Figure 8.1  Breaking out a script into multiple parts**

You also want to avoid building functionality into your tools that will be difficult to test. For example, you might decide to implement some error logging in a tool. That's great—but if that logging is going to a SQL Server database or a SIM tool, it will be trickier to test and make sure the logging is working as desired. Logging to a file might be easier because a file would be more accessible to check. Easier still would be to write a *separate tool* that handles logging. You could then test that tool independently and *use it* in your other tools. This gets back to the idea of having each tool do one thing, and one thing only, as a good design pattern.

## 8.3    *Tools are flexible*

You want to design tools that can be used in various scenarios. This often means wiring up parameters to accept pipeline input. For example, suppose you write a tool named `Set-MachineStatus` that changes some settings on a computer. You might specify a `-ComputerName` parameter to accept computer names. Will it accept one computer name or many? Where will those computer names come from? Always assume there will be more than one computer name, if you can, and don't worry about where they come from. From a design perspective, you want to enable a variety of approaches.

It can help to sit down and write some examples of using the command that you *intend to work*. These can become help-file examples later (covered in chapter 14), but in the design stage, they can help ensure you're designing to allow all of them. For example, you might want to be able to support these usage patterns:

```
Get-Content names.txt | Set-MachineStatus
Get-ADComputer -filter * | Select -Expand Name | Set-MachineStatus
Get-ADComputer -filter * | Set-MachineStatus
Set-MachineStatus -ComputerName (Get-Content names.txt)
```

That third example will require some careful design because you're not going to be able to pipe an AD computer object to the same `-ComputerName` parameter that also accepts a `String` object from `Get-Content`! You may have identified a need for two parameter sets, perhaps one using `-ComputerName <string[]>` and another using `-InputObject <ADComputer>`, to accommodate both scenarios. Creating two parameter sets will make the coding and the automated unit testing a bit harder—so you'll need to decide whether the tradeoff is worth it. Will that third example be used so frequently that it justifies the extra coding and test development, or will it be a rare enough scenario to exclude it and instead rely on a similar second example?

The point is that every design decision you make will affect your tool's code, its unit tests, and so on. It's worth thinking about those decisions up front, which is why it's called the *design phase*!

## 8.4    *Tools look native*

Finally, be careful with tool and parameter names. We went over this in part 1, but it's worth repeating because we see people get "creative" all the time. Tools should always adopt the standard PowerShell *verb-noun* pattern and should only use the most appropriate verb from the list returned by `Get-Verb`. Microsoft also publishes that list on Microsoft Learn (http://mng.bz/A8rE); the online list includes incorrect variations and explanations that you can use to check yourself. Don't beat yourself up *too* hard over fine distinctions between approved verbs, such as the difference between Get and Read. If you check out that website, you'll realize that `Get-Content` should probably be `Read-Content`; it's likely a distinction Microsoft came up with *after* `Get-Content` was already in the wild.

We also recommend that you get in the habit of using a short prefix on your command's noun. For example, if you work for Globomantics, Inc., you might design commands named Get-GloboSystemStatus rather than just Get-SystemStatus. The prefix helps prevent your command name from conflicting with those written by others and will make it easier to discover and identify commands and tools created for your organization.

> **NOTE**  One reason we went on about native patterns in part 1 of this book is that they're so important. Don't ever forget that the existing commands, particularly the core ones authored by the PowerShell team at Microsoft, represent their vision for how PowerShell works. Break with that vision at your peril!

Parameter names should also follow native PowerShell patterns. Whenever you need a parameter, look at a bunch of native PowerShell commands to see what parameter name they use for similar purposes. For example, if you needed to accept computer names, you'd use `-ComputerName` (notice it's singular!) and not some variation like "MachineName". If you need a filename, that's usually `-FilePath` or `-Path` on most native commands.

> ### The verb quandary
> One area where you can get a bit wound up is in choosing the correct verb for your command name. Honestly, Microsoft probably has too many verbs to choose from. Although we're sure someone in the company had a clear idea of their differences, that hasn't always been communicated well to the PowerShell public. For example, if you're writing a command that will retrieve information from a SQL Server database, is the command name Get-MyWhatever-Data or Read-My-WhateverData? The company offers guidance, stating, "The `Get` verb is used to retrieve a resource, such as a file. The `Read` verb is used to get information from a source, such as a file." This implies `Get` would be used to *get a file*, meaning an object representing the file itself, whereas `Read` would be used to retrieve *the file's contents*. Although `Get-Content` is a thing, Microsoft didn't even take its own advice.
>
> Our advice? Do what seems most consistent with whatever's already in PowerShell. If you're truly stuck, post a question in the forums at PowerShell.Org to get a little feedback from experienced pros.

## 8.5   *For example*

Before you can even start making design decisions, you must look at the business requirements. Then, try to translate those business requirements to usage examples so it's more apparent to you and your team how a tool might be used. If other stakeholders are involved—such as the people who might consume this tool once it's finished (i.e., help desk)—you can get them to sign off on this functional specification so that we can go into the design phase with clear, mutual expectations for the new tool. In addition, try to capture *problem statements* that this new tool is meant to solve because those sometimes offer a clearer business perspective than a specification that someone else may have written. Let's consider an example now.

Business Problem: We have a lot of different computers deployed in our company, which have other hardware vendors, different versions of Windows, different configurations, and so on. When users call the help desk, it's often difficult for the technicians to figure out what kind of computer they're dealing with. Users aren't always aware of details such as model numbers, OS versions, installed RAM, and so on. We have a configuration management system the help desk can check, but it isn't always up to date or accurate. We likely want a tool that the help desk can use to quickly query a computer, if it's online, and get some essential information about its OS and hardware configuration. In some cases, we have downtime and can query that information from multiple computers and double-check the accuracy of the configuration management system. The help desk can update that database if it needs updating.

> ### Be careful of context.
>
> When you start designing tools, making business-level problem statements is fine. That's a large part of what the design is for, after all! Statements like, "When users call the help desk, it's often difficult for the technicians to figure out what kind of computer they're dealing with," are fantastic.
>
> Stating desired outcomes, such as when we wrote, "We'd like a tool that the help desk can use to query a computer quickly," is also fine—it defines a business need. But not every business statement must be something you try to solve with a *single* tool or command. You may need a suite of tools, which could be packaged as a module . . . but we're getting ahead of ourselves.
>
> We've discussed the need for tools to be as detached as possible from a particular context. Yet, our business statement has provided a very clear context: "We want technicians to query things." That context leads to certain assumptions, like, "The output needs to be human-readable," and, maybe, "Our technicians aren't that experienced, so a GUI will be needed for them to operate this thing." This is good background information, but it doesn't mean you'll solve it all with a single tool.
>
> Our complete business statement implies creating a tool to retrieve data and perhaps a controller script to provide the help desk with an input/output interface. The *tool* doesn't need to worry about how the technician uses it or what the technician will see; the *controller* can worry about those context-specific things and use the *tool* under the hood to get the data.
>
> *Never* lose track of the tool/controller design pattern. Get used to reading business statements that will ultimately need tools *and* controllers, and understand which elements of a business solution will be best solved by each type of script.

Taking the last part of the previous sidebar to heart would lead us to more detailed questions, asking for specifics about what the tool needs to query. Suppose the answer came back as follows:

- Computer hostname
- Manufacturer
- Model
- OS version and build number
- Service pack version, if any
- Installed RAM
- Processor type
- Processor socket count
- Total core count
- Free space on the system drive (usually C:, but not always)

That's fine—we know we can get all that information somehow. We know we're going to write a tool called `Get-MachineInfo`, and it will probably have at least a `-Computer-Name` parameter that accepts one or more computer names as strings. Thinking ahead, we might also start making notes for an `Update-OrgCMDatabase` command, which could consume the output of `Get-MachineInfo` and automatically update the organization's configuration management database. Nobody *asked* for that, but it's implied in the business problem statements, and we can see them asking for it once we deliver the first tool—"Hey, because the tool gets all the data, is there any way we can have it just push that into the CM database?" We'll keep that in mind as we design the first tool—we want to ensure that the tool is outputting something that could be easily consumed by another command sometime in the future.

We'll assume that some computers won't respond to the query, so we'll design a way to deal with that situation. We'll also assume that we have some old versions of Windows out there, so we'll make sure the tool is designed to work with as old a version of Windows as possible, as well as the latest and greatest.

Our design usage examples might be pretty simple:

```
Get-MachineInfo -ComputerName CLIENT
Get-MachineInfo -ComputerName CLIENTA,CLIENTB
Get-MachineInfo -ComputerName (Get-Content names.txt)
Get-MachineInfo -ComputerName (Get-ADComputer -id CLIENTA |
Select -Expand name)
Get-Content names.txt | Get-MachineInfo
Get-ADComputer -id CLIENTA | Select -Expand name | Get-MachineInfo
```

The second chunk of examples will all require the same design elements, whereas the last chunk of examples will all be made possible by another set of design elements. That's no problem. The output of these should be pretty deterministic. Given a specific set of inputs, we should get the same output, which will make this a fairly straightforward design for which to write unit tests. Our command is only doing one thing with very few parameters, which gives us a good feeling about the design's tight scope.

> ### The beauty of usage examples in design
>
> Stating usage examples as part of your tool design is a *wonderful* idea. For one thing, it helps you ensure you're not bleeding from *tool* design into *controller* design. If your usage examples start to take up 10 sheets of paper and look complicated, then you know you're probably not scoping your tool's functionality tightly enough, and you might be looking at several instruments instead of just one.
>
> Usage examples can also become part of your eventual help file. There's a school of thought that you should *start* tool design by writing the help file. The help file can then exist as a functional specification, which you code to. Similarly, writing usage examples can help support *test-driven development* (TDD), in which you write auto-mated tests first to sort of specify how your tool should work, and then you write the code.

Writing usage examples first can also help you avoid bad design decisions. If you're struggling to write all the examples you need, and you still keep coming up with an overly long or overly complicated list, then you know you're on the wrong track entirely. It might be worth sitting down with a colleague to try and refactor the whole project to keep it simpler.

We'd return that set of examples to the team and ask what they think. Almost invariably, doing so will generate questions:

- How will we know if a machine fails?
- Will the tool keep going?
- Will the tool log that information anywhere?

Okay—we need to evolve the design a bit. We know that we need to keep going in the event of a failure and give the user the option to log failures to, perhaps, a text file:

```
Get-MachineInfo -ComputerName ONE,TWO,BUCKLE,SHOE `
➥  -LogFailuresToPath errorlog.txt
```

Provided the team is happy with a text file as the error log, we can include that in the design. If they wanted something more complicated—the option to log to a database or an event log—then we'd design a separate logging tool to do all of that. For the sake of argument, though, let's say they're okay with the text file. At this stage, we don't figure out *how* we'll do all that; right now, we're just designing the thing.

Let's say that the team is satisfied with these additions and that we have our desired usage examples locked down. We can now get into the coding. But before we do, why don't you take a stab at your design exercise?

**Designing sets of commands**

The foregoing discussion is great when you're writing a command to do something self-contained, such as retrieving management information from multiple computers. There's a slightly different discussion, however, when you start writing sets of commands to help manage a large system.

For example, suppose you want to write a set of commands to help manage a customer information-tracking application. What commands might you need to write?

Start by inventorying the *nouns* in the system. What are the things that the system works with? Users? Customers? Orders? Items in an order? Addresses? Write down that list somewhere.

Next, look at each noun, and decide what the system can *do* with it. For users, what tasks does the system offer? Creating new ones? Removing them? Modifying existing ones? Listing them all? Those give you your verbs—*New, Remove, Set,* and *Get,* in this case, yielding commands such as New-SystemUser, Remove-SystemUser, Set-SystemUser, and Get-SystemUser (assuming *System* is a useful prefix for your organization).

This little inventory exercise helps ensure you're not missing any key functionality. Having the command list doesn't automatically mean you're going to *write* all those commands, but it gives you a checklist to prioritize and work against.

## 8.6 Your turn

If you're working with a group, this will make a great discussion exercise. You won't need a computer, just a whiteboard or a pen and paper. The idea is to read through the business requirements and develop some usage examples that meet the requirements. We'll provide *all* the business requirements in a single statement so you don't have to "go back to the team" and gather more information.

### 8.6.1 Start here

Your team has asked you to design a PowerShell tool that will help them automate a repetitive, boring task. They're all skilled in *using* PowerShell, so they need a command or set of commands that will help automate this task.

You've been lazy about changing service logon passwords. Many have been switched over to group Managed Service Accounts (gMSA), so you don't need to, but you have a lot of services—many of which run on multiple computers in a cluster—that haven't had a password change in years. The native `Set-Service` command doesn't do it. You'd like a tool to let you change the logon user account and the password for a single service on one or more machines simultaneously. If any device fails, you must know how to handle it manually. Displaying onscreen and logging into a text file is okay.

This needs to run on a variety of Windows Server versions. You don't usually need to script this, so the password can be provided as a parameter in clear text on the command line as a parameter. You'd like the command to output something no matter what happens—such as the name of each computer and whether it succeeded, the service it was changing, and the logon account it's now using (whether that was changed or not). You'll usually want that output onscreen, in a simple HTML report, or in a CSV file you can load into Microsoft Excel.

### 8.6.2   *Your task*

You should design the tool to meet the team's business requirements. You're not writing any code at this point. When creating a new tool, you must consider who will use it, how they might use it, and their expectations. And, the user might be you! The end result of your design will be a list of command usage examples (like those we've shown you), which should illustrate how the tool will solve each of the team's business needs. Including existing PowerShell commands in your examples is fine if those commands play a role in meeting the requirements.

**TRY IT NOW**    Stop reading here, and complete the task before resuming.

### 8.6.3   *Our take*

We'll design the command name as Set-TMServiceLogon. The TM stands for *toolmaking* because we don't have a specific company or organizational name. We'll design the following use cases:

```
Set-TMServiceLogon -ServiceName LOBApp
                   -NewPassword "P@ssw0rd"
                   -ComputerName SERVER1,SERVER2
                   -ErrorLogFilePath failed.txt
                   -Verbose
```

We intend that -Verbose will generate onscreen warnings about failures and -ErrorLogFilePath will write failed computer names to a file. Notice that to make this specification easier to read, we've put each parameter on its line. The command won't *execute* exactly like that, but that's fine—clarity is the idea at this point:

```
Set-TMServiceLogon -ServiceName OurService
                   -NewPassword "P@ssw0rd"
                   -NewUser "COMPANY\User"
                   -ComputerName SERVER1,SERVER2
```

This example illustrates that -ErrorLogFilePath and -Verbose are optional, as is -NewUser; if a new user isn't specified, we'll leave that property alone. We also want to illustrate some of our flexible execution options:

```
Get-Content servers.txt |
  Set-TMServiceLogon -ServiceName TheService -NewPassword "P@ssw0rd"
```

This illustrates our ability to accept computer names from the pipeline.

Finally, we'll illustrate two more things with the following:

```
Import-CSV tochange.csv | Set-TMServiceLogon | ConvertTo-HTML
```

First, this shows we can accept an imported CSV file, assuming it has columns named ServiceName, NewPassword, ComputerName, and, optionally, NewUser. Second, our output is consumable by standard PowerShell commands such as `ConvertTo-HTML`, implying that `Format-` and `Export-` commands will also work.

---

**Big designs don't mean big coding**

We usually create initial designs that are all-encompassing. That doesn't mean we immediately start implementing the entire design. In software, there's a difference between *vision* and *execution*.

We're just talking about PowerShell commands, so there's perhaps no need to go all philosophical on you, but this is an important point. You may not want to implement error logging in your command right now, and that's fine. That doesn't mean you can't *plan* for it to someday exist. Planning—in other words, having a *vision* for your code— means you can take that into account as you write the code you *do* need right away.

If you have no plans to log failed computers right now, but you know you will someday, you can implement a code structure that'll be easier to add logging to in the future. Your execution today, in other words, doesn't have to be the entire vision. You can create your vision now and then execute it in increments as you have time and need.

---

## Summary

We dived into the fundamental principles of PowerShell tool design, emphasizing the importance of meticulous planning and adherence to best practices. This chapter emphasized the significance of tools performing singular tasks, avoiding the trap of multifunctional scripts that complicate coding, debugging, testing, and maintenance. Through detailed examples and discussions, we elucidated the essence of testability, flexibility, and native appearance in tool design, urging scripters to anticipate diverse scenarios and streamline their scripts accordingly. By articulating business requirements into clear usage examples, we equipped you with a structured approach to design, laying a solid foundation for effective PowerShell script development.

# Avoiding bugs:
# Start with a command

Before ever firing a script editor, we start in the basic PowerShell command-line window. This is your lowest common denominator for testing, and it's a perfect way to ensure the commands your tool will run are correct. It's way easier to debug or troubleshoot a single command from an interactive console than debugging an entire script. By "a single command," we mean a PowerShell expression—a single thing that we can manually type into the console to see if we've got the correct syntax. You'll start to notice a theme from here on out. Start small (with a single command), get that working, and start building from there. Don't try to write your entire script all at once. This will make it almost impossible to debug.

> **This is by design**
> One of the cool parts about PowerShell is that you can open a console, run commands, and get immediate results (good or bad). Traditionally, programmers have had to write code as best they could, compile it, and possibly even code up a test harness so that they could test their code. Take advantage of PowerShell's immediacy to reduce your overall workload!

## 9.1 What you need to run

If you've already read the previous chapter, then you know that in the example scenario, you've been asked to develop a tool that will query the following information:

- Computer hostname
- Manufacturer

- Model
- OS version and build number
- Service pack version, if any
- Installed RAM
- Processor type
- Processor socket count
- Total core count
- Free space on the system drive (usually C:, but not always)

It would be best if you planned on using a Common Information Model (CIM) because Windows Management Instrumentation (WMI) was deprecated in Windows PowerShell. You'll also need to log information to a text file as well. You'll need to do more regarding the tool itself, but these are the basic units of functionality you need to figure out.

At this point, we're in the design phase. The goal in this chapter, then, is to identify the *moving parts* of your script. Yeah, the script will involve some logic and stuff, which will control what commands are eventually executed, but we're not to that point yet. First, you want to figure out *which* commands to run, *how* to run them, and *whether* you've got the right syntax.

Speaking of goals, let's be specific about what you need to figure out:

- What command or commands will you need to run?
- What classes of data will you need to query?
- What modifications will you need to make to try both protocols?
- How do you log errors to a text file?

### The discovery process

We won't go through the whole process of how to find what command to run because about a quarter of *Learn PowerShell in a Month of Lunches, Fourth Edition* (Manning, 2022) is devoted to that process, and we assume you've read that or have equivalent education or experience.

But it's *super important* that you get good at the command-discovery process. If every toolmaking project you undertake has to start with a three-week Google-based investigation just to figure out what commands you'll need to make your tool work, you'll be inefficient and frustrated. Frankly, you need some more basic PowerShell experience before diving into toolmaking.

It's equally vital that you get comfortable *experimenting* at the command line. Read examples from the help files, and try things. In classes and at conference presentations, people always ask, "What if I try an IP address instead of a computer name?" Well, you're sitting in front of the computer—try it. See what happens. Playing around is how we learn half of what we know ("messing around" covered the other half), so get used to experimenting and don't worry about trashing your desktop. Spin up a test virtual machine (VM) with Windows 11 or Windows Server 2022, and go to town.

Sure, there's a *lot* that can go wrong here. That's part of the process. You might get the wrong command to start with. You might even use the wrong command, and that's okay as well. Once you find the correct command, you might make wrong assumptions about the results it creates—and those flawed assumptions will create bugs further down the line. The command might work fine locally but not against a remote computer—and you need to figure that out before you do anything else. The command might work against some versions of Windows but not others, and you need to solve that problem too. These are all things to get out of the way *before* you open a script editor. There would be far fewer bugs in the world if people just tested stuff thoroughly in an interactive console before they started coding.

> **NOTE**  Most .NET Framework developers like PowerShell because it lets them interactively play with .NET. They don't have to write a huge program, compile it, and run it to see whether they've got the right idea for their code—they can try it quickly in PowerShell, validate their assumptions, and code with confidence. It's the same thing for PowerShell scripters—test it in the console, get it working in every way it will need to work, and *then* start scripting. Don't worry—we'll go into more depth on debugging your script with Visual Studio Code (VS Code) later in this book.

## 9.2 *Breaking it down, and running it right*

If you don't already have the PowerShell console open, go ahead and do that (either with Windows Terminal or PowerShell console). Notice we didn't say VS Code. Let's take a good, concrete example. Suppose we hop into the PowerShell console and run this:

```
Get-CimInstance -ClassName Win32_ComputerSystem
```

> **TRY IT NOW**  By the way, feel free to follow along and try these commands. Nothing in this chapter will break anything, and it's a good experience.

Did it work? Have we successfully tested our command the way our script will use it? *No, we haven't!* That's because our script will need to run this command *against remote computers*, but we've only run it against the local computer here. It's not the same thing at all, and running against a remote computer brings in a lot more complexity.

Here's a better test in the console because it's closer to what our script will probably need to run (assuming SRV2 is a legitimate server name in our environment that we have admin access to, of course, or substitute your computer name):

```
Get-CimInstance -ClassName Win32_ComputerSystem -ComputerName SRV2
```

The point is to identify the moving parts of your script and make sure you're thinking about *how* your script will run them so that you can test them from the console exactly the same way. We should run this against a few computers with different versions of Windows too. (It pains me to say this, but I know a few of you are still running Windows

XP for whatever business reasons you may have. It'll fail if you're still using those dinosaurs, and now's the time to discover that fact.)

**TIP** We can't tell you how many times we've helped people in the forums at PowerShell.org who've started up a script editor and begun typing. We invariably end up asking them to run some command "from the console" so that they can more clearly see what they're doing wrong. You'll save a ton of time if you don't get ahead of yourself!

### The importance of a test environment
It would be best if you had a safe place to play.

Discovering how to use PowerShell commands invariably involves experimentation, and your organization's production network is likely not the best place for that to happen. That's why virtualization is so fantastic—using a product like VMware Workstation, VMware Fusion, VirtualBox, Parallels, Hyper-V, Azure Virtual Desktop, and so on, you can run multiple computers on a single machine and have your own test lab. You can also set up test labs (with permission) on your organization's virtual infrastructure, use cloud-based environments such as Microsoft Azure or Amazon Web Services (AWS), and so on.

We sometimes run into frustrated individuals trying to learn this stuff independently who can't afford an Azure or AWS subscription. They don't have an organization's resources to rely on, and perhaps their home computer doesn't have the juice to run two or three VMs. Unfortunately, that's kind of the price of admission. PowerShell and toolmaking comprise a business-class set of technologies that require business-class resources. It *can* be challenging to learn on your own, but there isn't always a super-inexpensive way to experiment with these kinds of tasks.

Once you have some decent hardware with 8–16 GB of RAM and good disk space, if it at least runs Windows 10 or Windows Server 2016, you can use the AutomatedLab project from https://AutomatedLab.org to make it easy to spin up preconfigured test environments.

There's more to it than just running commands and hoping you don't get any errors. You need to look at the *results* of those commands. Are you hoping the previous command returns a version number for Windows? Well—you should run the command and see what happens. Because many commands have a prettified default onscreen display, we always recommend piping the results to `fl *` (`Format-List *`) so that you can see the full, unadulterated output right in front of you. Which properties will you use? What do they contain? Do you know what those contents mean? Do they differ from computer to computer in any way that will affect the script you're planning to write?

## 9.3    *Running commands and digging deeper*

We'll assume that you already know how to run PowerShell commands. If that's not your strong suit, please stop and read *Learn PowerShell in a Month of Lunches, Fourth Edition* (Manning, 2022) because it's all about discovering and running commands. Our point is that you should test and ensure you know how to accomplish everything your tool needs to accomplish by manually running commands in the command-line window.

In this specific case, you also want to make sure you know how to retrieve all the information in your list reliably, which will involve more than one CIM class. You'll need `Win32_OperatingSystem` and `Win32_ComputerSystem` at the least. You'll also have to use one of those to determine which drive is the system drive and then retrieve its instance of `Win32_LogicalDisk` to get the free space. Again—you should know how to do these things already if you're reading this book, so we won't walk through that entire discovery process.

Our "discovery and test" process is about more than just finding what commands to run and what syntax to use. As suggested in the previous section, we also spend time looking at the output of those commands. In which exact property of `Win32_OperatingSystem` or `Win32_ComputerSystem` will you find the system drive? Is it formatted as C:, C, or C:\? Or is it a number, such as 0 or 1? What value will you need to use to get the corresponding `Win32_LogicalDisk` instance? The idea is to figure out *all* of your "How do I . . .?" questions up front, test your answers at the console, and go into the actual scripting process with working commands, notes, and everything else you need to do it right the first time.

> **TIP**   If you don't use a note-taking application, get one. As you start to figure out what you'll need to do in a script, it's incredibly valuable to have a place to jot down electronic notes. You'll often want to copy and paste things *from* those notes, which is why a big spiral notebook and a pen aren't as useful.

You're going to use `Get-CimInstance` to do the querying, and, because you'll eventually end up querying multiple classes, you'll need to make multiple queries. Might that be slow? We'd test it. We'd also take the time to read the help—the *full* help, including the examples—and in doing so, we'd discover a way to create and reuse a persistent connection, making multiple queries faster. We love faster! Therefore, you'll use `New-CimSession` and `Remove-CimSession` to create (and then remove), respectively, a persistent connection to each computer to run all the queries over one connection. You'll need to be able to detect errors if the connection doesn't work. Review the help for `New-CimSession` if you're unfamiliar with those tasks—it's time to figure it all out.

> **TRY IT NOW**   Seriously, read the help. Do it right now. How would you go about creating and removing a persistent session? *Try* it—see if you can make it work, and query an instance of `Win32_LogicalDisk` from a remote computer or two.

## 9.4    Process matters

We mentioned this at the beginning of the chapter as an aside, but it's so important that it bears reinforcement. The process of discovery, testing, and refining your command should continue throughout your development process. We've seen students in class spend an hour writing lines and lines of code in VS Code. Then they run it, and it fails. And they curse. Despite our best efforts, they ignore our advice to discover, test, and code *as* you write your script or tool. Discover/test/code is a great reason to use the PowerShell extension in VS Code. You can find the commands you need, enter them, and run them more easily within the editor. If it fails, you can fix it then and there, and repeat the process. Once you get it right, copy and paste the working code into your script, and you're on your way. Then, move on to the next part of your script. PowerShell is immediate. Please take advantage of it.

## 9.5    Know what you need

We've developed a little saying that isn't reassuring, but it's a hard truth you can't avoid: "PowerShell is easy. Windows is hard." The point is that many of us—thanks to years of being insulated from the operating system by a GUI—don't know what Windows is doing under the hood. Do you know the difference between a partition, a disk, a logical disk, and a disk volume? The OS knows, but it doesn't always surface those distinctions in its GUI. If you don't know the difference, then working from PowerShell—a lower-level form of control than the GUI—will be hard.

This comes up *all the time* in the forums on PowerShell.org. Someone will ask for help with a block of code, and they'll paste in what amounts to a C# program because they're using PowerShell to access a bunch of raw .NET Framework stuff. In that case, PowerShell isn't the question—it's all the esoteric .NET things. Or someone will ask something like, "Where can I find a list of events from USB device insertions?" That's a spot-on question. It's not a *PowerShell* question, but it highlights what is difficult: dealing with the underlying operating system.

This is why the discover/test/code process is so vital. First, you've got to figure out *what* to do and then *how* to do it, and the interactive PowerShell console is the place for that once you know *what* to do and *how* you can assemble what you've done into a script using your script editor.

## 9.6    Your turn

The previous chapter included an exercise for you, and this one picks up where it left off. This is where you'll get to practice what we've preached in this chapter: making sure you know how to accomplish everything your tool will need to do by starting in the PowerShell command-line window. If there's *anything* about the tasks you don't know how to do, figure it out *before* you leave this chapter.

### 9.6.1    *Start here*

Remember that you've designed a tool that will change service logon names and passwords. You won't be able to use `Set-Service` for this (it doesn't offer the ability to change those things); you'll need to use CIM.

### 9.6.2    *Your task*

Your main task is to discover the CIM class that will let you change a service's logon name and password. A search engine is probably the best way to start looking for this, and we'll give you one hint: the class name starts with `Win32_`.

You also need to make sure you can use this class to accomplish the task. You'll need to *invoke* something in CIM. Here's a tip: when experimenting with services, we usually play with the Background Intelligent Transfer Service (BITS) or the Print Spooler. Messing with it won't crash Windows, which is great. But if you're working on a non-lab computer, remember that BITS is what makes Windows Update and some other essential things work. After you've finished playing with BITS, reset it so it's logging on as LocalSystem with no password set.

**DO IT NOW**    Stop reading here, and complete the task before resuming.

### 9.6.3    *Our take*

We found that the `Win32_Service` class will do the trick. We learned this, honestly, by hopping on Google, entering the `change windows service password`, and looking for a Microsoft.com page (http://mng.bz/1noL) in the results.

We also ran `Get-Command -verb invoke` in PowerShell, given that *invoke* was a not-so-subtle hint in the lab assignment. We found `Invoke-CimMethod`, which we'll use. We read its help file and came up with the following command to change the startup username and password for the BITS service:

```
$CimMethodParameters = @{
    Query = "SELECT * FROM Win32_Service WHERE Name='BITS'"
    Method = "Change"
    Arguments = @{
        'StartName'     = 'DOMAIN\User'
        'StartPassword' = 'P@ssw0rd'
    }
    ComputerName = $env:computername
}
Invoke-CimMethod @CimMethodParameters
```

We won't lie—coming up with that took a bit of experimentation and searching (yay, Google!). We wound up using `-Query` because we need a specific instance of `Win32_Service`, not *all* the services on the computer. In addition, we noticed a `-Computer-Name` parameter that should be useful later when we're targeting remote machines. To make sure we're using it properly, we'll use the environment variable for the local computer name. This should verify the complete syntax we'll eventually incorporate into our tool.

DOMAIN is valid in our test environment, but obviously, you'd need to use a proper username in that *DOMAIN\USERNAME* form. We noted that the command returned an object, and ReturnValue was 0 for success and 22 when we provided an invalid username. The Change method's web page, which we gave a link to earlier, includes all the valid return codes. We could capture that return object into a variable to ensure each computer succeeds when we write our tool.

We were, by the way, careful to reset the service:

```
Invoke-CimMethod -Query "SELECT * FROM Win32_Service WHERE Name='BITS'"
                 -Method Change
                 -Arguments @{'StartName'='LocalSystem'}
```

Take the time to follow the process. You must start building some PowerShell toolmaking muscle memory.

## Summary

In this chapter, we emphasized the importance of starting small and testing thoroughly in PowerShell before diving into scripting. By beginning with single commands in the essential PowerShell command-line window, you can ensure the correctness of your commands and reduce the likelihood of bugs in your scripts. We also outlined the essential units of functionality needed for a tool development project, such as querying system information and logging data to a text file.

The discovery process of finding the proper commands to run is crucial, and we encouraged you to become proficient in it. Experimenting at the command line, trying different scenarios, and understanding the output of commands are essential steps in this process. Additionally, having a test environment, whether through virtualization or cloud-based solutions, provides a safe space for experimentation without impacting production systems.

Throughout the chapter, we stressed the iterative nature of script development, where discovery, testing, and refining commands should continue throughout the process. By leveraging PowerShell's immediacy and interactive nature, developers can build confidence in their scripts and avoid common pitfalls.

Finally, we had you practice the concepts discussed in the chapter, such as discovering CIM classes and testing commands, to solidify your understanding and build essential skills in PowerShell toolmaking.

# Building a basic
# function and script module

Remember the tool we made back in chapter 8? Well, go ahead and fire up Visual Studio Code (VS Code) and open that .ps1 file. In this chapter, we'll take the tool you designed in chapter 8 and turn that into a reusable tool for others to use. It's important to understand that this chapter isn't going to attempt to have you build the entire tool or solve the entire business statement from chapter 8. We'll take things one step at a time because it's the process of toolmaking that we want to demonstrate for you.

## 10.1 Starting with a basic function

Basic functions have been a part of PowerShell since day one, and they're one of the many types of *commands* that PowerShell understands (some of the others being cmdlets, applications, etc.). Functions make a great unit of work for toolmaking as long as you follow the basic principle of *keeping your function tightly scoped and self-contained.* We've already written about the need to have tightly scoped functions—functions that do just one thing. *Self-contained* means the function needs to live in its own little world and become a kind of black box. Practically speaking, that means two things:

- Information inside the function should come only from declared input parameters. Of course, some functions may look up data from elsewhere, such as a database or a registry, and that's fine if it's what the function does. But functions shouldn't rely on external variables or sources other than intrinsic items such as PSDrives to the filesystem or environmental variables. You want them to be as self-contained as possible.

- Output from a function should be to the PowerShell pipeline *only*. Stuff like creating a file on disk, updating a database, and others aren't *output*, they are *actions*. A function can perform one of those actions *if that's what the function does*.

> ## Designing function output
>
> We're going to harp on this for a moment because it's one of the first things people get wrong. PowerShell's `Write-Output` command is the shell's *default command.* That is, if you give the shell some expression all by itself, the shell uses `Write-Output`. For example, hop into the shell, type 5+5, and press Enter. You see the result on the screen. Well, in reality, the shell ran something like `Write-Output (5+5)` and sent the result to the pipeline (because that's what `Write-Output` does); because there was nothing else in the pipeline, the formatting system took over and created an onscreen display of whatever was in the pipeline (hopefully, 10).
>
> That means your script should never use `Write-Output` for anything except your intended output. And your intended output should always be either nothing, if appropriate, or some structured data—objects—that can be passed to another command.
>
> `Write-Output` should never be used for little status messages that tell you what the script is doing. It should never output plain, preformatted text (unless that's the output or result of your command). We're going to walk through this output design process throughout several chapters. Still, for now, keep in mind that *output matters* and that PowerShell's foundational design has certain expectations for the output's form and content.

### 10.1.1  Designing the input parameters

Looking back through the design, what information will the function need? The usage examples already provide clear guidance about what parameters you'll have to create, which is one reason you create usage examples as your primary design deliverable. Now, let's create basic versions of those parameters:

```
function Get-MachineInfo {
 Param(
   [string[]]$ComputerName,
   [string]$LogFailuresToPath,
   [string]$Protocol = "wsman",
   [switch]$ProtocolFallback
 )}
```

Notice how careful we're being with the formatting of this code? To conserve space throughout this book, we're only indenting the code a little within the function and within the `Param()` block, but you'll typically indent four spaces (which, in most code editors, is what the Tab key inserts). *Don't* get lazy about your code formatting. Lazy formatting is a sign of the devil and an indication of code that probably has bugs—and will be hard to debug.

**TIP**  Formatting is important! VS Code will auto-format your PowerShell document for you. Just type `Format Document` into the command palette.

In the `Param()` block, you declare four parameters. These are simple declarations, and you'll build on them in upcoming chapters. For now, here are some things to notice:

- Data types are enclosed in square brackets. Common data types include `[string]`, `[int]`, and `[datetime]`. You'll notice `[switch]` here, which defines a parameter containing `$True` if the command is run with the parameter or `$False` if not.
- Parameters become variables inside the function, meaning their names are preceded by a `$`. And for goodness' sake, don't try to create a parameter name with spaces!
- In the `Param()` section, a comma separates each parameter from the next. You don't *have* to put them one per line as we've done, but when you start building on these, it'll be a lot easier to read if they're broken out one per line.
- The `-ComputerName` parameter will accept zero or more values in an *array*, which is what `[string[]]` denotes.
- The `$Protocol` variable will contain "Wsman" unless someone explicitly specifies something else. You're not limiting a user's choices to "Wsman" or "Dcom," but you eventually will.

### 10.1.2  *Writing the code*

Now let's insert some basic functional code in Listing 10.1. Again, this won't complete the tool's *entire* mission—you're just getting started, and we want to walk you through each step. We also encourage you to pay attention to the process and not necessarily the result. All of our samples are intended to be educational, not necessarily the absolute best way to accomplish a task.

---

**Listing 10.1  Basic functional code**

```
#You may need to run Enable-PSRemoting or Winrm QC to enable remoting
function Get-MachineInfo {
 Param(
  [string[]]$ComputerName,
  [string]$LogFailuresToPath,
  [string]$Protocol = "Wsman",
  [switch]$ProtocolFallback
 )
 foreach ($computer in $computername) {          Processes each
                                                  computer
  # Establish session protocol
  if ($protocol -eq 'Dcom') {                     If construct
   $option = New-CimSessionOption -Protocol Dcom
  } else {
   $option = New-CimSessionOption -Protocol Wsman
  }
  # Connect session
  $session = New-CimSession -ComputerName $computer -SessionOption $option
  # Query data
```

```
$os = Get-CimInstance -ClassName Win32_OperatingSystem -CimSession $session
# Close session
$session | Remove-CimSession
# Output data
# TODO
} #foreach                          Closes the
} #function                         function
```

**TIP**  Notice that we tagged a #function comment on the closing bracket of the function. That's a good habit to get into when you have a closing bracket because it can help remind you which construct the bracket closes. You should also learn the commands for your scripting editor of choice to find matching brackets. If your editor supports code folding, that, too, will be helpful. People run into more than a few bugs due to a missing or misplaced closing bracket.

The If construct will help prevent problems if someone specifies an illegal protocol for the -Protocol parameter; if they specify "Dcom," you'll set up a distributed component object model (DCOM) session. Otherwise, you'll go with a Web Services Management (WSMan) session if they specify anything else.

You're querying only one of the classes that you'll ultimately need to query; the point is to start, test, and then add more once everything's working. This is a conservative coding approach; although it adds little development time, it will help you prevent complex bugs from creeping into the code. If you test as you go, you'll probably have only a couple of lines to debug whenever a bug crops up.

### 10.1.3  Designing the output

Finally, it would help if you had the command output something, as in the following listing:

**Listing 10.2   Adding output**

```
function Get-MachineInfo {
 Param(
  [string[]]$ComputerName,
  [string]$LogFailuresToPath,
  [string]$Protocol = "Wsman",
  [switch]$ProtocolFallback
 )
 foreach ($computer in $computername) {
  # Establish session protocol
  if ($protocol -eq 'Dcom') {
   $option = New-CimSessionOption -Protocol Dcom
  } else {                                                    Connects the
   $option = New-CimSessionOption -Protocol Wsman                session
  }
  $session = New-CimSession -ComputerName $computer -SessionOption $option
  # Query data
  $os = Get-CimInstance -ClassName Win32_OperatingSystem -CimSession
➠ $session
  # Close session                                          Queries for OS data
```

```
    $session | Remove-CimSession
    # Output data
    $os | Select-Object -Prop @{n='ComputerName';e={$computer}},
                        Version,ServicePackMajorVersion
  } #foreach
} #function
```
**Writes the output using
Select-Object**

This isn't an especially complex output—you're just grabbing the computer name and the two OS properties you specified in the design. Eventually, this output will become more complex as you add queries to the mix and incorporate their properties into your output.

> **NOTE** Again, notice that you're outputting a data structure—an *object*—to the pipeline. You haven't explicitly used `Write-Output`, but it's implicitly there because you didn't assign the results of that expression to a variable, nor did you explicitly pipe your object anyplace else. You piped $os to `Select-Object`, and the result of that expression will end up in the pipeline.

## 10.2   *Creating a script module*

The last step will be to save all of this code as a *script module*. Modules can be saved in a variety of places but the best place is in the default directory for modules. You can find this listed in the `PSModulePath` environment variable ($env:PSModulePath -split ";"). On Windows PowerShell and later, that path, by default, includes C:\Program Files\ WindowsPowerShell\Modules, and on PowerShell v7 and later, that path, by default, includes C:\Program Files\PowerShell\7\Modules, so that's where you'll create the module, under a subfolder called ScriptingMOL. Specifically, save it as ScriptingMOL.psm1. Notice that the *subfolder name* and the *filename* must match for PowerShell to discover the module and load it on demand automatically.

> **TIP** Actually, when we're just playing around, we usually save our module to the path under the Documents folder. That makes it feel personal. We generally reserve the Program Files location for production modules that are ready to go. In this case, we want you to get used to that location existing and being where "real" modules go when you're finished with them.

We've included our module, such as it is at this point, in the code samples for this book (arranged by chapter and downloadable from http://mng.bz/rjgE). To load the module, you must manually run `Import-Module` and provide the full path to the .psm1 file on your computer from the extracted zip file. That's because the code samples include multiple versions of the module, and you aren't installing the code samples in one of the locations where PowerShell automatically looks for modules. Providing the full path to `Import-Module` ensures that you're loading the right version of the module for your purposes. When you're finished, you should use `Remove-Module` (or close the console and open a new one) to ensure you've cleaned up before loading a subsequent version of the same module. You can also use the `-Force` parameter with `Import-Module` to forcibly overwrite existing commands.

**TIP**  Depending on how you download the zip file, its file header may be flagged, indicating that it came from the internet. Again, depending on how you unzip it, the individual files may also be flagged. Many PowerShell execution policies block downloaded files from running. Newer versions of PowerShell include an `Unblock-File` command, which removes that "downloaded" flag, clearing the script for execution (or for loading as a module).

## 10.3  Prereq check

Before you test the command, especially if you're planning to run it yourself and follow along, you need to check a few things:

- Make sure your PowerShell window always says Administrator in the title bar. If it doesn't, run the shell with the As Administrator option by right-clicking the PowerShell Task Bar icon and selecting the option.
- Run `Get-ExecutionPolicy`; the result should be `RemoteSigned`, `Bypass`, or `Unrestricted`. If not, use `Set-ExecutionPolicy` to change the setting to one of those (we use `Bypass`, and we've covered in chapter 7 why you might pick one or another).
- Run `Get-CimInstance win32_service -computername localhost` to ensure that the Common Information Model (CIM) is set up and working.

If any of these aren't confirmed on your system, *stop*. You'll need to fix them. We've covered the first two; the last item should be a problem only on older versions of Windows (pre-Windows 8), where CIM isn't enabled by default. You can usually correct this by installing a more recent version of PowerShell (v3 or later should do it), and you may need to restart afterward. But rest assured that if you don't get these three items working, nothing else in this book will work either.

## 10.4  Running the command

Now for the actual test. First, close your PowerShell window to ensure that the test is in a clean PowerShell environment. Then, open a new one (make sure it's As Administrator), and run this command:

```
Get-MachineInfo -ComputerName localhost
```

### No shortcuts

We assume you've been following along and creating your module from scratch, not just testing with our provided sample code. As we explained previously, running `Get-MachineInfo` won't work automatically unless you've created a .psm1 file in the correct magic location that PowerShell looks in. Our code samples will *not* be in the correct magic location.

Don't try to take shortcuts here by running our samples—follow along and write your code. It's the best way to learn.

If you get the error message, The client cannot connect to the destination specified in the request, that means you don't have remoting enabled. To fix this you can run the command Winr QuickConfig or Enable-PSRemoting. Then, try again.

It would be best if you got some output from running the command. You should be able to type Get-Machi, press Tab, type a space, type –Comp, press Tab, and then type a space and localhost. If Tab completion isn't working, double-check your script for proper filenames, any typos in the code (indicated in VS Code by red squiggly underlines), and so on. In addition, make sure you've used a path that's in your machine's PSModulePath environment variable:

```
$env:PSModulePath
```

If the command runs without trouble, then you're good to go. Take some time to ensure that you understand *why* each line of code is in the command and that you can explain the reason for each step you've performed to this point.

If you *make any changes* to your module, it's important to understand that Power-Shell won't "see" those changes. That's because it loaded the module into memory when you first ran your command; afterward, it runs entirely from memory and doesn't reload from disk. So, if you make any changes to your code, you need to do one of three things:

- Close the PowerShell console window you've been testing, and open a new one. This is a surefire way to ensure you get a fresh start every time.
- Unload your module, and then rerun your command to reload the module. In this case, that means running Remove-Module ScriptingMOL because ScriptingMOL is the module name (as defined by the subfolder name and the .psd1 filename).
- Try manually forcing PowerShell to reimport the module with the command Import-Module ScriptingMOL -force.

You'll also notice that we tend to test our commands in a standard PowerShell console window, even though we're developing in something like VS Code. That's because development environments sometimes have a slightly different way of running scripts, and the console window represents the standard way your script will run in production. The console represents the production environment, so that's where we test.

## 10.5 *Your turn*

Let's return to the tool we asked you to design in chapter 8. It's time to start coding it up.

### 10.5.1 *Start here*

To review, you've designed the command name as Set-TMServiceLogon. The *TM* stands for *toolmaking* because you don't have a specific company or organizational name to use. You'll design the following use cases:

```
Set-TMServiceLogon -ServiceName LOBApp
                   -NewPassword "P@ssw0rd"
                   -ComputerName SERVER1,SERVER2
                   -ErrorLogFilePath failed.txt
                   -Verbose
```

The intent is that -Verbose will generate onscreen warnings about failures, whereas -ErrorLogFilePath will write failed computer names to a file. Notice that we've put each parameter on its own line to make this specification easier to read. The command won't *execute* exactly like that, but that's fine—clarity is the idea at this point.

The following example illustrates that -ErrorLogFilePath and -Verbose are optional, as is -NewUser; if a new user isn't specified, you'll leave that property alone:

```
Set-TMServiceLogon -ServiceName OurService
                   -NewPassword "P@ssw0rd"
                   -NewUser "COMPANY\User"
                   -ComputerName SERVER1,SERVER2
```

We also want to show some flexible execution options:

```
Get-Content servers.txt |
➥ Set-TMServiceLogon -ServiceName TheService -NewPassword "P@ssw0rd"
```

This illustrates your ability to accept computer names from the pipeline. Finally, you'll demonstrate two more things here:

```
Import-CSV tochange.csv | Set-TMServiceLogon | ConvertTo-HTML
```

First, this shows that you can accept an imported CSV file, assuming it has columns named ServiceName, NewPassword, and ComputerName, and, optionally, NewUser. Second, the output is also consumable by standard PowerShell commands such as ConvertTo-HTML, which implies that Format- commands and Export- commands will also work.

### 10.5.2   *Your task*

Create a basic function named Set-TMServiceLogon. Specify all the parameters that are listed in the design, although right now, you might not use all of them. Write enough code so that given a computer name, service name, and new password, the function can change the password. If a new username is specified, that should be set as well. You'll use both an If and a ForEach construct. Right now, make sure these two usage examples will work:

```
Set-TMServiceLogon -ServiceName OurService
                   -NewPassword "P@ssw0rd"
                   -NewUser "COMPANY\User"
                   -ComputerName SERVER1,SERVER2
Set-TMServiceLogon -ServiceName OurService
                   -NewPassword "P@ssw0rd"
                   -ComputerName SERVER1,SERVER2
```

Create the function in a script module named `MolTools`. Test your function against the Background Intelligent Transfer Service (BITS) on your local host. Remember, you should have run the necessary commands in the previous lab to discover the correct syntax. For now, assume that a WSMan (CIM) connection is all you need to implement. Additionally, for now, don't worry about logging or other features specified in the design.

Keep in mind what you've learned from the previous chapter regarding the output of `Invoke-CimMethod`. For now, it's okay to output the computer name and its return code; you can create that output using `Select-Object` and custom properties as you did in the `Get-MachineInfo` example. Later, you'll work on getting the output closer to the design specification.

Test your command in the PowerShell console rather than in the ISE or VS Code, and bear in mind the caveats we pointed out about unloading your module after making changes.

### 10.5.3  *Our take*

Here's our solution for you to compare to your own. Minor variations shouldn't be cause for concern, provided your command works when you run it.

Listing 10.3    Our solution

```
function Set-TMServiceLogon {
    Param(
        [string]$ServiceName,
        [string[]]$ComputerName,
        [string]$NewPassword,
        [string]$NewUser,
        [string]$ErrorLogFilePath                          Uses
    )                                            PSBoundParameters
    ForEach ($computer in $ComputerName) {
        $option = New-CimSessionOption -Protocol Wsman
        $session = New-CimSession -SessionOption $option `
                                -ComputerName $Computer
        If ($PSBoundParameters.ContainsKey('NewUser')) {        <--
            $args = @{'StartName'=$NewUser;
                    'StartPassword'=$NewPassword}
        } Else {
            $args = @{'StartPassword'=$NewPassword}
        }
        Invoke-CimMethod -ComputerName $computer `                 CIM query
                    -MethodName Change `
                    -Query "SELECT * FROM Win32_Service WHERE Name =   <--
    ⟱  '$ServiceName'" `
                    -Arguments $args |
        Select-Object -Property @{n='ComputerName';e={$computer}},   <--
                        @{n='Result';e={$_.ReturnValue}}
        $session | Remove-CimSession
    } #foreach                                  Method result piped to
} #function                                          Select-Object
```

Notice that we didn't include a `Verbose` parameter. That's intentional, and you'll see why in the next couple of chapters.

In addition, notice our use of `$PSBoundParameters` to see whether the `NewUser` parameter was specified. This is kind of a trick that we didn't expect you to know—you may have done something like `If ($NewUser -ne "")` or `if (-Not $NewUser)` to see whether `$NewUser` contains anything, and that's fine. `$PSBoundParameters` is a hash table containing all the parameters the command was run with. It's created automatically. You don't have to do anything. Using its `ContainsKey()` method, we can see whether `NewUser` is among the parameters used. This is considered a better way to test whether a parameter is used. But you can see how the `If` construct is used to build the CIM arguments hash table, either with just a password or with a password and a new username. We're in trouble if someone doesn't specify a new password, but we'll deal with that possibility as we evolve the function.

In our CIM query (which may get truncated in the book; check the code samples to see the whole thing), we use PowerShell's double-quotes trick to insert `$Service-Name` into the query. We pipe the result of `Invoke-CimMethod`—which, in the previous chapter, you learned returns an object having a `ReturnValue` property—to `Select-Object` so that we can construct our output. We created a manifest for this too:

```
New-ModuleManifest -Path TMTools.psd1
                   -RootModule .\TMTools.psm1
                   -FunctionsToExport Set-TMServiceLogon
                   -ModuleVersion 1.0.0.0
```

To this point, we've included our solution in the code samples for this book in the corresponding chapter folder (http://mng.bz/rjgE). To load the module, you'll need to manually run `Import-Module` and provide the full path to our .psd1 file on your computer. In the code samples for this chapter, the module name is `MoLTools-Prelim` to avoid conflicting with the "real" `MoLTools` module that you're building on your own. Finally, reset the BITS service after testing your function, as you did in the previous chapter.

## Summary

In this chapter, you learned how to transform a PowerShell script into a reusable tool by building a basic function and script module. Starting with a basic function, you learned the importance of tightly scoped and self-contained functions, ensuring that they only rely on declared input parameters and output to the PowerShell pipeline. Designing input parameters and output data structures was emphasized, along with writing functional code and formatting it properly. You also delved into creating a script module, saving it in the appropriate directory, and ensuring that PowerShell recognizes and loads it. The chapter culminated in a hands-on exercise where you created a function named `Set-TMServiceLogon`, specifying parameters for changing service logon credentials, and testing it against the Background Intelligent Transfer Service (BITS) on your local host. Throughout, attention to detail in coding practices and understanding the PowerShell environment was emphasized to ensure the creation of effective tools.

# *Getting started with advanced functions*

We're almost there, we promise, but before we can start writing our own advanced functions, we'll focus entirely on the Param() block of the example function in this chapter and discuss some of the cool things you can do with it.

## 11.1 About CmdletBinding and common parameters

What's the difference between a simple function and an advanced function? It may surprise you to know that it's just a single line of code—the CmdletBinding() attribute. This attribute adds so much functionality—let's take a look. To illustrate the first major difference, let's start with a basic function:

```
function test {
    Param(
    [string]$ComputerName
    )
}
```

That's it—no code at all. Now ask PowerShell for help with that function:

```
PS C:\> help test
NAME
    test
SYNTAX
    test [[-ComputerName] <string>]
ALIASES
    None
```

That's what we'd expect—PowerShell is producing the best help it can, given the complete nonexistence of anything. Now, let's make one change to the code:

```
function test {
    [CmdletBinding()]
    Param(
        [string]$ComputerName
    )
}
```

Again, ask for help:

```
PS C:\> help test
NAME
    test
SYNTAX
    test [[-ComputerName] <string>]  [<CommonParameters>]
ALIASES
    None
```

Adding the `[CmdletBinding()]` attribute, PowerShell added the common parameters to our function. If you read the `about_CommonParameters` help file, you'll discover that *all* PowerShell commands support this set of parameters. The number has grown through the subsequent versions of PowerShell, and there are now 11 parameters. Cmdlet authors don't need to do anything to make these work—PowerShell takes care of everything. And because we added `[CmdletBinding()]`, the function will support all of these common parameters as well. Some of the cooler ones (with availability differing based on your version of PowerShell) include the following:

- `-Verbose`—Enables the output of `Write-Verbose` in your function, overriding the global `$VerbosePreference` variable.
- `-Debug`—Enables the use of `Write-Debug` in your function.
- `-ErrorAction`—Modifies your function's behavior in the event of an error and overrides the global `$ErrorActionPreference` variable.
- `-ErrorVariable`—Lets you specify a variable name in which PowerShell will capture any errors your function generates.
- `-InformationAction`—Overrides the global `$InformationPreference` variable and enables `Write-Information` output. This was added in PowerShell v5.
- `-InformationVariable`—Specifies a variable in which output from `Write-Information` will be captured. This, too, was added in PowerShell v5.
- `-OutVariable`—Specifies a variable in which PowerShell will place copies of your function's output while also sending copies into the main pipeline.
- `-PipelineVariable`—Specifies a variable in which PowerShell will store a copy of the current pipeline element. We'll cover this more in a later chapter.

There are others, and we'll discuss almost all of them in more detail in upcoming chapters.

### 11.1.1  Accepting pipeline input

If you remember the original design for the example tool, we specified a need to capture input from the pipeline. This requires a modification to the parameters and the code of the function. As a reminder, listing 11.1 shows where you're starting after the previous chapter, and listing 11.2 gives the modified function.

**Listing 11.1   Original `Get-MachineInfo` function**

```
function Get-MachineInfo {
    Param(
        [string[]]$ComputerName,
        [string]$LogFailuresToPath,
        [string]$Protocol = "Wsman",
        [switch]$ProtocolFallback
    )
    foreach ($computer in $computername) {          Establishes session
        if ($protocol -eq 'Dcom') {          ◀───┘ protocol
            $option = New-CimSessionOption -Protocol Dcom
        } else {
            $option = New-CimSessionOption -Protocol Wsman
        }                                                         Connects the
        $session = New-CimSession -ComputerName $computer   ◀──┘ session
        ➥ -SessionOption $option
        #                                                         Queries data
        $os = Get-CimInstance -ClassName Win32_OperatingSystem  ◀─┘
        ➥ -CimSession $session                             Closes the
        $session | Remove-CimSession          ◀────────────── session
        $os | Select-Object -Prop @{n='ComputerName';e={$computer}},  ◀─
                            Version,ServicePackMajorVersion
    } #foreach                                        Outputs the data
} #function
```

**Listing 11.2   Modified `Get-MachineInfo`**

```
function Get-MachineInfo {
    [CmdletBinding()]          ◀──┘ Added cmdletbinding
    Param(
        [Parameter(ValueFromPipeline=$True)]   ◀─┐ Added a
        [string[]]$ComputerName,                  │ [Parameter]
        [string]$LogFailuresToPath,               │ decorator
        [string]$Protocol = "Wsman",
        [switch]$ProtocolFallback
    )
    BEGIN {}                  ◀────────┘ Added script blocks
    PROCESS {
        foreach ($computer in $computername) {
            # Establish session protocol
            if ($protocol -eq 'Dcom') {
                $option = New-CimSessionOption -Protocol Dcom
            } else {
                $option = New-CimSessionOption -Protocol Wsman
            }
```

```
        # Connect session
        $session = New-CimSession -ComputerName $computer `
                                -SessionOption $option
        # Query data
        $os = Get-CimInstance -ClassName Win32_OperatingSystem `
                                -CimSession $session
        # Close session
        $session | Remove-CimSession
        # Output data
        $os | Select-Object -Prop @{n='ComputerName';e={$computer}},
                                Version,ServicePackMajorVersion
    } #foreach
} #PROCESS
END {}
} #function
```

Here's what we did:

- We added [CmdletBinding()] to the Param() block.
- We added a [Parameter()] *decorator*, or *attribute*, to the $ComputerName parameter. Although we physically placed it on the preceding line, PowerShell will read those two lines as one.
- We added BEGIN{}, PROCESS{}, and END{} script blocks.

Understanding how all this fits together requires you to remember that you want the function to run in two distinct modes and that each mode has slightly different requirements from PowerShell.

### RUNNING COMMANDS IN NON-PIPELINE MODE

Imagine running the command like this:

```
Get-MachineInfo -ComputerName ONE,TWO,THREE
```

In this mode, PowerShell will ignore the BEGIN{}, PROCESS{}, and END{} *labels*, but it won't ignore the *code within those labels*. In other words, it's like the labels never existed. $ComputerName will contain an array, or collection, of three [string] objects: ONE, TWO, and THREE. The entire command will run once, from the first line of code to the last. The ForEach loop will be executed three times.

### RUNNING COMMANDS IN PIPELINE MODE

Now, imagine running the command this way:

```
"ONE","TWO","THREE" | Get-MachineInfo
```

First, PowerShell will construct a three-element array because that's what comma-separated lists do in PowerShell. It will then scan ahead in the pipeline and execute the BEGIN{} block for each command in the pipeline. That's true for both advanced functions and compiled cmdlets. The Begin block (which doesn't *have* to be all uppercase and can be omitted if you don't have any code to stick in) is a good place to do setup tasks, such as opening database connections, setting up log files, or initializing arrays. Any variables you create in the Begin block will continue to exist elsewhere in your function.

Next, PowerShell will start feeding the elements from that three-element array down the pipeline, *one at a time*. So, it will insert `"ONE"` into `$ComputerName` and then run the `PROCESS{}` block. The `ForEach` loop will execute, but only once—it's redundant in this mode, but we need it for the non-pipeline mode. PowerShell will then feed `"TWO"` into `$ComputerName` and run `PROCESS{}` again. It'll then put `"THREE"` into `$ComputerName` and run `PROCESS{}` one last time.

Finally, after all the objects have been sent through the pipeline, PowerShell will rescan the pipeline and ask everyone to run their `END{}` blocks. Again, you can omit this if you don't have anything to put in there, but for visual purposes, we like to include it even if it's empty. One suggestion is to insert a comment into empty `Begin` and `End` blocks, so you don't think something is missing:

```
End {
 Write-Output "All Done"
}
```

### VALUES AND PROPERTYNAMES

Notice that the example uses this decorator:

```
[Parameter(ValueFromPipeline=$True)]
```

This enables `ByValue` binding of pipeline input. You can enable this for only one parameter per data type. Because `$ComputerName` is a `[string]`, it's the only `[string]` parameter we can mark as accepting pipeline input `ByValue`.

You can also enable input `ByPropertyName`:

```
[Parameter(ValueFromPipeline=$True,ValueFromPipelineByPropertyName=$True)]
```

Now, if the object in the pipeline isn't a `System.String`, but it has a `ComputerName` *property*, the `$ComputerName` variable will pick that up as well.

If you're not deeply familiar with pipeline parameter input `ByValue` and `ByProperty-Name`, we urge you to read *Learn PowerShell in a Month of Lunches, Fourth Edition* (Manning, 2022) and learn all about it. It's a crucial feature in Windows PowerShell.

### 11.1.2 *Mandatory-ness*

Because the function can't run correctly without a computer name, you want to ensure that at least one is always provided. Here's the revised set of parameters:

```
Param(
    [Parameter(ValueFromPipeline=$True,
             Mandatory=$True)]
    [string[]]$ComputerName,
    [string]$LogFailuresToPath,
    [string]$Protocol = "Wsman",
    [switch]$ProtocolFallback
)
```

Here are some notes on our decision-making process:

- Making $ComputerName mandatory makes sense. If a value isn't provided, Power-Shell will prompt for it and then fail with an error if one still isn't given. It's important to remember that if you make a parameter mandatory, you can't also provide a default value, as we do with the Protocol parameter.

- Making $LogFailuresToPath mandatory doesn't make sense because you don't want to force people to log errors. We'll check to see if this is provided and enable logging accordingly.

- Although $Protocol is technically mandatory, we're providing a default value of "Wsman", so there's no need to force people to manually provide a value, which is what Mandatory=$True would do. We're happy with someone not specifying a protocol because we have a useful default value.

- You never make a [switch] parameter mandatory because you're essentially forcing it to be $True (or forcing someone to run -ProtocolFallback:$false to turn it off, which is awkward).

- You can make as many parameters mandatory as you require.

### 11.1.3 *Parameter validation*

The $Protocol parameter has a weakness in that it will accept any string whatsoever. The code is a little protected from incorrect values, due to the way the If construct is written, but it would be nice to prevent incorrect values altogether. It would also be nice to provide users with a clue as to what the valid values are. You can do both in one step:

```
[CmdletBinding()]
Param(
    [Parameter(ValueFromPipeline=$True,
            Mandatory=$True)]
    [string[]]$ComputerName,
    [string]$LogFailuresToPath,
    [ValidateSet('Wsman','Dcom')]
    [string]$Protocol = "Wsman",
    [switch]$ProtocolFallback
)
```

You add a [ValidateSet()] attribute to the $Protocol parameter. PowerShell will disallow any values not in the list, display valid values in the help it automatically generates, and even tab-complete those values for users. There are other validation methods available as well; read about_functions_advanced_parameters for a full list.

### 11.1.4 *Parameter aliases*

Finally, although you've followed native PowerShell patterns in using -ComputerName as a parameter name, you might also find value in this addition:

```
[CmdletBinding()]
Param(
```

```
    [Parameter(ValueFromPipeline=$True,
            Mandatory=$True)]
    [Alias('CN','MachineName','Name')]
    [string[]]$ComputerName,
    [string]$LogFailuresToPath,
    [ValidateSet('Wsman','Dcom')]
    [string]$Protocol = "Wsman",
    [switch]$ProtocolFallback
)
```

Here, you define three aliases for the parameter, making `-CN`, `-MachineName`, and `-Name` valid alternatives.

---

**Going further**

Parameters can get almost infinitely complex, especially as you move into the more cutting-edge features of newer versions of PowerShell. Although we've covered those in more advanced books (*PowerShell in Depth* [Manning, 2014], *The PowerShell Scripting & Toolmaking Book* [independently published, 2022]), we don't cover them here because they're outside the realm of "getting started with toolmaking" that this book focuses on. That said, we do want you to be aware of the possibilities!

One thing you can do is define multiple *parameter sets*. Parameter sets often share certain parameters that are common to all of them, while reserving other parameters for mutually exclusive sets. Your `CmdletBinding` attribute can even define which set is the default.

Another topic—and one that could almost be its own book—is *dynamic parameters*. These parameters magically come into existence—or go out of existence—based on the exact situation in which the command finds itself. You might expose certain parameters when a command is in a local disk drive but hide them when it's in a network drive. The possibilities are nearly limitless, making these things tricky to work with.

PowerShell's parameters provide a ton of depth to support a wide range of sophisticated scenarios. You'll be ready to explore even further when you've mastered the basics we've covered here.

---

### 11.1.5 Supporting –Confirm and –WhatIf

There are two more additional pieces of functionality that come with the `[Cmdlet-Binding()]` attribute: the `-WhatIf` and `-Confirm` parameters. Let's step out of our running example for a moment and discuss this often-misunderstood, but deeply valuable option. Consider this parameter block:

```
Function Set-Something {
  [CmdletBinding(SupportsShouldProcess=$True,ConfirmImpact='Low')]
  Param(
  )
} #function
```

The CmdletBinding attribute has gotten a bit more complex. It has declared that it supports ShouldProcess, a PowerShell feature enabling the function's -WhatIf and -Confirm parameters. This is appropriate for functions that plan to make some change to the system. If someone runs our command with -WhatIf, and we've taken the proper steps, then the command won't do anything—it will just show what it would have done had we let it. Or, if someone runs the command with -Confirm, and we've again taken the proper steps in the code, then PowerShell will ask the user to confirm each operation, essentially asking them, "Are you sure?"

It's worth noting that the -WhatIf and -Confirm switches are inherited by commands inside our function. That is, we don't have to do *anything* if all we're doing is running some other command that itself supports -WhatIf and -Confirm. Running *our* function with one or both parameters will pass them to the commands inside. But suppose we want to run some command that doesn't support -WhatIf and -Confirm—maybe a raw .NET Framework class that might blow up the system:

```
Function Invoke-InfoTechExplosion {
  [CmdletBinding(SupportsShouldProcess=$True,ConfirmImpact='Low')]
  Param(
    [Parameter(Mandatory=$True)]
    [string[]] $DomainNameToCrash
  )
  ForEach ($Domain in $DomainNameToCrash) {
    If ($PSCmdlet.ShouldProcess($Domain)) {
      [System.Directory]::GetDomain($Domain).Destroy()
    }
  }
} #function
```

This example is fun, but you hopefully get the idea. When we call $PSCmdlet .ShouldProcess() and pass a description of what we're about to target, here's what PowerShell does:

- If the command wasn't run with either -WhatIf or -Confirm, then the method returns True, and whatever we've put inside the If construct runs.
- If the command was run with -WhatIf, a message is displayed, the method returns False, and our dangerous code never runs.
- If the command was run with -Confirm, a prompt is produced, and the method returns True or False based on the response to that prompt, determining whether our dangerous code runs.

The ConfirmImpact setting plays into the built-in $ConfirmPreference variable in the shell, which defaults to "High". We can specify "Low", "Medium", or "High". Here's the deal: if the specified ConfirmImpact setting is *equal to or greater than* the content of $ConfirmPreference, then the -Confirm parameter is automatically used, even if we don't explicitly type it.

As a best practice, you should support the ShouldProcess feature in any command that might modify the system. Typically, commands with a Get verb wouldn't do that, but commands like Set, Invoke, Remove, Add, and so on might—and should support this feature set. If you provide comment-based help with your command (which we'll discuss briefly), you don't need to document –WhatIf and –Confirm; they'll be automatically documented for you.

As a secondary best practice, *don't* declare support for ShouldProcess unless you *implement* that support. As we've noted, sometimes you don't need to do anything other than let –WhatIf or –Confirm fall through to the commands you're already running. But *test that*—nothing is more dangerous than someone running your command with –WhatIf, only to discover that you coded it wrong, and whatever dangerous thing your command did *actually happened*! Whoops.

## 11.2   Your turn

Okay, let's return to the command you built in the previous chapter and start making some improvements.

### 11.2.1   Start here

Here's where we finished up after the previous chapter. You can use this as a starting point for your lab result.

> **Listing 11.3   Set-TMServiceLogon**

```
function Set-TMServiceLogon {
    Param(
        [string]$ServiceName,
        [string[]]$ComputerName,
        [string]$NewPassword,
        [string]$NewUser,
        [string]$ErrorLogFilePath
    )
    ForEach ($computer in $ComputerName) {
        $option = New-CimSessionOption -Protocol Wsman
        $session = New-CimSession -SessionOption $option `
                               -ComputerName $Computer
        If ($PSBoundParameters.ContainsKey('NewUser')) {
            $args = @{'StartName'=$NewUser;
                      'StartPassword'=$NewPassword}
        } Else {
            $args = @{'StartPassword'=$NewPassword}
        }
        Invoke-CimMethod -ComputerName $computer `
                         -MethodName Change `
                         -Query "SELECT * FROM Win32_Service WHERE Name =
➡ '$ServiceName'" `
                         -Arguments $args |
        Select-Object -Property @{n='ComputerName';e={$computer}},
                                @{n='Result';e={$_.ReturnValue}}
        $session | Remove-CimSession
    } #foreach
} #function
```

### 11.2.2   Your task

Go ahead and make this an advanced function and accomplish the following:

- Ensure that `ServiceName`, `ComputerName`, and `NewPassword` are mandatory. Don't make `NewUser` mandatory.
- Ensure that `ComputerName` can accept pipeline input `ByValue`.
- Ensure that `ServiceName`, `ComputerName`, `NewPassword`, and `NewUser` can accept pipeline input `ByPropertyName`.

### 11.2.3   Our take

Listing 11.4 shows what we came up with. Notice especially the PROCESS{} label addition in the body of the code.

> **NOTE**   We didn't implement `ShouldProcess` here, although we probably should because this command is modifying the system. Notice that our change is being made by using `Invoke-CimMethod`. Does *it* support Should-Process? That is, does it support `-WhatIf` and `-Confirm`? If so, how must we pass that through from our command? Give it a try as a bonus exercise, and see if you can figure it out!

**Listing 11.4   Modified** `Set-TMServiceLogon`

```
function Set-TMServiceLogon {
    [CmdletBinding()]
    Param(
        [Parameter(Mandatory=$True,
                   ValueFromPipelineByPropertyName=$True)]
        [string]$ServiceName,
        [Parameter(Mandatory=$True,
                   ValueFromPipelineByPropertyName=$True,
                   ValueFromPipeline=$True)]
        [string[]]$ComputerName,
        [Parameter(Mandatory=$True,
                   ValueFromPipelineByPropertyName=$True)]
        [string]$NewPassword,
        [Parameter(ValueFromPipelineByPropertyName=$True)]
        [string]$NewUser,
        [string]$ErrorLogFilePath
    )
BEGIN{}
PROCESS{
    ForEach ($computer in $ComputerName) {
        $option = New-CimSessionOption -Protocol Wsman
        $session = New-CimSession -SessionOption $option `
                                  -ComputerName $Computer
        If ($PSBoundParameters.ContainsKey('NewUser')) {
            $args = @{'StartName'=$NewUser
                      'StartPassword'=$NewPassword}
        } Else {
            $args = @{'StartPassword'=$NewPassword}
        }
```

```
       Invoke-CimMethod -ComputerName $computer `
                        -MethodName Change `
                        -Query "SELECT * FROM Win32_Service WHERE Name =
 ➡  '$ServiceName'" `
                        -Arguments $args |
       Select-Object -Property @{n='ComputerName';e={$computer}},
                               @{n='Result';e={$_.ReturnValue}}
       $session | Remove-CimSession
    } #foreach
} #PROCESS
END{}
} #function
```

To this point, we've included our solution in the code samples for this book at http://mng.bz/rjgE.

Finally, reset the Background Intelligent Transfer Service (BITS), as you did in the previous chapter, after testing your function. You don't want BITS messed up!

```
Get-Service Bits | Start-service
Get-Service Bits | Set-Service -StartupType Automatic
```

## Summary

This chapter delved into the intricacies of advanced PowerShell functions, focusing on understanding and utilizing the `CmdletBinding()` attribute. By adding this attribute to a function, common parameters such as `-Verbose`, `-Debug`, `-ErrorAction`, and others are automatically enabled, enhancing the functionality and usability of the function. The chapter explored various aspects of advanced functions, including accepting pipeline input, setting parameters as mandatory, parameter validation, parameter aliases, and supporting `-Confirm` and `-WhatIf` parameters. You also learned how to elevate your PowerShell scripting skills through examples and explanations by creating more versatile and powerful functions. Additionally, we encouraged further exploration of dynamic parameters and parameter sets for more advanced scripting scenarios, providing resources for continued learning and improvement.

*Objects:*
*The best kind of output*

Remember back in chapter 8 when we created our initial design for Get-MachineInfo? So far, we're querying for some information but not for everything we want it to do. That was a deliberate decision we made so that you could get some structure around the tool first. We've also held off because once you start querying a bunch of information, you need to take a specific approach to combine it, and we wanted to tackle that approach in a single chapter.

Right now, the "functional" part of the tool looks like this:

```
# Query data
$Session = New-CIMSession -ComputerName SRV1
$os = Get-CimInstance -ClassName Win32_OperatingSystem `
                      -CimSession $session
# Close session
$session | Remove-CimSession
# Output data
$os | Select-Object -Prop @{n='ComputerName';e={$computer}},
                    Version,ServicePackMajorVersion
```

We're using Select-Object to produce the pieces of output we want. Some might call this the lazy way, but we're just reducing the information we gathered, which someone could have done entirely alone. Let's go back to the list of the information we originally wanted and add where we'll get the information from:

- Computer hostname (you have this from the parameter).
- Manufacturer (Win32_ComputerSystem).
- Model (Win32_ComputerSystem).

107

- OS version and build number (`Win32_OperatingSystem`; `Version` and `Build-Number`).
- Service pack version, if any (`Win32_OperatingSystem`; `ServicePackMajor-Version`).
- Installed RAM (`Win32_ComputerSystem`; `TotalPhysicalMemory` is in bytes).
- Processor type (`Win32_Processor`; `AddressWidth` is either 32 or 64).
- Processor socket count (`Win32_ComputerSystem`; `NumberOfProcessors`).
- Total core count (`Win32_ComputerSystem`; `NumberOfLogicalProcessors`).
- Free space on the system drive (usually C:, but not always). This one's harder. `Win32_OperatingSystem` has a `SystemDrive` property that's something like "C:"; you'd need to query `Win32_LogicalDisk`, where the `DeviceId` property matches, and then look at its `FreeSpace`, which is in bytes.

Now let's start assembling that information.

## 12.1  *Assembling the information*

We'll avoid using backticks in some places to keep the code's column width under the 80-character count that fits well in this book. Instead, we'll start using a technique called *splatting*. With this technique, you construct a hash table whose keys are parameter names and whose values are the corresponding parameter values. You can call the hash table variable anything you'd like. We tend to use a meaningful name, for example:

```
$params = @{'ClassName'='Win32_OperatingSystem'
            'ComputerName'='CLIENT1'}
```

Put each parameter on a new line. For switch parameters, assign a value of `$True`:

```
$params = @{'ClassName'='Win32_OperatingSystem'
            'ComputerName'='CLIENT1'
            'Verbose' = $True}
```

You then feed those values to the command by prefixing the variable name with @ instead of $:

```
Get-CimInstance @params
```

There, now you can tell your family you splatted today!

So, here's the revised chunk of code that queries the information you need into variables:

```
# Query data
$os_params = @{'ClassName'='Win32_OperatingSystem'
               'CimSession'=$session}
$os = Get-CimInstance @os_params
$cs_params = @{'ClassName'='Win32_ComputerSystem'
               'CimSession'=$session}
```

```
$cs = Get-CimInstance @cs_params
$sysdrive = $os.SystemDrive                          ◁─┐  Gets just the
$drive_params = @{'ClassName'='Win32_LogicalDisk'        SystemDrive value
                 'Filter'="DeviceId='$sysdrive'"
                 'CimSession'=$session}
$drive = Get-CimInstance @drive_params
$proc_params = @{'ClassName'='Win32_Processor'
                 'CimSession'=$session}                  Selects the first
$proc = Get-CimInstance @proc_params |                   processor
        Select-Object -first 1                       ◁─┘
```

Here's a couple of notes to consider:

- Notice where you're getting the system drive letter into `$sysdrive` and then using `$sysdrive` as part of a filter in `Get-CimInstance`. This will ensure that `$drive` contains only one object.

- Notice that you're using `Select-Object` to ensure that `$proc` contains only one object. The processors in a computer can't have a different `AddressWidth`, so limiting the query to one result will make that result a bit easier to work with as you assemble information.

## 12.2 Constructing and emitting output

What you *want to avoid doing* at this point is output *text*. It would be best never to use `Write-Host` for tool output because that output is sent to the information stream and spit out to the console. You couldn't reuse, redirect, or re-anything that output, which is the opposite of the point of a reusable tool. Instead, your tools should *always* output structured data in the form of objects, the way PowerShell commands were designed to do:

```
# Output data
$props = @{'ComputerName'=$computer
           'OSVersion'=$os.version
           'SPVersion'=$os.servicepackmajorversion
           'OSBuild'=$os.buildnumber
           'Manufacturer'=$cs.manufacturer
           'Model'=$cs.model
           'Procs'=$cs.numberofprocessors
           'Cores'=$cs.numberoflogicalprocessors
           'RAM'=($cs.totalphysicalmemory / 1GB)
           'Arch'=$proc.addresswidth
           'SysDriveFreeSpace'=$drive.freespace}
$obj = New-Object -TypeName PSObject -Property $props
Write-Output $obj
```

Again, here are some notes for you to consider:

- You're constructing a hash table in the `$props` variable, unlike when splatting, that holds your output. Each key in the hash table is a property name you want to output, and each value is the corresponding data for that property.

- We've used shorter property names for the output than usual, mainly to help the code fit into this book. For example, we'd generally use `Architecture` instead of `Arch` because it's more straightforward. The hash table key will eventually become the property name. It would be best if you didn't try to use names with spaces, and names with underscores ( _ ) look amateurish.
- You use `New-Object` to construct a blank object and attach your properties and values from the hash table.
- You don't *need* to save the object in `$obj`, but we tend to do that because you'll modify the object later, so having it in a variable is useful.
- You output the object *immediately* to the pipeline, using `Write-Output`, rather than accumulating it in an array or something to output later. The whole point of the pipeline is to accumulate objects for you and pass them on to whatever's next in the pipeline.

## 12.3   *A quick test*

After importing the module and running the command, we got the following output:

```
OSVersion         : 10.0.22621
SPVersion         : 0
SysDriveFreeSpace : 16500285440
Procs             : 1
Manufacturer      : HyperV
Cores             : 12
ComputerName      :
RAM               : 31.5475044250488
OSBuild           : 22621
Model             : 20MDCTO1WW
Arch              : 64
```

Notice that *these properties aren't in the right order!* That's because we used a normal hash table to construct the property list, and .NET memory optimizes that storage, which can result in reordering. That's fine. At this tool level, you shouldn't be worried about what the output looks like—you could always use a `Format` command or `Select-Object` to specify an order. It *is* possible to construct an `[ordered]` hash table instead, but we rarely do so. Worrying about the raw output of a script is counterproductive and counter to native PowerShell patterns. Swallow your OCD, and let the output fall where it may!

> **NOTE**   We deliberately left `SysDriveFreeSpace` in bytes because it will be useful for showing you another trick later.

Here's the code.

---
**Listing 12.1   `Get-MachineInfo`**
---

```
function Get-MachineInfo {
    [CmdletBinding()]
```

```
    Param(
        [Parameter(ValueFromPipeline=$True,
                   Mandatory=$True)]
        [Alias('CN','MachineName','Name')]
        [string[]]$ComputerName,
        [string]$LogFailuresToPath,
        [ValidateSet('Wsman','Dcom')]
        [string]$Protocol = "Wsman",
        [switch]$ProtocolFallback
    )
BEGIN {}
PROCESS {
    foreach ($computer in $computername) {
        # Establish session protocol
        if ($protocol -eq 'Dcom') {
            $option = New-CimSessionOption -Protocol Dcom
        } else {
            $option = New-CimSessionOption -Protocol Wsman
        }
        # Connect session
        $session = New-CimSession -ComputerName $computer `
                                 -SessionOption $option
        # Query data
        $os_params = @{'ClassName'='Win32_OperatingSystem'
                       'CimSession'=$session}
        $os = Get-CimInstance @os_params
        $cs_params = @{'ClassName'='Win32_ComputerSystem'
                       'CimSession'=$session}
        $cs = Get-CimInstance @cs_params
        $sysdrive = $os.SystemDrive
        $drive_params = @{'ClassName'='Win32_LogicalDisk'
                          'Filter'="DeviceId='$sysdrive'"
                          'CimSession'=$session}
        $drive = Get-CimInstance @drive_params
        $proc_params = @{'ClassName'='Win32_Processor'
                         'CimSession'=$session}
        $proc = Get-CimInstance @proc_params |
                Select-Object -first 1
        # Close session
        $session | Remove-CimSession
        # Output data
        $props = @{'ComputerName'=$computer
                   'OSVersion'=$os.version
                   'SPVersion'=$os.servicepackmajorversion
                   'OSBuild'=$os.buildnumber
                   'Manufacturer'=$cs.manufacturer
                   'Model'=$cs.model
                   'Procs'=$cs.numberofprocessors
                   'Cores'=$cs.numberoflogicalprocessors
                   'RAM'=($cs.totalphysicalmemory / 1GB)
                   'Arch'=$proc.addresswidth
                   'SysDriveFreeSpace'=$drive.freespace}
        $obj = New-Object -TypeName PSObject -Property $props
        Write-Output $obj
    } #foreach
```

```
} #PROCESS
END {}
} #function
```

## 12.4    *An object alternative*

By this point in the book, we hope you've gotten the memo that PowerShell is all about the objects. Using `New-Object`, as we've demonstrated, is useful. But as an alternative, you can also use a type accelerator, `[pscustomobject]`. You can use this in front of a hash table definition, and PowerShell will create a custom object, just as if you'd used `New-Object`:

```
[pscustomobject]@{
Name = 'James'
Department = 'IT'
ComputerName = 'Laptop-QTP097'
Expires = (Get-Date).AddDays(90)
}
```

This will create an object as follows:

```
Name   Department ComputerName  Expires
----   ---------- ------------  -------
James  IT         Laptop-QTP097 3/30/2023 1:23:33 PM
```

We find it handy to use `[pscustomobject]` in the console when testing pipeline binding because we can create a simple object on the fly:

```
[pscustomobject]@{Name='bits';computername='Laptop-256'} | get-service
```

As a bonus, the type accelerator will use the hash table as an ordered hash table. This means your property names will be displayed in the order you list them. As we said earlier, this is something you shouldn't worry too much about, but sometimes it comes in handy.

Now, the question we hope you're asking is, "Which technique do I use?" Using a cmdlet like `New-Object` is probably preferred because if someone new to PowerShell is looking at your code, they can get help for `New-Object`. Because you're using full parameter names, the syntax is more intuitive. Using `[pscustomobject]` can make your code a little more cryptic, but if you insert a comment explaining what you're doing, there's probably nothing wrong with using it.

## 12.5    *Enriching objects*

In the running example, you're using custom objects to combine information from other objects you've obtained. That's not the only use case in which you'll find yourself, though, so we wanted to briefly step out of the running example and explore a different scenario.

Suppose that you're writing a command to retrieve computer accounts from Active Directory that match the provided filter criteria. Your goal is to produce all the original information that Active Directory has for each computer account. Still, you also want to return the Windows build number that each computer is running—at least for those online computers that you have permission to query.

You *could* follow the same model we've followed thus far and create a brand-new object containing the combined information. But those Active Directory computer objects have a *lot* of properties, which would require a *lot* of code to copy over. And all you want to do is add one teeny little property. Can't you add it to the existing computer object? Yup. Check out the following listing.

> **Listing 12.2** `Add-ADComputerWindowsBuild` **function**

```
function Add-ADComputerWindowsBuild {
    [CmdletBinding()]
    Param(
        [Parameter(ValueFromPipeline=$True)]
        [object[]]$InputObject
    )
    PROCESS {
        ForEach ($comp in $inputobject) {
            $os = Get-CimInstance -ComputerName $comp.name `
                                  -Class Win32_OperatingSystem
            $comp | Add-Member -MemberType NoteProperty `
                               -Name OSBuild `
                               -Value $os.BuildNumber
        } #foreach
    } #process
} #function
```

This is pretty bare-bones—we haven't dealt with a situation where a computer isn't online, for example. The key functionality here is the `Add-Member` cmdlet. When you pipe an object to this cmdlet, it lets you add a property. In this case, we're adding a `Note-Property`, which is a static value. We've named the new property `OSBuild` and populated it with the operating system build number we just queried from the Common Information Model (CIM). `Add-Member` automatically modifies the object and then passes it through the pipeline. Because we didn't "capture" that output, it becomes the function's output. We would run this like so:

```
Get-ADComputer -filter * | Add-ADComputerWindowsBuild
```

We're still using the core `Get-ADComputer` command to do what it does best; we're just piping that to a second command that enriches the objects by adding new information to them. Again, this isn't much different from producing a new object and copying whatever we want to it, but in this case, adding one thing is a lot easier than copying dozens or hundreds of things. This add-a-member technique can also be *faster* because you don't have to produce a new object and copy a bunch of data.

We'll point out, however, that from a purist software development perspective, what we've done is probably horrifying. Objects (well, more properly, *classes*, which define what a class looks like) are meant to be *contracts*. They're fixed, unchanging, and reliable. By tacking stuff on as we've done, we've—well, maybe not *broken* the contract, but indeed scribbled with a crayon in the margins. But it's okay—PowerShell's Extensible Type System (ETS, the thing that makes Add-Member work) was *designed* for this purpose. PowerShell enriches objects of all kinds daily, and you've probably never even noticed. So, use this technique when it helps you solve your problems!

## 12.6   *Your turn*

As with the previous chapters, let's focus on the service-changing tool. You may be thinking that tool doesn't produce any output, but you'd be wrong. If you revisit the original design, you want it to *produce output* for each computer, *success or failure*. Right now, you're probably just producing a minimal set of output using Select-Object:

```
Select-Object -Property @{n='ComputerName';e={$computer}},
@{n='Result';e={$_.ReturnValue}}
```

But that's about to change!

### 12.6.1  *Start here*

Here's where we left off with our version of this function. Use this, or your own work from the previous chapter, as a starting point.

**Listing 12.3   Set-TMServiceLogon**

```
function Set-TMServiceLogon {
    [CmdletBinding()]
    Param(
        [Parameter(Mandatory=$True,
                   ValueFromPipelineByPropertyName=$True)]
        [string]$ServiceName,
        [Parameter(Mandatory=$True,
                   ValueFromPipeline=$True,
                   ValueFromPipelineByPropertyName=$True)]
        [string[]]$ComputerName,
        [Parameter(ValueFromPipelineByPropertyName=$True)]
        [string]$NewPassword,
        [Parameter(ValueFromPipelineByPropertyName=$True)]
        [string]$NewUser,
        [string]$ErrorLogFilePath
    )
BEGIN{}
PROCESS{
    ForEach ($computer in $ComputerName) {
        $option = New-CimSessionOption -Protocol Wsman
        $session = New-CimSession -SessionOption $option `
                               -ComputerName $Computer
        If ($PSBoundParameters.ContainsKey('NewUser')) {
```

```
                $args = @{'StartName'=$NewUser
                          'StartPassword'=$NewPassword}
            } Else {
                $args = @{'StartPassword'=$NewPassword}
            }
            Invoke-CimMethod -ComputerName $computer `
                             -MethodName Change `
                             -Query "SELECT * FROM Win32_Service WHERE Name =
➡ ?'$ServiceName'" `
                             -Arguments $args |
            Select-Object -Property @{n='ComputerName';e={$computer}},
                                    @{n='Result';e={$_.ReturnValue}}
            $session | Remove-CimSession
        } #foreach
    } #PROCESS
END{}
} #function
```

### 12.6.2  *Your task*

Modify your function to output an object for each computer it operates against. The output should include the computer name and status. Revisit the status codes at http://mng.bz/c05L, and make it so that 0 displays "Success" in your output, 22 displays "Invalid Account," and anything else displays "Failed: *XX*," where *XX* is the numeric return value. As a challenge, try not to add more If constructs to your code— look into the Switch construct instead. It would be best if you also looked for places to use splatting.

### 12.6.3  *Our take*

Here's our version (remember, you can get the code file in the downloadable samples).

Listing 12.4  Our version of Set-TMServiceLogon

```
function Set-TMServiceLogon {
    [CmdletBinding()]
    Param(
        [Parameter(Mandatory=$True,
                   ValueFromPipelineByPropertyName=$True)]
        [string]$ServiceName,
        [Parameter(Mandatory=$True,
                   ValueFromPipeline=$True,
                   ValueFromPipelineByPropertyName=$True)]
        [string[]]$ComputerName,
        [Parameter(ValueFromPipelineByPropertyName=$True)]
        [string]$NewPassword,
        [Parameter(ValueFromPipelineByPropertyName=$True)]
        [string]$NewUser,
        [string]$ErrorLogFilePath
    )
BEGIN{}
PROCESS{
    ForEach ($computer in $ComputerName) {
```

```
        $option = New-CimSessionOption -Protocol Wsman
        $session = New-CimSession -SessionOption $option `
                                -ComputerName $Computer
        If ($PSBoundParameters.ContainsKey('NewUser')) {
            $args = @{'StartName'=$NewUser
                    'StartPassword'=$NewPassword}
        } Else {
            $args = @{'StartPassword'=$NewPassword}
        }
        $params = @{'CimSession'=$session
                    'MethodName'='Change'
                    'Query'="SELECT * FROM Win32_Service
                        ➥ WHERE Name = '$ServiceName'"
                    'Arguments'=$args}
        $ret = Invoke-CimMethod @params
        switch ($ret.ReturnValue) {
            0  { $status = "Success" }
            22 { $status = "Invalid Account" }
            Default { $status = "Failed: $($ret.ReturnValue)" }
        }
        $props = @{'ComputerName'=$computer
                    'Status'=$status}
        $obj = New-Object -TypeName PSObject -Property $props
        Write-Output $obj
        $session | Remove-CimSession
    } #foreach
} #PROCESS
END{}
} #function
```

Hopefully, you noticed a few things:

- We changed to using the CIM session instead of a computer name. Bet you were wondering about that, right? Well, we hope you were. Why did we do it? To see if you were paying attention.

- We switched to splatting in line 29, and used the `$params` hash table in line 34. Notice how much more intuitive this is when compared to listing 12.3, line 29.

- Notice our use of the `switch` construct to construct the status message. You can also see that we used the + symbol when defining the query. We only did this to format the code to fit properly on the page. Normally, you would write out the query as a single line: `SELECT * FROM Win32_Service WHERE Name = '$Service-Name'`, and that's what you'll see in the code download.

Accumulating a lot of results will make your command block the pipeline; outputting objects one at a time allows the pipeline to run multiple commands in parallel.

## Summary

In this chapter, we delved deeper into constructing and emitting structured output in PowerShell, emphasizing the importance of producing objects rather than text output. We revisited our `Get-MachineInfo` tool, refining it to assemble comprehensive information about a system's hardware and software. Using techniques like splatting and `New-Object`, we created custom objects with properties representing various system attributes. Additionally, we explored alternative methods for creating objects, such as using `[pscustomobject]`. We then discussed enriching objects by adding properties dynamically, demonstrating how to incorporate additional information, such as the Windows build number, to existing objects. Finally, we applied these concepts to enhance the `Set-TMServiceLogon` function, modifying it to output structured data for each computer processed, utilizing the switch construct for status determination and splatting for parameter handling. By focusing on producing structured output in the form of objects, our PowerShell tools become more versatile, reusable, and conducive to pipeline processing.

# *Using all the streams*

You may need to flip back a few chapters and refamiliarize yourself with the [CmdletBinding()] keyword. We can add this to a Param() block, which turns our function into an advanced function that enables the commands for verbose, warning, informational, and other output. Well, it's time to put that to use and demonstrate why you'd want to use them.

## 13.1 Knowing the seven output streams

It's helpful to understand that PowerShell has seven *output streams* rather than the one we normally think of. First up, and the one you're most familiar with, is the *Success* stream, which you're used to thinking of as "the end of the pipeline." This gets some special treatment from the PowerShell engine. For example, it's the pipeline used to pass objects from command to command. Additionally, at the end of the pipeline, PowerShell sort of invisibly adds the Out-Default cmdlet, which runs any objects in the pipeline through PowerShell's formatting system. Whatever hosting application you're using—the PowerShell console, Visual Studio Code (VS Code), and so on—is responsible for dealing with that output by placing it onto the screen or doing something else.

There are seven streams in all:

1. Success, which we just discussed
2. Error
3. Warning
4. Verbose
5. Debug

6 Information

7 Progress

Those numbers correspond with how PowerShell references each pipeline for redirection purposes.

Each pipeline represents a discrete, independent way of passing information. Each hosting application decides how to deal with each pipeline. For example, the console host displays items from pipeline 4 (Verbose) in yellow text, prefixed by "VERBOSE:". Other hosts might log that output to an event log or ignore it.

Additionally, the shell defines several *preference* variables that control each pipeline's output. `$VerbosePreference` controls pipeline 4, `$WarningPreference` controls 3, and so on. Setting a preference to `SilentlyContinue` will suppress that pipeline's output; setting it to `Continue` will display the output in whatever way the host application defines. The common parameters override the preference variables on a per-command basis. For example, adding `-Verbose` to your command when you run it will enable `Write-Verbose` output in the command.

## 13.2 Adding verbose and warning output

Verbose output is disabled by default, but warning output is enabled. With that in mind, we do the following with those two output forms.

> **Listing 13.1 Adding output**

```
function Get-MachineInfo {
    [CmdletBinding()]                              ◁──  [CmdletBinding()] is
    Param(                                              added just prior to
        [Parameter(ValueFromPipeline=$True,             the param block.
                Mandatory=$True)]
        [Alias('CN','MachineName','Name')]
        [string[]]$ComputerName,
        [string]$LogFailuresToPath,
        [ValidateSet('Wsman','Dcom')]
        [string]$Protocol = "Wsman",
        [switch]$ProtocolFallback
    )
 BEGIN {}
 PROCESS {
    foreach ($computer in $ComputerName) {
        if ($protocol -eq 'Dcom') {
            $option = New-CimSessionOption -Protocol Dcom
        } else {
            $option = New-CimSessionOption -Protocol Wsman
        }
        Write-Verbose "Connecting to $computer over $protocol"   ◁──  Uses verbose
        $session = New-CimSession -ComputerName $computer `            messages
                            -SessionOption $option
        Write-Verbose "Querying from $computer"
        $os_params = @{'ClassName'='Win32_OperatingSystem'
                    'CimSession'=$session}
        $os = Get-CimInstance @os_params
```

```
        $cs_params = @{'ClassName'='Win32_ComputerSystem'
                       'CimSession'=$session}
        $cs = Get-CimInstance @cs_params
        $sysdrive = $os.SystemDrive
        $drive_params = @{'ClassName'='Win32_LogicalDisk'
                          'Filter'="DeviceId='$sysdrive'"
                          'CimSession'=$session}
        $drive = Get-CimInstance @drive_params
        $proc_params = @{'ClassName'='Win32_Processor'
                         'CimSession'=$session}
        $proc = Get-CimInstance @proc_params |
                Select-Object -first 1
        Write-Verbose "Closing session to $computer"
        $session | Remove-CimSession
        Write-Verbose "Outputting for $computer"
        $obj = [pscustomobject]@{'ComputerName'=$computer   <──┐  Uses
                    'OSVersion'=$os.version                      [pscustomobject]
                    'SPVersion'=$os.servicepackmajorversion
                    'OSBuild'=$os.buildnumber
                    'Manufacturer'=$cs.manufacturer
                    'Model'=$cs.model
                    'Procs'=$cs.numberofprocessors
                    'Cores'=$cs.numberoflogicalprocessors
                    'RAM'=($cs.totalphysicalmemory / 1GB)
                    'Arch'=$proc.addresswidth
                    'SysDriveFreeSpace'=$drive.freespace}
        Write-Output $obj
    } #foreach
} #PROCESS
END {}
} #function
```

Sharp-eyed readers will notice two things:

- We sneaked in a change to the New-Object creation. This is mainly to show you a new technique that you may run across. Rather than defining a hash table of properties and passing it to New-Object, we used the [pscustomobject] type accelerator to do the same job in a bit less space. We touched on this type of accelerator in the previous chapter.

- We've replaced a lot of our inline comments with verbose output. This lets the same message be seen by someone *running* the code, provided they add -Verbose when doing so. If the command is run without -Verbose, the Write-Verbose lines will still be run, but you won't see the output.

You haven't added any warning output yet because you haven't needed it. But you will, eventually—so keep Write-Warning in the back of your brain. Eventually, you'll add statements like this:

```
write-warning "Danger, Danger!"
```

## 13.3 Doing more with -Verbose

If you take a moment to think about it, you'll realize that incorporating `Write-Verbose` statements into your tools makes a lot of sense. We recommend that you include the statements from the beginning. Please don't wait to add them until after you've finished scripting. Add them first! Insert verbose messages throughout your script highlighting what action your command is performing or the values of key variables. This will help you troubleshoot and debug during the development process because you can run your command with `-Verbose`. The verbose messages can also double as internal documentation. Finally, if someone is trying to run your tool and is encountering problems, you can have them start a transcript, run the command with `-Verbose`, and then close the transcript and send it to you. If you've written good verbose messages, you can track what's happening and, hopefully, identify the problem.

Consider adding verbose messages like this at the beginning of your command:

```
Write-Verbose "Execution Metadata:"
Write-Verbose "User = $($env:userdomain)\$($env:USERNAME)"
$id = [System.Security.Principal.WindowsIdentity]::GetCurrent()
$IsAdmin = [System.Security.Principal.WindowsPrincipal]::new($id).IsInRole(
  'administrators')
Write-Verbose "Is Admin = $IsAdmin"
Write-Verbose "ComputerName = $env:COMPUTERNAME"
Write-Verbose "OS = $((Get-CimInstance Win32_Operatingsystem).Caption)"
Write-Verbose "Host = $($host.Name)"
Write-Verbose "PSVersion = $($PSVersionTable.PSVersion)"
Write-Verbose "Runtime = $(Get-Date)"
```

When this is executed, you'll get potentially useful information:

```
VERBOSE: Execution Metadata:
VERBOSE: User = Win10Laptop\James
VERBOSE: Is Admin = False
VERBOSE: ComputerName = Win10Laptop
VERBOSE: Perform operation 'Enumerate CimInstances' with following
parameters, ''namespaceName' = root\cimv2,'className' =
Win32_Operatingsystem'.
VERBOSE: Operation 'Enumerate CimInstances' complete.
VERBOSE: OS = Microsoft Windows 10.0 Professional
VERBOSE: Host = Microsoft Studio Code Host
VERBOSE: PSVersion = 7.3.2
VERBOSE: Runtime = 02/01/2023 13:57:25
```

Remember, when using `-Verbose`, any cmdlets supporting `-Verbose` (e.g., `Get-CimInstance`) called within your command will also generate their own verbose output. As such, your verbose output will contain more than what your `Write-Verbose` statements generate.

Another tip is to add a prefix to each verbose message that indicates what script block is being called:

```
Function TryMe {
[cmdletbinding()]
Param(
[string]$ComputerName
)
Begin {
    Write-Verbose "[BEGIN  ] Starting: $($MyInvocation.Mycommand)"
    Write-Verbose "[BEGIN  ] Initializing array"
    $a = @()
} #begin
Process {
    Write-Verbose "[PROCESS] Processing $ComputerName"
    # code goes here
} #process
End {
    Write-Verbose "[END    ] Ending: $($MyInvocation.Mycommand)"
} #end
} #function
```

See how there's a block-comment effect? This makes it easier to know exactly where your command is. Note the use of padded spaces. We did this to make the verbose output easier to read in the console:

```
PS C:\> tryme -ComputerName FOO -Verbose
VERBOSE: [BEGIN  ] Starting: TryMe
VERBOSE: [BEGIN  ] Initializing array
VERBOSE: [PROCESS] Processing FOO
VERBOSE: [END    ] Ending: TryMe
```

Consider including a timestamp. This is especially useful for long-running commands:

```
Function TryMe {
[cmdletbinding()]
Param(
[string]$ComputerName
)
Begin {
    Write-Verbose "[$((get-date).TimeOfDay.ToString()) BEGIN  ] Starting:
     $($MyInvocation.Mycommand)"
    Write-Verbose "[$((get-date).TimeOfDay.ToString()) BEGIN  ] `
    Initializing array"
    $a = @()
} #begin
Process {
    Write-Verbose "[$((get-date).TimeOfDay.ToString()) PROCESS] Processing
 $ComputerName"
    # code goes here
} #process
End {
    Write-Verbose "[$((get-date).TimeOfDay.ToString()) END    ] Ending:
 $($MyInvocation.Mycommand)"
} #end
} #function
```

You'll get verbose output like this:

```
VERBOSE: [15:18:55.3840626 BEGIN  ] Starting: TryMe
VERBOSE: [15:18:55.4040871 BEGIN  ] Initializing array
VERBOSE: [15:18:55.4080634 PROCESS] Processing FOO
VERBOSE: [15:18:55.4090586 END    ] Ending: TryMe
```

There's no limit to how you can use verbose messages. It's up to you to decide what information would be helpful to you. With that in mind, our last tip is to include a verbose message indicating your command's name. That's what the line `$myinvocation` `.mycommand` provided. The built-in variable `$MyInvocation` can provide useful information; the `MyCommand` property indicates the name of your command. This is especially helpful if your command is calling other commands. Including the type of verbose information we've suggested makes it much easier to trace the flow of your PowerShell expression.

## 13.4 Information output

The sixth stream was introduced in PowerShell v5, which more or less did away with its original `Write-Host` cmdlet and turned `Write-Host` into a wrapper around `Write-Information`. The Information stream is a bit different from other pipelines that can carry messages because it's designed to carry *structured* messages. It requires a bit of preplanning to use well. But there's still an `$InformationPreference` variable that can suppress or allow the output of this stream, and it's set to `SilentlyContinue`, or `Off`, by default. When you run a command, you can specify `-InformationAction Continue` to enable that command's informational output.

   `$InformationPreference` and `-InformationAction` are automatically set to `Continue` when you use `Write-Host` so that `Write-Host` behaves as it did in previous versions of PowerShell.

   On a basic level, using `Write-Information` isn't any different than using `Write-Verbose`. The `-MessageData` parameter is in the first position, so you can often skip using the parameter name and add whatever message you want to include—the same as we did with `Write-Verbose`. But messages can also be *tagged*, usually with a keyword such as *information, instructions,* or whatever you decide. The Information stream can then be *searched* based on those tags. You can also run commands using the `-InformationVariable` parameter to have informational messages added to a variable that you designate. This can help keep the information messages from cluttering up your normal output. Here's an example:

```
Function Example {
    [CmdletBinding()]
    Param()
    Write-Information "First message" -tag status
    Write-Information "Note that this had no parameters" -tag notice
    Write-Information "Second message" -tag status
}
Example -InformationAction Continue -InformationVariable x
```

Using `Continue` this way makes it apply to all `Write-Information` commands *inside* the `Example` function. If you run this (in PowerShell v5 or later), you'll see that the informational messages do indeed appear. If you examine $x, you'll find its messages too. Contrast the previous example with this:

```
function Example {
    [CmdletBinding()]
    Param()
    Write-Information "First message" -tag status
    Write-Information "Note that this had no parameters" -tag notice
    Write-Information "Second message" -tag status
}
Example -InformationAction SilentlyContinue -IV x
```

This time, the messages don't appear because we used `SilentlyContinue`. But *the* commands still run and work, and if you were to examine $x, you'd find all three messages. Notice that we shortened `-InformationVariable` to its `-IV` alias to save some room.

Let's now go one step further:

```
function Example {
    [CmdletBinding()]
    Param()
    Write-Information "First message" -tag status
    Write-Information "Note that this had no parameters" -tag notice
    Write-Information "Second message" -tag status
}
Example -InformationAction SilentlyContinue -IV x
$x | where tags -in @('notice')
```

In this example, only the second message, "Note that this had no parameters", will display because we filtered that out of $x by using the `Tags` property of the messages.

### 13.4.1 A detailed Information stream example

Like verbose output, effectively using the Information stream requires some planning. You have to figure out what needs to be logged and how it might be used, and you need to implement your `Write-Information` commands when creating your tool. Here's a simple function to illustrate how you might use `Write-Information`. You can find a file with these test functions in the code folder for this chapter at http://mng .bz/rjgE.

**Listing 13.2  Using an information variable**

```
Function Test-Me {
[cmdletbinding()]
Param()
Write-Information "Starting $($MyInvocation.MyCommand) " -Tags Process
Write-Information "PSVersion = $($PSVersionTable.PSVersion)" -Tags Meta
Write-Information "OS = $((Get-CimInstance Win32_operatingsystem).Caption)"`
-Tags Meta
```

```
Write-Verbose "Getting top 5 processes by WorkingSet"
Get-process | sort WS -Descending | select -first 5 -OutVariable s
Write-Information ($s[0] | Out-String) -Tags Data
Write-Information "Ending $($MyInvocation.MyCommand) " -Tags Process
}
```

Running the command normally will give you the top five processes by working set. Now, run it like this:

```
PS C:\> test-me -InformationAction Continue
Starting Test-Me
PSVersion =  7.3.2
OS = Microsoft Windows 10 Pro Insider Preview
Handles  NPM(K)     PM(K)      WS(K) VM(M)   CPU(s)     Id  SI ProcessName
-------  ------     -----      ----- -----   ------     --  -- -----------
   2145     249    856976     883488  1931 7,151.38   5948   1 firefox
   2692     126    769444     396928 ...86 1,531.13   8552   1 PowerShell
    373      59    310584     390504  1421   446.03   7172   1 slack
    395      55    186628     361964  1391   590.89   7508   1 slack
   1181      95    335932     317060  1216   375.38   1004   1 PowerShell...
Handles  NPM(K)     PM(K)      WS(K) VM(M)   CPU(s)     Id  SI ProcessName
-------  ------     -----      ----- -----   ------     --  -- -----------
   2145     249    856976     883488  1931 7,151.38   5948   1 firefox
Ending Test-Me
```

By setting the common parameter -InformationAction to Continue, you turn on the Information stream, which also displays the information. This can be useful when you're building messages and want to see what they will do.

Next, run the command using the -InformationVariable parameter:

```
PS C:\> test-me -InformationVariable inf
```

You won't get the information messages because the command is running with the default SilentlyContinue setting for information messages, suppressing them. Instead, they're directed to the variable inf:

```
PS C:\> $inf
Starting Test-Me
PSVersion =  7.3.2
OS = Microsoft Windows 10 Pro
Handles  NPM(K)     PM(K)      WS(K) VM(M)   CPU(s)     Id  SI ProcessName
-------  ------     -----      ----- -----   ------     --  -- -----------
   2142     248    857768     883332  1904 7,155.00   5948   1 firefox
Ending Test-Me
```

You get back a very rich object:

```
PS C:\> $inf | get-member
   TypeName: System.Management.Automation.InformationRecord
Name             MemberType Definition
----             ---------- ----------
Equals           Method     bool Equals(System.Object obj)
```

```
GetHashCode       Method      int GetHashCode()
GetType           Method      type GetType()
ToString          Method      string ToString()
Computer          Property    string Computer {get;set;}
ManagedThreadId   Property    uint32 ManagedThreadId {get;set;}
MessageData       Property    System.Object MessageData {get;}
NativeThreadId    Property    uint32 NativeThreadId {get;set;}
ProcessId         Property    uint32 ProcessId {get;set;}
Source            Property    string Source {get;set;}
Tags              Property    System.Collections.Generic.List[string] Tags...
TimeGenerated     Property    datetime TimeGenerated {get;set;}
User              Property    string User {get;set;}
```

This means you can work with the data however you like:

```
PS C:\> $inf.where({$_.tags -contains 'meta'}) |
select Computer,Messagedata
Computer    MessageData
--------    -----------
Win10-01    PSVersion = 7.3.2
Win10-01    OS = Microsoft Windows 10 Pro Insider Preview
```

The key takeaway is that the information parameters are irrelevant if your command doesn't have any `Write-Information` commands.

But as we mentioned earlier, in PowerShell v5, `Write-Host` was refactored as a conduit for `Write-Information`. Check this revised version of the function.

##### Listing 13.3   Revised function

```
Function Test-Me2 {
[cmdletbinding()]
Param()
Write-Host "Starting $($MyInvocation.MyCommand) " -foreground green
Write-Host "PSVersion = $($PSVersionTable.PSVersion)" -foreground green
Write-Host "OS = $((Get-CimInstance Win32_operatingsystem).Caption)"
 -foreground green
Write-Verbose "Getting top 5 processes by WorkingSet"
Get-Process | sort WS -Descending | select -first 5 -OutVariable s
Write-Host ($s[0] | Out-String) -foreground green
Write-Host "Ending $($MyInvocation.MyCommand) " -foreground green
}
```

One benefit of using `Write-Host` is the ability to colorize the output. Unfortunately, even if you run the command as

```
test-me2 -InformationVariable inf2
```

the information output will be saved to `$inf2`. But the informational messages will also be written to the host in green. This may not be desirable. This technique also loses the ability to add tags.

Here's one final version that's more a proof of concept than anything. You need to run it for yourself to see the results.

**Listing 13.4 Proof of concept**

```
Function Test-Me3 {
[cmdletbinding()]
Param()
if ($PSBoundParameters.ContainsKey("InformationVariable")) {
 $Info = $True
 $infVar = $PSBoundParameters["InformationVariable"]
}
if ($info) {
 Write-Host "Starting $($MyInvocation.MyCommand) " -foreground green
 (Get-Variable $infVar).value[-1].Tags.Add("Process")
 Write-Host "PSVersion = $($PSVersionTable.PSVersion)" -foreground green
 (Get-Variable $infVar).value[-1].Tags.Add("Meta")
 Write-Host "OS = $((Get-CimInstance Win32_operatingsystem).Caption)"
 -foreground green
 (Get-Variable $infVar).value[-1].Tags.Add("Meta")
}
Write-Verbose "Getting top 5 processes by WorkingSet"
Get-process | sort WS -Descending | select -first 5 -OutVariable s
if ($info) {
 Write-Host ($s[0] | Out-String) -foreground green
 (Get-Variable $infVar).value[-1].Tags.Add("Data")
 Write-Host "Ending $($MyInvocation.MyCommand) " -foreground green
 (Get-Variable $infVar).value[-1].Tags.Add("Process")
}
}
```

This function tests whether –InformationVariable was specified; if so, a variable ($Info) is switched on. When information is needed via Write-Host, the Write-Host lines are called if $Info is True. Immediately after each line, a tag is added to the information variable:

```
test-me3 -InformationVariable inf3
```

This displays the information messages in green and generates the information variable:

```
PS C:\> $inf3 | Group {$_.tags -join "-"}
Count Name                        Group
----- ----                        -----
    2 PSHOST-Process              {Starting Test-Me3 , Ending Test-Me3 }
    2 PSHOST-Meta                 {PSVersion =  7.3.2, OS = Mi...}
    1 PSHOST-Data                 {...
```

Before moving on, don't forget that information variables are just object types. You could export the variable using Export-Clixml, store the results in a database, or create a custom text log file from the different properties.

Verbose output is still a good choice when you're using PowerShell versions before v5. Once you're using PowerShell v5, it may make sense to start migrating to information messages instead, given their flexibility, tags, and searchability. For now, because we aim for more excellent compatibility, we're sticking with verbose output in our examples.

## 13.5   *Your turn*

As you might imagine, you'll add some verbose output to your tool.

### 13.5.1   *Start here*

Here's where we left off after the previous chapter. You can start here (or use our code sample from the download), or begin with your result from the previous chapter.

Listing 13.5   `Set-TMServiceLogon`

```
function Set-TMServiceLogon {
    [CmdletBinding()]
    Param(
        [Parameter(Mandatory=$True,
                   ValueFromPipelineByPropertyName=$True)]
        [string]$ServiceName,
        [Parameter(Mandatory=$True,
                   ValueFromPipeline=$True,
                   ValueFromPipelineByPropertyName=$True)]
        [string[]]$ComputerName,
        [Parameter(ValueFromPipelineByPropertyName=$True)]
        [string]$NewPassword,
        [Parameter(ValueFromPipelineByPropertyName=$True)]
        [string]$NewUser,
        [string]$ErrorLogFilePath
    )
BEGIN{}
PROCESS{
    ForEach ($computer in $ComputerName) {
        $option = New-CimSessionOption -Protocol Wsman
        $session = New-CimSession -SessionOption $option `
                                  -ComputerName $Computer
        If ($PSBoundParameters.ContainsKey('NewUser')) {
            $args = @{'StartName'=$NewUser
                      'StartPassword'=$NewPassword}
        } Else {
            $args = @{'StartPassword'=$NewPassword}
        }
        $params = @{'CimSession'=$session
                    'MethodName'='Change'
                    'Query'="SELECT * FROM Win32_Service " +
                            "WHERE Name = '$ServiceName'"
                    'Arguments'=$args}
        $ret = Invoke-CimMethod @params
        switch ($ret.ReturnValue) {
            0  { $status = "Success" }
```

```
                22 { $status = "Invalid Account" }
                Default { $status = "Failed: $($ret.ReturnValue)" }
            }
            $props = @{'ComputerName'=$computer
                      'Status'=$status}
            $obj = New-Object -TypeName PSObject -Property $props
            Write-Output $obj
            $session | Remove-CimSession
        } #foreach
    } #PROCESS
END{}
} #function
```

### 13.5.2  *Your task*

Add some meaningful verbose output to your tool. If you see an opportunity to add warning output, feel free to add that as well.

### 13.5.3  *Our take*

Here's what we came up with.

---
**Listing 13.6   Our solution**

```
function Set-TMServiceLogon {
    [CmdletBinding()]
    Param(
        [Parameter(Mandatory=$True,
                   ValueFromPipelineByPropertyName=$True)]
        [string]$ServiceName,
        [Parameter(Mandatory=$True,
                   ValueFromPipeline=$True,
                   ValueFromPipelineByPropertyName=$True)]
        [string[]]$ComputerName,
        [Parameter(ValueFromPipelineByPropertyName=$True)]
        [string]$NewPassword,
        [Parameter(ValueFromPipelineByPropertyName=$True)]
        [string]$NewUser,
        [string]$ErrorLogFilePath
    )
BEGIN{}
PROCESS{
    ForEach ($computer in $ComputerName) {
        Write-Verbose "Connect to $computer on WS-MAN"
        $option = New-CimSessionOption -Protocol Wsman
        $session = New-CimSession -SessionOption $option `
                                  -ComputerName $Computer
        If ($PSBoundParameters.ContainsKey('NewUser')) {
            $args = @{'StartName'=$NewUser
                      'StartPassword'=$NewPassword}
        } Else {
            $args = @{'StartPassword'=$NewPassword}
            Write-Warning "Not setting a new user name"
        }
```

```
        Write-Verbose "Setting $servicename on $computer"
        $params = @{'CimSession'=$session
                    'MethodName'='Change'
                    'Query'="SELECT * FROM Win32_Service " +
                            "WHERE Name = '$ServiceName'"
                    'Arguments'=$args}
        $ret = Invoke-CimMethod @params
        switch ($ret.ReturnValue) {
            0  { $status = "Success" }
            22 { $status = "Invalid Account" }
            Default { $status = "Failed: $($ret.ReturnValue)" }
        }
        $props = @{'ComputerName'=$computer
                   'Status'=$status}
        $obj = New-Object -TypeName PSObject -Property $props
        Write-Output $obj
        Write-Verbose "Closing connection to $computer"
        $session | Remove-CimSession
    } #foreach
} #PROCESS
END{}
} #function
```

Add as much verbose output as you need to provide meaningful feedback or information. It costs you nothing to add the `Write-Verbose` commands, and they won't be
activated until you run the command with `-Verbose`.

## Summary

In this chapter, we looked into the intricacies of using all the output streams in Power-
Shell beyond just the Success stream that we are accustomed to. We explored the seven
output streams: Success, Error, Warning, Verbose, Debug, Information, and Progress.
Each stream serves a distinct purpose and can be controlled using preference variables and common parameters. We learned how to add verbose and warning output
to functions, enabling us to provide additional information and alerts during script
execution. Additionally, we discussed the importance of incorporating verbose messages
from the outset of script development for easier troubleshooting and debugging.
Finally, we explored the Information stream, which was introduced in PowerShell v5,
and its capabilities for structured messaging. Through examples and exercises, we
gained a deeper understanding of how to leverage these output streams effectively in
our PowerShell scripts, enhancing both functionality and user experience.

# *Simple help:*
# *Making a comment*

One of the things we all love about PowerShell is its help system. Like Linux's man pages, PowerShell's help files can provide information, examples, instructions, and more. So, we want to provide help with the tools we create—and you should too. You have two ways of doing so.

First is the easiest solution, which is comment-based help. You simply put the help files at the top of your scripts and functions, and PowerShell will interpret these as the help files. Second, an external help file is generally written in Markdown format. You can use modules such as PlatyPS to help create these files. For now, we'll use the simpler, single-language, comment-based help inside your function.

## 14.1  *Where to put your help*

There are three defined places where PowerShell will look for your specially formatted comments to turn them into help displays:

- *Just before your function's opening function keyword, with no blank lines between the last comment line and the function.* We don't like this spot because we prefer the next option in this list.
- *Just inside the function, after the opening* function *declaration, and before your* [CmdletBinding()] *or* Param *parts.* We love this spot because it's easier to move your help with the function if you're copying and pasting your code someplace else. Your comments will also collapse into the function if you use an editor with code-folding features. This is where you'll find that most people stick their help.

131

- *As the last thing in your function before the closing* }. We're not fans of this spot either, because having your comments at the top of the function helps better document the function for someone reading the code.

## 14.2   Getting started

As you'll see, there's nothing incredibly complicated about any of this. The best way to understand is to dive in and look at an example.

### Listing 14.1   Comment-based help

```
function Get-MachineInfo {
<#
.SYNOPSIS
Retrieves specific information about one or more computers using WMI or
CIM.
.DESCRIPTION
This command uses either WMI or CIM to retrieve specific information about
one or more computers. You must run this command as a user with
permission to query CIM or WMI on the machines involved remotely. You can
specify a starting protocol (CIM by default), and specify
that the other protocol be used on a per-machine basis in the event of a
failure
.PARAMETER ComputerName
One or more computer names. When using WMI, this can also be IP addresses.
IP addresses may not work for CIM.
.PARAMETER LogFailuresToPath
A path and filename to write failed computer names to. If omitted, no log
will be written.
.PARAMETER Protocol
Valid values: Wsman (uses CIM) or Dcom (uses WMI). It will be used for all
machines. "Wsman" is the default.
.PARAMETER ProtocolFallback
Specify this to try the other protocol if a machine fails automatically.
.EXAMPLE
Get-MachineInfo -ComputerName ONE,TWO,THREE
This example will query three machines.
.EXAMPLE
Get-ADComputer -filter * | Select -Expand Name | Get-MachineInfo
This example will attempt to query all machines in AD.
#>
    [CmdletBinding()]
    Param(
        [Parameter(ValueFromPipeline=$True,
                   Mandatory=$True)]
        [Alias('CN','MachineName','Name')]
        [string[]]$ComputerName,
        [string]$LogFailuresToPath,
        [ValidateSet('Wsman','Dcom')]
        [string]$Protocol = "Wsman",
        [switch]$ProtocolFallback
    )
    BEGIN {}
```

```
PROCESS {
    foreach ($computer in $computername) {
        if ($protocol -eq 'Dcom') {
            $option = New-CimSessionOption -Protocol Dcom
        } else {
            $option = New-CimSessionOption -Protocol Wsman
        }
        Write-Verbose "Connecting to $computer over $protocol"
        $session = New-CimSession -ComputerName $computer `
                                  -SessionOption $option
        Write-Verbose "Querying from $computer"
        $os_params = @{'ClassName'='Win32_OperatingSystem'
                       'CimSession'=$session}
        $os = Get-CimInstance @os_params
        $cs_params = @{'ClassName'='Win32_ComputerSystem'
                       'CimSession'=$session}
        $cs = Get-CimInstance @cs_params
        $sysdrive = $os.SystemDrive
        $drive_params = @{'ClassName'='Win32_LogicalDisk'
                          'Filter'="DeviceId='$sysdrive'"
                          'CimSession'=$session}
        $drive = Get-CimInstance @drive_params
        $proc_params = @{'ClassName'='Win32_Processor'
                         'CimSession'=$session}
        $proc = Get-CimInstance @proc_params |
                Select-Object -first 1
        Write-Verbose "Closing session to $computer"
        $session | Remove-CimSession
        Write-Verbose "Outputting for $computer"
        $obj = [pscustomobject]@{'ComputerName'=$computer
                   'OSVersion'=$os.version
                   'SPVersion'=$os.servicepackmajorversion
                   'OSBuild'=$os.buildnumber
                   'Manufacturer'=$cs.manufacturer
                   'Model'=$cs.model
                   'Procs'=$cs.numberofprocessors
                   'Cores'=$cs.numberoflogicalprocessors
                   'RAM'=($cs.totalphysicalmemory / 1GB)
                   'Arch'=$proc.addresswidth
                   'SysDriveFreeSpace'=$drive.freespace}
        Write-Output $obj
    } #foreach
} #PROCESS
END {}
} #function
```

The help here reflects what we believe is the bare minimum for inclusion in the race of upright human beings. Here are some notes to consider:

- You don't have to use all-uppercase letters, but the period preceding each help keyword (.SYNOPSIS, .DESCRIPTION) must be in the first column.
- We used a block comment (<#....#>); you could also use line-by-line words—each line preceded by a # character. The block comment looks nicer and is considered a collapsible region in some scripting editors.

- .SYNOPSIS is meant to concisely describe what your command does.
- .DESCRIPTION is a longer description full of details, instructions, and insights.
- .PARAMETER is followed by the parameter name and then a description of the parameters used. You don't need to provide a listing for every single parameter.
- .EXAMPLE should be followed immediately by the example itself; PowerShell will add a PowerShell prompt in front of this line when the help is displayed. If your tool takes advantage of different providers, such as the registry, you can insert an appropriate prompt to illustrate your example. The subsequent text can explain the example.
- You can put blank comment lines between these settings to make it all easier to read in code.
- You normally don't need to worry about line length. PowerShell will wrap lines as necessary, depending on the console size of the current host. But if you want to manually break lines, a width of 80 characters is your best bet:

```
<#
.SYNOPSIS
Retrieves specific information about one or more computers using WMI or
CIM.
.DESCRIPTION
This command uses either WMI or CIM to retrieve specific information about
one or more computers. You must run this command as a user who has
permission
to remotely query CIM or WMI on the machines involved. You can
specify a starting protocol (CIM by default) and specify that, in the
event of a failure, the other protocol be used on a per-machine basis.
.PARAMETER ComputerName
One or more computer names. When using WMI, this can also be IP addresses.
IP addresses may not work for CIM.
.PARAMETER LogFailuresToPath
A path and filename to write failed computer names to. If omitted, no log
will be written.
.PARAMETER Protocol
Valid values: Wsman (uses CIM) or Dcom (uses WMI). It will be used for all
machines. "Wsman" is the default.
.PARAMETER ProtocolFallback
Specify this to try the other protocol if a machine fails automatically.
.EXAMPLE
Get-MachineInfo -ComputerName ONE,TWO,THREE
This example will query three machines.
.EXAMPLE
Get-ADUser -filter * | Select -Expand Name | Get-MachineInfo
This example will attempt to query all machines in AD.
#>
```

As we wrote, these elements are the bare minimum. You can do more—a lot more.

## 14.3   Going further with comment-based help

You can use an .INPUTS section to list .NET class types, one per line, that your command accepts as input from the pipeline. This is useful for helping others understand what kinds of input your command can deal with:

```
.INPUTS
System.String
```

Similarly, .OUTPUTS lists the type names that your script outputs. Because ours presently only outputs a generic PSObject, there's not much point in listing anything.

A .NOTES section can list additional information, which is only displayed when the full help is requested by the user:

```
.NOTES
version      : 1.0.0
last updated: 1 February, 2023
```

A .LINK heading, followed by a topic name or a URL, appears as a Related Topic in the help. Use one .LINK keyword for each related topic; don't put multiples under a single .LINK:

```
.LINK
https://powershell.org/forums/
.LINK
Get-CimInstance
.LINK
Get-WmiObject
```

There's more too—read the about_comment_based_help topic in PowerShell for the complete list. We'll include a few additional inputs in upcoming chapters as we add functionality to those help keywords, so be on the lookout.

## 14.4   Broken help

PowerShell is very particular about help formatting and syntax. Get just one thing wrong, and none of the help will work, *and* you won't get an error message or explanation. So, if you're not getting the help display you expect, carefully review your help keyword spelling, period locations, and other details.

## 14.5   Beyond comments

Comment-based help has more than a few limitations, but it's essential to understand why it exists. Initially, PowerShell only supported external help, stored in XML-based files written in a Microsoft Assistance Markup Language (MAML) dialect. MAML is incomprehensible—like, seriously unreadable to a human—but it offers advantages over comment-based help. Although it's harder to create, it offers the following:

- It's separated from your code to be updated independently and is the basis for how PowerShell's `Update-Help` command works.
- It can be delivered in multiple languages, allowing PowerShell to offer localized help content to different audiences.
- It's parsed by PowerShell into an object hierarchy, providing additional features and functionality to help create valuable content across a broader range of situations.

So, if MAML is so cool but so hard to make, what do you do? Back then, many different folks made tools to copy and paste the content into a GUI that spits out MAML files for you. It's easier, but super time-consuming. Today, all the cool kids are using an open source project called PlatyPS. PlatyPS lets you write your help content in Markdown, a simple markup language. Markdown is the native markup language of GitHub, meaning your help files can be easily read and edited on that website if you're hosting a project there. PlatyPS can then take that Markdown and produce a valid MAML file. Other tools can consume Markdown and produce HTML if you want to have web-based help for some reason. Markdown becomes the source format for your help (it's easy to read and edit with any text editor—you don't need a dedicated Markdown editor, although VS Code has excellent Markdown plugins you can try), and you produce everything else from there.

If you've never written help for your code, PlatyPS can examine the code and create a framework, or *stub*, for your Markdown help files. The stub will include all of your parameters, with as much data as PlatyPS can figure out already filled in—like which parameters are mandatory, which ones accept pipeline input, and so on. PlatyPS can help you *maintain* your help files too. Say you add a parameter, or change one, or whatever. PlatyPS can look at your code, figure that out, and update your existing help files with stubs, which you can then fill in to document whatever's new and changed in your code fully.

We *love* PlatyPS and Markdown. Although they're more extensive topics than we were ready to tackle for this book, we wanted to give you some direction for future exploration.

## 14.6   Your turn

It's time to add some comment-based help to your function.

### 14.6.1   Start here

Here's where we left off after chapter 13. You can use this as a starting point or use your result from that chapter.

Listing 14.2   `Set-TMServiceLogon`

```
function Set-TMServiceLogon {
    [CmdletBinding()]
    Param(
        [Parameter(Mandatory=$True,
```

```
                                ValueFromPipelineByPropertyName=$True)]
            [string]$ServiceName,
            [Parameter(Mandatory=$True,
                        ValueFromPipeline=$True,
                        ValueFromPipelineByPropertyName=$True)]
            [string[]]$ComputerName,
            [Parameter(ValueFromPipelineByPropertyName=$True)]
            [string]$NewPassword,
            [Parameter(ValueFromPipelineByPropertyName=$True)]
            [string]$NewUser,
            [string]$ErrorLogFilePath
        )
BEGIN{}
PROCESS{
    ForEach ($computer in $ComputerName) {
        Write-Verbose "Connect to $computer on WS-MAN"
        $option = New-CimSessionOption -Protocol Wsman
        $session = New-CimSession -SessionOption $option `
                                    -ComputerName $Computer
        If ($PSBoundParameters.ContainsKey('NewUser')) {
            $args = @{'StartName'=$NewUser
                        'StartPassword'=$NewPassword}
        } Else {
            $args = @{'StartPassword'=$NewPassword}
            Write-Warning "Not setting a new user name"
        }
        Write-Verbose "Setting $servicename on $computer"
        $params = @{'CimSession'=$session
                    'MethodName'='Change'
                    'Query'="SELECT * FROM Win32_Service " +
                            "WHERE Name = '$ServiceName'"
                    'Arguments'=$args}
        $ret = Invoke-CimMethod @params
        switch ($ret.ReturnValue) {
            0  { $status = "Success" }
            22 { $status = "Invalid Account" }
            Default { $status = "Failed: $($ret.ReturnValue)" }
        }
        $props = @{'ComputerName'=$computer
                    'Status'=$status}
        $obj = New-Object -TypeName PSObject -Property $props
        Write-Output $obj
        Write-Verbose "Closing connection to $computer"
        $session | Remove-CimSession
    } #foreach
} #PROCESS
END{}
} #function
```

### 14.6.2 *Your task*

At a minimum, add the following to your tool:

- Synopsis
- Description

- Parameter descriptions
- Two examples, including descriptions

Import your module, and test your help (e.g., `Help Set-TMServiceLogon -ShowWindow`) to make sure it works.

### 14.6.3  *Our take*

Here's the help we came up with. As always, you'll find this in the code downloads at http://mng.bz/rjgE, under this chapter's folder.

---

**Listing 14.3  Our solution**

```
function Set-TMServiceLogon {
<#
.SYNOPSIS
Sets service login name and password.
.DESCRIPTION
This command uses either CIM (default) or WMI to
set the service password, and optionally the logon
user name, for a service, which can be running on
one or more remote machines. You must run this command
as a user who has permission to perform this task,
remotely, on the computers involved.
.PARAMETER ServiceName
The name of the service. Query the Win32_Service class
to verify that you know the correct name.
.PARAMETER ComputerName
One or more computer names. Using IP addresses will
fail with CIM; they will work with WMI. CIM is always
attempted first.
.PARAMETER NewPassword
A plain-text string of the new password.
.PARAMETER NewUser
Optional; the new logon user name, in DOMAIN\USER
format.
.PARAMETER ErrorLogFilePath
If provided, this is a path and filename of a text
file where failed computer names will be logged.
#>
    [CmdletBinding()]
    Param(
        [Parameter(Mandatory=$True,
                   ValueFromPipelineByPropertyName=$True)]
        [string]$ServiceName,
        [Parameter(Mandatory=$True,
                   ValueFromPipeline=$True,
                   ValueFromPipelineByPropertyName=$True)]
        [string[]]$ComputerName,
        [Parameter(ValueFromPipelineByPropertyName=$True)]
        [string]$NewPassword,
        [Parameter(ValueFromPipelineByPropertyName=$True)]
        [string]$NewUser,
```

```
            [string]$ErrorLogFilePath
    )
BEGIN{}
PROCESS{
    ForEach ($computer in $ComputerName) {
        Write-Verbose "Connect to $computer on WS-MAN"
        $option = New-CimSessionOption -Protocol Wsman
        $session = New-CimSession -SessionOption $option `
                                    -ComputerName $Computer
        If ($PSBoundParameters.ContainsKey('NewUser')) {
            $args = @{'StartName'=$NewUser
                        'StartPassword'=$NewPassword}
        } Else {
            $args = @{'StartPassword'=$NewPassword}
            Write-Warning "Not setting a new user name"
        }
        Write-Verbose "Setting $servicename on $computer"
        $params = @{'CimSession'=$session
                    'MethodName'='Change'
                    'Query'="SELECT * FROM Win32_Service " +
                            "WHERE Name = '$ServiceName'"
                    'Arguments'=$args}
        $ret = Invoke-CimMethod @params
        switch ($ret.ReturnValue) {
            0  { $status = "Success" }
            22 { $status = "Invalid Account" }
            Default { $status = "Failed: $($ret.ReturnValue)" }
        }
        $props = @{'ComputerName'=$computer
                    'Status'=$status}
        $obj = New-Object -TypeName PSObject -Property $props
        Write-Output $obj
        Write-Verbose "Closing connection to $computer"
        $session | Remove-CimSession
    } #foreach
} #PROCESS
END{}
} #function
```

Adding comment-based help doesn't have to be a tedious chore. Use the snippets feature of your scripting editor to create a template.

Before we sign off, here's a quick pro tip: comment-based help tolerates extra whitespace. So instead of

```
.SYNOPSIS
Sets service login name and password.
.DESCRIPTION
This command uses either CIM (default) or WMI to
set the service password, and optionally the logon
user name for a service which can be running on
one or more remote machines. You must run this command
as a user who has permission to perform this task,
remotely, on the computers involved.
.PARAMETER ServiceName
```

```
The name of the service. Query the Win32_Service class
to verify that you know the correct name.
```

you could do this:

```
.SYNOPSIS
Sets service login name and password.

.DESCRIPTION

This command uses either CIM (default) or WMI to
set the service password and, optionally, the logon
user name for a service, which can run on
one or more remote machines. You must run this command
as a user who has permission to perform this task
remotely on the computers involved.

.PARAMETER ServiceName
The name of the service. Query the Win32_Service class
to verify that you know the correct name.
```

Those extra blank lines go a *long* way toward making your code more readable, and they don't affect the help file created from your comments.

## Summary

In this chapter, we looked into the significance of incorporating help documentation into PowerShell scripts and functions using comment-based help, essential for users to comprehend tool usage effectively. It underscores two approaches: comment-based help and external help files. Comment-based help entails inserting specially formatted comments at the start of scripts or functions, which PowerShell interprets as help files. We detailed the three designated places where PowerShell searches for these comments within functions. We offered a practical demonstration of integrating comment-based help into a function, exemplified by Get-MachineInfo, featuring sections like SYNOPSIS, DESCRIPTION, PARAMETER, and EXAMPLE for a holistic understanding of function purpose, parameters, and usage. Emphasis was placed on correct formatting, including uppercase letters for help keywords, block comments, and proper spacing for code readability. Advanced topics like .INPUTS, .OUTPUTS, .NOTES, and .LINK sections were introduced for added information and related topics, alongside addressing broken help formatting. Furthermore, we briefly introduced PlatyPS, enabling help content composition in Markdown format, convertible into valid MAML files, for enhanced flexibility and ease of use. While PlatyPS and Markdown offer more advanced features, they are explored beyond the chapter's scope.

Chapter 14 furnished a thorough overview of comment-based help in PowerShell scripting, accentuating its significance, furnishing practical illustrations, and exploring advanced concepts and tools for augmenting help documentation.

# Errors and how
# to deal with them

You have much functionality yet to write in the tool you've been building, and we've been deferring a lot of it to this point. In this chapter, we'll focus on capturing, dealing with, logging, and otherwise handling errors the tool may encounter.

> **NOTE** PowerShell.org offers a free e-book, *The Big Book of PowerShell Error Handling*, which dives into this topic from a more technical reference perspective (https://PowerShell.org/free-resources/). We recommend checking it out once you've completed this tutorial-focused chapter.

## 15.1 Understanding errors and exceptions

PowerShell defines two broad types of bad situations: errors and exceptions. Because most PowerShell commands are designed to deal with multiple things at once, and because a problem with one thing doesn't mean you want to stop dealing with all the other things, PowerShell tries to err on the side of "keep going until it breaks." So, PowerShell will often emit an error when something goes wrong in a command and keep going. For example:

```
Get-Service -Name BITS, Nobody, WinRM
```

No service is called `Nobody`, so PowerShell will emit an error on that second item (notice the grayed-out text in figure 15.1. But, by default, PowerShell continues processing the third item in the list. When PowerShell is in this "keep-going" mode, you *can't* have your code respond to the problem condition. If you want to do something about the problem, you must change PowerShell's default response to this *-terminating error.*

```
PS C:\tools> Get-Service -Name BITS, Nobody, WinRM
Get-Service: Cannot find any service with service name 'Nobody'.

Status   Name         DisplayName
------   ----         -----------
Stopped  BITS         Background Intelligent Transfer Servi…
Running  WinRM        Windows Remote Management (WS-Managem…
```

**Figure 15.1   Error message for Nobody service**

At a global level, PowerShell defines an $ErrorActionPreference variable, which tells PowerShell what to do in the event of a nonterminating error. This variable tells PowerShell what to do when a problem arises, but PowerShell can keep going. The default value for this variable is Continue, which is described here along with the other options:

- Continue—Emits an error message and keeps going. Your code can't detect that a problem occurred, so you can't do anything else.
- SilentlyContinue—Doesn't emit an error message and keeps going. Again, you can't detect the problem or respond to it yourself.
- Inquire—Displays a prompt and asks the user whether to continue or stop.
- Stop—Turns the nonterminating *error* into a *terminating exception* and stops running the command. This is something your code can detect and respond to.
- Ignore—Not a value for this preference variable, but it can be used on the -Error-Action parameter, which we'll cover in a moment. Its behavior is similar to SilentlyContinue.
- Suspend—Only applies to errors in a PowerShell workflow, which is outside the scope of this book.

**TRY IT NOW**   Run $ErrorActionPreference from a PowerShell prompt. You should be set to Continue unless it has been changed already.

It's considered best practice to leave $ErrorActionPreference as is. Instead, you'll typically want to specify a behavior per command. You can do this using the -ErrorAction common parameter or its alias (-EA, used here to save space in this book), which exists on every PowerShell command—even the ones you write yourself that include [CmdletBinding()]. For example, try running these commands, and note the different behaviors:

```
Get-Service -Name BITS, Nobody, WinRM -EA Continue
Get-Service -Name BITS, Nobody, WinRM -EA SilentlyContinue
Get-Service -Name BITS, Nobody, WinRM -EA Inquire
Get-Service -Name BITS, Nobody, WinRM -EA Ignore
Get-Service -Name BITS, Nobody, WinRM -EA Stop
```

Remember that you *can't* handle exceptions in your code *unless* PowerShell generates an exception. Unless you run them with the Stop error action, most commands won't generate an exception. One of the biggest mistakes people make is forgetting to add -EA Stop to a command where they want to handle the problem.

## 15.2  Bad handling

We see people engage in two fundamentally bad practices. These aren't *always, always, always* bad, but they're *usually* bad, so we want to bring them to your attention.

First up is globally setting the preference variable right at the top of a script or function:

```
$ErrorActionPreference='SilentlyContinue'
```

In the olden days of VBScript, people used On Error Resume Next. This says, "I don't want to know if anything is wrong with my code." People do this misguidedly to suppress possible errors that they know won't matter. For example, attempting to delete a file that doesn't exist will cause an error—but you probably don't care because the mission is accomplished either way, right? But to suppress that unwanted error, you should use -EA SilentlyContinue on the Remove-Item command instead of globally suppressing *all* errors in your script.

The other bad practice is slightly more subtle and can arise in the same situation. Suppose you run Remove-Item with -EA SilentlyContinue, and then suppose you try to delete a file that does exist but doesn't have permission to delete. You'll suppress the error and wonder why the file still exists.

Before you start suppressing errors, make sure you've thought it through. Nothing is more vexing than spending hours debugging a script because you suppressed an error message that would have told you where the problem was. We can't tell you how often this comes up in forum questions.

## 15.3  Two reasons for exception handling

There are two broad reasons to handle exceptions in your code. (Notice that we're using their official name and exceptions to differentiate them from the non-handleable *errors* we wrote about previously.)

Reason 1 is that you plan to run your tool out of your view. Perhaps it's a scheduled task, or maybe you're writing tools that remote customers will use. In either case, you want to make sure you have evidence for any problems that occur to help you with debugging. In this scenario, you might globally set $ErrorActionPreference to stop at the top of your script and wrap the entire script in an error-handling construct. Any errors, even unanticipated ones, can be trapped and logged for diagnostic purposes. Although this scenario is valid, it isn't the one we'll focus on in this book.

We'll focus on reason 2: you're running a command where you can anticipate a certain kind of problem *and* want to deal with that problem actively. This might be a failure to connect to a computer, a failure to log on to something, or another scenario. Let's dig into that with the tool you've been building.

## 15.4   *Handling exceptions in your tool*

In the tool you've been building, you can anticipate the New-CimSession command running into problems: a computer might be offline or nonexistent, or the computer might not work with the selected protocol. You want to catch that condition and, depending on the parameters you ran with, log the failed computer name to a text file and/or try again using the other protocol. You'll start by focusing on the command that could cause the problem and making sure it will generate a *terminating exception* if it runs into trouble. To do so, change

```
Write-Verbose "Connecting to $computer over $protocol"
$session = New-CimSession -ComputerName $computer `
                          -SessionOption $option
```

to

```
Write-Verbose "Connecting to $computer over $protocol"
$params = @{'ComputerName'=$Computer
            'SessionOption'=$option
            'ErrorAction'='Stop'}
$session = New-CimSession @params
```

It's important to notice that you've already constructed the command so that it only attempts to connect to one computer at a time using the ForEach loop. Any time you'll be handling errors, it's crucial that you construct things so that only *one thing* can fail at a time. That's because you're telling PowerShell *not* to continue. If you attempted five computers at once, a failure in any of them would result in the rest of them never being attempted. Make sure you understand why this design principle is so important!

Just changing the error action to Stop isn't enough, though. You also need to wrap your code in a Try/Catch construct. If an exception occurs in the Try block, then all the subsequent code in the Try block will be skipped, and the Catch block will execute instead. So the PROCESS{} block of the function now looks like this:

```
PROCESS {
    ForEach ($computer in $ComputerName) {
        if ($protocol -eq 'Dcom') {
            $option = New-CimSessionOption -Protocol Dcom
        } else {
            $option = New-CimSessionOption -Protocol Wsman
        }
        Try {                                              ◁─┐ Try script
            Write-Verbose "Connecting to $computer over $protocol"      block
            $params = @{'ComputerName'=$Computer
                        'SessionOption'=$option
                        'ErrorAction'='Stop'}
            $session = New-CimSession @params
            Write-Verbose "Querying from $computer"
            $os_params = @{'ClassName'='Win32_OperatingSystem'
                           'CimSession'=$session}
            $os = Get-CimInstance @os_params
            $cs_params = @{'ClassName'='Win32_ComputerSystem'
```

```
                         'CimSession'=$session}
        $cs = Get-CimInstance @cs_params
        $sysdrive = $os.SystemDrive
        $drive_params = @{'ClassName'='Win32_LogicalDisk'
                         'Filter'="DeviceId='$sysdrive'"
                         'CimSession'=$session}
        $drive = Get-CimInstance @drive_params
        $proc_params = @{'ClassName'='Win32_Processor'
                         'CimSession'=$session}
        $proc = Get-CimInstance @proc_params |
                Select-Object -first 1
        Write-Verbose "Closing session to $computer"
        $session | Remove-CimSession
        Write-Verbose "Outputting for $computer"
        $obj = [pscustomobject]@{'ComputerName'=$computer
                    'OSVersion'=$os.version
                    'SPVersion'=$os.servicepackmajorversion
                    'OSBuild'=$os.buildnumber
                    'Manufacturer'=$cs.manufacturer
                    'Model'=$cs.model
                    'Procs'=$cs.numberofprocessors
                    'Cores'=$cs.numberoflogicalprocessors
                    'RAM'=($cs.totalphysicalmemory / 1GB)
                    'Arch'=$proc.addresswidth
                    'SysDriveFreeSpace'=$drive.freespace}
        Write-Output $obj
    } Catch {                      ⊲─┐  Catch script
    } #try/catch                     │  block
  } #foreach
} #PROCESS
```

The idea is that if a problem happens with New-CimSession, *everything else* is abandoned. That should make sense because without a session, you can't execute queries. Without queries, you can't generate results. Without results, you can't produce output. If one thing goes wrong, you need to quit.

Now, let's focus on what you'll do if an error—sorry, an *exception*—does occur:

```
} Catch {
    Write-Warning "FAILED $computer on $protocol"      ⊲─┐  Writes a warning
    # Did we specify protocol fallback?                  │  message
    # If so, try again. If we specified logging,
    # we won't log a problem here - we'll let
    # the logging occur if this fallback also
    # fails
    If ($ProtocolFallback) {           ⊲─┐  Tests for a
        If ($Protocol -eq 'Dcom') {      │  parameter
            $newprotocol = 'Wsman'
        } else {
            $newprotocol = 'Dcom'
        } #if protocol
        Write-Verbose "Trying again with $newprotocol"
        $params = @{'ComputerName'=$Computer
                    'Protocol'=$newprotocol
```

```
                    'ProtocolFallback'=$False}
        If ($PSBoundParameters.ContainsKey('LogFailuresToPath')){
            $params += @{'LogFailuresToPath'=$LogFailuresToPath}
        } #if logging
        Get-MachineInfo @params
    } #if protocolfallback
    # if we didn't specify fallback, but we
    # did specify logging, then log the error,
    # because we won't be trying again
    If (-not $ProtocolFallback -and
        $PSBoundParameters.ContainsKey('LogFailuresToPath')){
        Write-Verbose "Logging to $LogFailuresToPath"
        $computer | Out-File $LogFailuresToPath -Append
    } # if write to log
} #try/catch
```

**No protocol
fallback,
but logging
requested**

Here's what's happening:

1   Within the `Catch` block, you can write out a warning message for the user's benefit. They can suppress these by adding `-Warning-Action SilentlyContinue` when running the command.

2   You look to see whether `-ProtocolFallback` was specified. If it was, you set `$newprotocol` to be whatever protocol you *weren't* already running with. You then set up a parameter hash table with your current computer name and that new protocol, and you specify `$False` for `ProtocolFallback`. Because you've *already fallen back* on the protocol, there's no sense in doing it again and falling into an endless loop. If you're running with `-LogFailuresToPath`, add that parameter to your hash table, and—here's the fun part—*call your function* using these parameters. Its output will become part of *your* output, giving you an easy way to try the other protocol without duplicating a bunch of code.

3   Look to see if you *aren't* running with `-ProtocolFallback`, but *are* running with `-LogFailuresToPath` so that you can log the failed computer name. Why don't you log the computer name to begin with? If the *current* protocol fails, but you're asked to use protocol fallback, your self-call to `Get-MachineInfo` will take care of the logging if *it* fails with the second protocol.

This is some complex logic—go through it a few times to make sure you understand it!

## 15.5  *Capturing the exception*

The example so far hasn't cared what problem happened with `New-CimSession`; you have the same response to any possible failure. In some cases, you may want to know what exception happened. An easy way to do this is to specify the `-ErrorVariable`, or `-EV`, parameter and provide the name of a variable (remembering that $ isn't part of a variable's name, so you omit the $ here). Whatever exception happens will be placed in the specified variable for you to work with.

## 15.6 Handling exceptions for non-commands

What if you're running something—like a .NET Framework method—that doesn't have an -ErrorAction parameter? In *most* cases, you can run it in a Try block as is because *most* of these methods will throw trappable, terminating exceptions if something goes wrong. The nonterminating exception thing is unique to PowerShell commands like functions and cmdlets.

But you *still* may have instances when you need to do this:

```
Try {
    $ErrorActionPreference = "Stop"
    # run something that doesn't have -ErrorAction
    $ErrorActionPreference = "Continue"
} Catch {
    # ...
}
```

This is your error handling of last resort. You're temporarily modifying $ErrorActionPreference for the duration of the one command (or whatever) for which you want to catch an exception. This isn't a common situation in our experience, but we figured we should point it out.

## 15.7 Going further with exception handling

It's possible to have multiple Catch blocks after a given Try block, with each Catch dealing with a specific type of exception. For example, if a file deletion failed, you could react differently for a File Not Found or an Access Denied situation. To do this, you'll need to know the .NET Framework type name of each exception you want to call out separately. *The Big Book of PowerShell Error Handling* e-book (https://PowerShell .org/free-resources/) lists common type names and advice for figuring these out (e.g., generating the error on your own in an experiment and then figuring out what the exception type name was). Broadly, the syntax looks like this:

```
Try {
    # something here generates an exception
} Catch [Exception.Type.One] {
    # deal with that exception here
} Catch [Exception.Type.Two] {
    # deal with the other exception here
} Catch {
    # deal with anything else here
} Finally {
    # run something else
}
```

Also shown in that example is the optional Finally block, which will always run after the Try or the Catch, whether or not an exception occurs.

**Deprecated exception-handling**

In your internet travels, you may run across a `Trap` construct in PowerShell. This dates back to v1, when the PowerShell team frankly didn't have time to get `Try/Catch` working, and `Trap` was the best short-term fix they could come up with. `Trap` is *deprecated*, meaning it's left in the product for backward compatibility, but you're not intended to use it in newly written code. For that reason, we're not covering it here. It *does* have some uses in global, "I want to catch and log any possible error" situations, but `Try/Catch` is considered a more structured, professional approach to exception handling, and we recommend that you stick with it.

## 15.8   Your turn

It's time to deal with errors in your code.

### 15.8.1   Start here

This is where we left off at the end of chapter 14. You can use this as a starting point or use your own results from that chapter.

Listing 15.1   Set `TMServiceLogon`

```
function Set-TMServiceLogon {
<#
.SYNOPSIS
Sets service login name and password.
.DESCRIPTION
This command uses either CIM (default) or WMI to
set the service password and, optionally, the logon
user name, for a service that can run on
one or more remote machines. You must run this command
as a user with permission to perform this task,
remotely on the computers involved.
.PARAMETER ServiceName
The name of the service. Query the Win32_Service class
to verify that you know the correct name.
.PARAMETER ComputerName
One or more computer names. Using IP addresses will
fail with CIM; they will work with WMI. CIM is always
attempted first.
.PARAMETER NewPassword
A plain-text string of the new password.
.PARAMETER NewUser
Optional; the new logon user name, in DOMAIN\USER
format.
.PARAMETER ErrorLogFilePath
If provided, this is a path and filename of a text
file where failed computer names will be logged.
#>
    [CmdletBinding()]
    Param(
        [Parameter(Mandatory=$True,
```

```
                            ValueFromPipelineByPropertyName=$True)]
            [string]$ServiceName,
            [Parameter(Mandatory=$True,
                       ValueFromPipeline=$True,
                       ValueFromPipelineByPropertyName=$True)]
            [string[]]$ComputerName,
            [Parameter(ValueFromPipelineByPropertyName=$True)]
            [string]$NewPassword,
            [Parameter(ValueFromPipelineByPropertyName=$True)]
            [string]$NewUser,
            [string]$ErrorLogFilePath
        )
    BEGIN{}
    PROCESS{
        ForEach ($computer in $ComputerName) {
            Write-Verbose "Connect to $computer on WS-MAN"
            $option = New-CimSessionOption -Protocol Wsman
            $session = New-CimSession -SessionOption $option `
                                      -ComputerName $Computer
            If ($PSBoundParameters.ContainsKey('NewUser')) {
                $args = @{'StartName'=$NewUser
                          'StartPassword'=$NewPassword}
            } Else {
                $args = @{'StartPassword'=$NewPassword}
                Write-Warning "Not setting a new user name"
            }
            Write-Verbose "Setting $servicename on $computer"
            $params = @{'CimSession'=$session
                        'MethodName'='Change'
                        'Query'="SELECT * FROM Win32_Service " +
                                "WHERE Name = '$ServiceName'"
                        'Arguments'=$args}
            $ret = Invoke-CimMethod @params
            switch ($ret.ReturnValue) {
                0  { $status = "Success" }
                22 { $status = "Invalid Account" }
                Default { $status = "Failed: $($ret.ReturnValue)" }
            }
            $props = @{'ComputerName'=$computer
                       'Status'=$status}
            $obj = New-Object -TypeName PSObject -Property $props
            Write-Output $obj
            Write-Verbose "Closing connection to $computer"
            $session | Remove-CimSession
        } #foreach
    } #PROCESS
    END{}
    } #function
```

### 15.8.2 *Your task*

Your job is to add error handling to your tool. Remember, in the event of an error, the design calls for you to try the distributed component object model (DCOM) protocol automatically because you're always starting with the Web Services Management

(WSman) protocol. If a computer fails, you should log it *only* if logging was specified and *only* after *both* protocols have been attempted.

Your task is made a little more difficult because the parameter design doesn't include a parameter for the protocol. That means you can't just call your own function again with a different protocol parameter! Instead, you'll have to write a *loop* that will execute your code up to two times. One such loop might look something like this:

```
Do {
    # code goes here
} Until ($something -eq 'else')
```

This kind of loop will always execute its contents at least once. It will continue executing *until* the condition specified at the end of the loop is $True. See if you can find the necessary logic to add to your script.

### 15.8.3 *Our take*

Here's what we came up with.

---

**Listing 15.2  Our solution**

```
function Set-TMServiceLogon {
<#
.SYNOPSIS
Sets service login name and password.
.DESCRIPTION
This command uses either CIM (default) or WMI to
set the service password, and optionally the logon
user name, for a service, which can be running on
one or more remote machines. You must run this command
as a user who has permission to peform this task,
remotely, on the computers involved.
.PARAMETER ServiceName
The name of the service. Query the Win32_Service class
to verify that you know the correct name.
.PARAMETER ComputerName
One or more computer names. Using IP addresses will
fail with CIM; they will work with WMI. CIM is always
attempted first.
.PARAMETER NewPassword
A plain-text string of the new password.
.PARAMETER NewUser
Optional; the new logon user name, in DOMAIN\USER
format.
.PARAMETER ErrorLogFilePath
If provided, this is a path and filename of a text
file where failed computer names will be logged.
#>
    [CmdletBinding()]
    Param(
        [Parameter(Mandatory=$True,
                   ValueFromPipelineByPropertyName=$True)]
```

```
        [string]$ServiceName,
        [Parameter(Mandatory=$True,
                  ValueFromPipeline=$True,
                  ValueFromPipelineByPropertyName=$True)]
        [string[]]$ComputerName,
        [Parameter(ValueFromPipelineByPropertyName=$True)]
        [string]$NewPassword,
        [Parameter(ValueFromPipelineByPropertyName=$True)]
        [string]$NewUser,
        [string]$ErrorLogFilePath
    )
BEGIN{}
PROCESS{
    ForEach ($computer in $ComputerName) {
        Do {
            Write-Verbose "Connect to $computer on WS-MAN"
            $protocol = "Wsman"
            Try {
                $option = New-CimSessionOption -Protocol $protocol
                $session = New-CimSession -SessionOption $option `
                                         -ComputerName $Computer `
                                         -ErrorAction Stop
                If ($PSBoundParameters.ContainsKey('NewUser')) {
                    $args = @{'StartName'=$NewUser
                              'StartPassword'=$NewPassword}
                } Else {
                    $args = @{'StartPassword'=$NewPassword}
                    Write-Warning "Not setting a new user name"
                }
                Write-Verbose "Setting $servicename on $computer"
                $params = @{'CimSession'=$session
                            'MethodName'='Change'
                            'Query'="SELECT * FROM Win32_Service " +
                                    "WHERE Name = '$ServiceName'"
                            'Arguments'=$args}
                $ret = Invoke-CimMethod @params
                switch ($ret.ReturnValue) {
                    0  { $status = "Success" }
                    22 { $status = "Invalid Account" }
                    Default { $status = "Failed: $($ret.ReturnValue)" }
                }
                $props = @{'ComputerName'=$computer
                           'Status'=$status}
                $obj = New-Object -TypeName PSObject -Property $props
                Write-Output $obj
                Write-Verbose "Closing connection to $computer"
                $session | Remove-CimSession
            } Catch {
                # change protocol - if we've tried both
                # and logging was specified, log the computer
                Switch ($protocol) {
                    'Wsman' { $protocol = 'Dcom' }
                    'Dcom'  {
                        $protocol = 'Stop'
```

```
                              if              ($PSBoundParameters.ContainsKey(
    'ErrorLogFilePath')) {
                                   Write-Warning "$computer failed; logged to
⇒ $ErrorLogFilePath"
                                   $computer | Out-File $ErrorLogFilePath -Append
                         } # if logging
                      }
                  } #switch
             } # try/catch
         } Until ($protocol -eq 'Stop')
     } #foreach
} #PROCESS
END{}
} #function
```

Again, apologies for any word-wrapping; consult the downloadable code samples at http://mng.bz/rjgE for a well-formatted version.

In this revision, we changed New-CimSessionOption to use a variable for the protocol. We manually set this to "Wsman" to begin with, but in the event of a failure, we switch it to "Dcom". If it fails again, we set the protocol to Stop, which triggers an exit from the Do loop; we also take the opportunity to log the computer name if we're asked to do so.

## Summary

In Chapter 15, we shifted focus to error handling within the tool being developed, addressing how to capture, manage, and log errors encountered during execution. We introduced the distinction between errors and exceptions in PowerShell and discussed PowerShell's default behavior of continuing execution despite encountering errors. We also emphasized the importance of understanding and modifying the $ErrorActionPreference variable to control PowerShell's response to errors. Various options for managing errors, such as Stop, Continue, and SilentlyContinue, were explored, along with practical examples demonstrating their usage. Additionally, we delved into best practices for error handling, including avoiding global suppression of errors and carefully considering error logging. Advanced concepts like exception handling and specifying error actions for non-PowerShell commands were also covered, providing you with a comprehensive understanding of error management in PowerShell scripting. Finally, we presented you with a task to implement error handling within some code, accompanied by a detailed solution that illustrated how to handle errors gracefully while executing commands across multiple computers. Through these discussions and examples, you gained the necessary skills to enhance the robustness and reliability of your PowerShell scripts by effectively managing errors.

# *Filling out a manifest*

Up to this point, you've been relying on the PowerShell magic to make your commands—within a module—run. It's worth digging into this magic a bit because you can do much more with it.

## 16.1 *Module execution order*

When PowerShell looks for modules, it first enumerates all the folders listed in the `PSModulePath` environment variable. Each folder under each of those paths is considered a potential module.

Within a module folder, PowerShell looks for the following:

1 A .psd1 file with the same filename as the module's folder name. This module manifest tells the shell what else needs to be loaded.
2 A .dll file with the same filename as the module's folder name. This is a *compiled* or *binary* module, usually written in C#.
3 A .psm1 file with the same filename as the module's folder name. This is a *script module.*

You've been using number 3 on that list. If you create a file named \Documents\ PowerShell\Modules\MyPSModule\MyPSModule.psm1, then you've created a script module named "MyPSModule," and whatever functions are in that .psm1 file will become commands that PowerShell can run. This is a super quick and easy way to get a module up and running, but it has some disadvantages.

First, the module can't easily handle things such as versioning, establishing prerequisites, and loading supporting files (e.g., custom formatting views, which we'll get to later in this book). As your modules become more complex and you iterate them over time, you'll need them all.

Second, as it becomes larger and contains more commands, a script module alone can slow down PowerShell—even if you're not using the module—because, at launch time, PowerShell has to figure out what modules you have and what commands they contain. For a standalone script module, that means loading and parsing the *entire file* to see what functions are lurking within. That parsing takes time, and for large modules, or if you have many of them, that time can become significant—and it's a hit every time you open a new PowerShell window.

A manifest—which takes advantage of item 1 on the earlier list—solves these problems because it allows you to specify a great deal of additional information about your module. When used correctly, a manifest can vastly speed up PowerShell's module-discovery time.

## 16.2   *Creating a new manifest*

Creating a new, very basic manifest is easy. Just change to your module folder, and run `New-ModuleManifest`. Specify a filename for the manifest (which should be the same as the module folder's name, followed by the .psd1 filename extension), and specify your existing .psm1 script module as the *root module*:

```
New-ModuleManifest -Path MyModule.psd1 -Root ./MyModule.psm1
```

> **WARNING**   PowerShell does exactly nothing to verify that what you've typed is correct. A typo in either of these paths will create a nonfunctional manifest and can prevent your entire module from loading until you fix your mistakes.

That example assumes you're in a `MyModule` directory, making the official name of the module `MyModule`. The result is something like the following (which you can and should create to follow along). The automatically generated comments for each section help explain:

```
#
# Module manifest for module 'MyModule'
#
# Generated by: User
#
# Generated on: 7/23/2023
#

@{

# Script module or binary module file associated with this manifest.
RootModule = './MyModule.psm1'

# Version number of this module.
ModuleVersion = '0.0.1'

# Supported PSEditions
# CompatiblePSEditions = @()
```

```
# ID used to uniquely identify this module
GUID = 'ce7775f9-e168-48d6-8e8f-f4c04696d673'

# Author of this module
Author = 'User'

# Company or vendor of this module
CompanyName = 'Unknown'

# Copyright statement for this module
Copyright = '(c) User. All rights reserved.'

# Description of the functionality provided by this module
# Description = ''

# Minimum version of the PowerShell engine required by this module
# PowerShellVersion = ''

# Name of the PowerShell host required by this module
# PowerShellHostName = ''

# Minimum version of the PowerShell host required by this module
# PowerShellHostVersion = ''

# Minimum version of Microsoft .NET Framework required by this module.
This prerequisite is valid for the PowerShell Desktop edition only.
# DotNetFrameworkVersion = ''

# Minimum version of the common language runtime (CLR)
required by this module. This prerequisite is valid for the
PowerShell Desktop edition only.
# ClrVersion = ''

# Processor architecture (None, X86, Amd64) required by this module
# ProcessorArchitecture = ''

# Modules that must be imported into the global environment
prior to importing this module
# RequiredModules = @()

# Assemblies that must be loaded prior to importing this module
# RequiredAssemblies = @()

# Script files (.ps1) that are run in the caller's environment
prior to importing this module.
# ScriptsToProcess = @()

# Type files (.ps1xml) to be loaded when importing this module
# TypesToProcess = @()

# Format files (.ps1xml) to be loaded when importing this module
# FormatsToProcess = @()

# Modules to import as nested modules of the module specified
in RootModule/ModuleToProcess
# NestedModules = @()
```

```
# Functions to export from this module, for best performance,
do not use wildcards and do not delete the entry, use an empty
array if there are no functions to export.
FunctionsToExport = '*'

# Cmdlets to export from this module, for best performance,
do not use wildcards and do not delete the entry, use an
empty array if there are no cmdlets to export.
CmdletsToExport = '*'

# Variables to export from this module
VariablesToExport = '*'

# Aliases to export from this module, for best performance,
do not use wildcards and do not delete the entry, use an
empty array if there are no aliases to export.
AliasesToExport = '*'

# DSC resources to export from this module
# DscResourcesToExport = @()

# List of all modules packaged with this module
# ModuleList = @()

# List of all files packaged with this module
# FileList = @()

# Private data to pass to the module specified in RootModule/ModuleToProcess.
    This may also contain a
PSData hashtable with additional module metadata used by PowerShell.
PrivateData = @{

    PSData = @{

        # Tags applied to this module. These help with module
discovery in online galleries.
        # Tags = @()

        # A URL to the license for this module.
        # LicenseUri = ''

        # A URL to the main website for this project.
        # ProjectUri = ''

        # A URL to an icon representing this module.
        # IconUri = ''

        # ReleaseNotes of this module
        # ReleaseNotes = ''

        # Prerelease string of this module
        # Prerelease = ''

        # Flag to indicate whether the module requires explicit
user acceptance for install/update/save
        # RequireLicenseAcceptance = $false
```

```
        # External dependent modules of this module
        # ExternalModuleDependencies = @()

    } # End of PSData hashtable

} # End of PrivateData hashtable

# HelpInfo URI of this module
# HelpInfoURI = ''

# Default prefix for commands exported from this module.
Override the default prefix using Import-Module -Prefix.
# DefaultCommandPrefix = ''

}
```

> **NOTE** We're assuming you'll do this on a PowerShell system. The same holds for Windows PowerShell, but the manifest that is created may look a little different, so don't be alarmed.

## 16.3   Examining the manifest

Let's take a look at a few critical sections in a bit more detail. It's worth mentioning that almost everything here can be specified in advance using the parameters of New-ModuleManifest. Often, though, we create the bare-bones manifest shown here and then edit it in Visual Studio Code (VS Code) when we want to add things to the module.

### 16.3.1   Metadata

You'll notice a great deal of *metadata*, or data about the module itself, in the manifest:

- ModuleVersion is something you should get in the habit of filling out using the standard Microsoft W.X.Y.Z version notation. If you plan to submit modules to the PowerShell Gallery (www.PowerShellGallery.com), this is mandatory in your manifest.
- A globally unique identifier (GUID) is a requirement generated automatically. This uniquely identifies your module.
- Author should be your name, and CompanyName should be your organization, if appropriate. If you're submitting to the PowerShell Gallery, Author is mandatory.
- Copyright and Description are optional, but you should include a Description for PowerShell Gallery submissions (it may become mandatory at some point).
- ModuleList is a list of all your module's submodules—basically, the names of any .psm1 files. This doesn't *do* anything—it's just here for documentation purposes, and it's rare to see this used.
- FileList is similar to ModuleList—it's just a way to document all the files included in the module.

### 16.3.2  *The root module*

This is the .psm1 file containing all of your functions or code to dot source the required script files. The .psm1 file is assumed to be in the same directory as the manifest. Power-Shell won't complain if you leave this empty, but your module won't behave as expected.

### 16.3.3  *Prerequisites*

Several manifest properties help PowerShell figure out whether your module can be run on a given computer:

- `CompatiblePSEditions`—This tells the engine if this module can run in Power-Shell or Windows PowerShell. The two options are `Core` and `Desktop`.
- `PowerShellVersion`—This specifies the minimum version of PowerShell needed for the module to run.
- `PowerShellHostName` and `PowerShellHostVersion`—These describe the host application and version in which your module runs. This can restrict modules to only certain hosting situations, such as `"Console-Host"` or another environment.
- `DotNetFrameworkVersion` and `CLRVersion`—These describe any minimum version requirements of the .NET Framework or the Framework's Common Language Runtime (CLR).
- `ProcessorArchitecture`—This documents platform dependencies, such as X86 or Amd64.
- `RequiredModules`. This is an array of module names that must be imported *before* your module's commands are loaded. PowerShell will attempt to load these for you and will fail—and refuse to load your module—if it can't load these prerequisites for some reason.
- `NestedModules`—This is a little different from `RequiredModules`. Modules included in `RequiredModules` are loaded into the global session, which means they won't unload when your module is unloaded. Modules in `NestedModules` are visible *only* to your module and can't be seen or used by the person who loaded your module (unless that person also manually imports them).

### 16.3.4  *Scripts, types, and formats*

You can specify a number of supporting elements for your module. These are loaded and unloaded along with the module. Each of these elements is an array, which means you can specify zero or more elements to load:

- `ScriptsToProcess`—This lists PowerShell scripts (.ps1 files) that should be run *before* your module is loaded. This is a little unusual, but you can use it to run things such as setup tasks. It's also possible to put those setup commands into the module .psm1 file, although breaking them into a separate preload script can help make the code easier to read and maintain.
- `TypesToProcess`—This is a list of PowerShell Extensible Type System (ETS) extensions—usually .ps1xml files—that your module needs to load.

- `FormatsToProcess`—This is a list of PowerShell formatting view files—usually .format.ps1xml files—that your module needs to load. We'll cover these later in this book.

Although you can provide full paths to any of these, the convention is to include each supporting element in the module's folder and to refer to `./filename` in the array.

### 16.3.5   Exporting members

This is where you can save PowerShell some load time. Rather than forcing it to parse your entire script module and figure out what functions exist, you can declare those functions as being exported from the module. There's a side effect: any functions you *don't* export become private to the module. That means anything else within the module can see and use those functions, but the person who loaded your module *won't* see them or be able to use them. You can use this feature to create helper functions that are used by other commands in your module but that aren't exposed to anyone else.

You can export five types of things. Each of these is an array within the manifest:

- `FunctionsToExport`—Holds functions you want people to be able to use as commands.
- `CmdletsToExport`—Won't be used in a script module—this is the equivalent of `FunctionsToExport` when publishing a compiled module.
- `VariablesToExport`—Holds module-level variables you want added to the global scope. This is a good way to publish variables that set things such as log filenames, database connection strings, and so on.
- `AliasesToExport`—Holds aliases that you define in your module (using `New-Alias`) and that you want to be exposed when your module is loaded.
- `DscResourcesToExport`—A special list related to building Desired State Configuration (DSC) resource modules. This is a special type of PowerShell tool that we aren't covering in this book.

As a note, it's legal for most of these to specify `*`, meaning "export everything." Sadly, that doesn't help PowerShell in a performance sense because it still forces PowerShell to open and parse the entire script module to see exactly what "everything" entails. As a best practice, avoid using `*`, and take the time to list exported items explicitly.

---

**Exporting exceptions**

You need to be aware of a few exporting exceptions. If you're creating a script module instead of a binary, compiled module—which is exporting and needs to export variables and aliases—then you must use `Export-ModuleMember` at the end of your .psm1 file. There's no harm in using `Export-ModuleMember` to list your functions here as well as in the manifest. You might have a line like this at the end of your .psm1 file:

```
Export-modulemember -function Get-Foo,Set-Foo -variable myfoo -alias gf,sf
```

> **(continued)**
>
> For consistency, you might get into the habit of using `Export-ModuleMember` and the manifest. PowerShell is a very active product, and you never know when a future version will allow exporting variables and aliases in a manifest. Cover all your bases.

## 16.4    Your turn

We'll give you a module (as a .psm1 file) and ask you to create a corresponding manifest. This shouldn't take long!

### 16.4.1    Start here

The following listing shows the contents of `MyTools.psm1`, a script module.

**Listing 16.1    `MyTools.psm1` script module**

```
function Get-TMIPInfo {
    [CmdletBinding()]
    Param(
        [Parameter(Mandatory=$True,
                   ValueFromPipeline=$True)]
        [string[]]$ComputerName
    )
    BEGIN {}
    PROCESS {
        ForEach ($comp in $ComputerName) {
            Write-Verbose "Connecting to $comp"
            $s = New-CimSession -ComputerName $comp
            $adapters = Get-NetAdapter -CimSession $s |
                      Where Status -ne 'Disconnected'
            ForEach ($adapter in $adapters) {
                Write-Verbose "  Interface $($adapter.interfaceindex)"
                $addresses = Get-NetIPAddress
   -InterfaceIndex $adapter.InterfaceIndex `
                                          -CimSession $s
                ForEach ($address in $addresses) {
                    $props = @{'ComputerName'=$Comp
                               'Index'=$adapter.interfaceindex
                               'Name'=$adapter.interfacealias
                               'MAC'=$adapter.macaddress
                               'IPAddress'=$address.ipaddress}
                    New-Object -TypeName PSObject -Property $props
                } #foreach address
            } #adapter
            $s | Remove-CimSession
        } #foreach computer
    } #process
    END {}
} #function
```

We assume you've saved this as \Documents\PowerShell\Modules\MyTools\MyTools.psm1.

### 16.4.2   Your task

Create a manifest for the `MyTools` module. In it, do the following:

- Specify at least a version, a description, and an author.
- Specify `MyTools.psm1` as the root module.
- Export the `Get-TMIPInfo` function.

### 16.4.3   Our take

We ran this command (we've prettied up the formatting here for readability; we typed it as one long line of text):

```
New-ModuleManifest -Path MyTools.psd1
                   -RootModule ./MyTools.psm1
                   -ModuleVersion 1.0.0.0
                   -Author 'Jeff and Don'
                   -Description 'A test module'
                   -FunctionsToExport @('Get-TMIPInfo')
```

For the sake of the book, we've truncated some of the comments. The result is something like this:

```
#
# Module manifest for module 'MyModule'
#
# Generated by: User
#
# Generated on: 6/19/2017
#
@{
# Script module or binary module file associated with this manifest.
RootModule = 'MyModule.psm1'
# Version number of this module.
ModuleVersion = '1.0'
# Supported PSEditions
# CompatiblePSEditions = @()
# ID used to uniquely identify this module
GUID = 'ea4d119b-6bcf-4540-a389-67cf7d261726'
# Author of this module
Author = 'User'
# Company or vendor of this module
CompanyName = 'Unknown'
# Copyright statement for this module
Copyright = '(c) 2017 User. All rights reserved.'
# Description of the functionality provided by this module
# Description = ''
# Minimum version of the Windows PowerShell engine required by this module
# PowerShellVersion = ''
# Name of the Windows PowerShell host required by this module
# PowerShellHostName = ''
# Minimum version of the Windows PowerShell host required by this module
# PowerShellHostVersion = ''
# Minimum version of Microsoft .NET Framework required by this module. ...
```

```
# DotNetFrameworkVersion = ''
# Minimum version of the common language runtime (CLR) required by this ...
# CLRVersion = ''
# Processor architecture (None, X86, Amd64) required by this module
# ProcessorArchitecture = ''
# Modules that must be imported into the global environment prior ...
# RequiredModules = @()
# Assemblies that must be loaded prior to importing this module
# RequiredAssemblies = @()
# Script files (.ps1) that are run in the caller's environment prior...
# ScriptsToProcess = @()
# Type files (.ps1xml) to be loaded when importing this module
# TypesToProcess = @()
# Format files (.ps1xml) to be loaded when importing this module
# FormatsToProcess = @()
# Modules to import as nested modules of the module specified in ...
# NestedModules = @()
# Functions to export from this module, for best performance, do not ...
FunctionsToExport = @('Get-TMIIPInfo')
# Cmdlets to export from this module, for best performance, do not ...
CmdletsToExport = '*'
# Variables to export from this module
VariablesToExport = '*'
# Aliases to export from this module, for best performance, do not ...
AliasesToExport = '*'
# DSC resources to export from this module
# DscResourcesToExport = @()
# List of all modules packaged with this module
# ModuleList = @()
# List of all files packaged with this module
# FileList = @()
# Private data to pass to the module specified in ...
PrivateData = @{
    PSData = @{
        # Tags applied to this module. These help with module discovery ...
        # Tags = @()
        # A URL to the license for this module.
        # LicenseUri = ''
        # A URL to the main website for this project.
        # ProjectUri = ''
        # A URL to an icon representing this module.
        # IconUri = ''
        # ReleaseNotes of this module
        # ReleaseNotes = ''
    } # End of PSData hashtable
} # End of PrivateData hashtable
# HelpInfo URI of this module
# HelpInfoURI = ''
# Default prefix for commands exported from this module. Override ...
# DefaultCommandPrefix = ''
}
```

## *Summary*

In this chapter, we looked into the intricacies of module management in PowerShell, particularly focusing on the creation and utilization of module manifests. Module manifests, denoted by .psd1 files, offer a structured approach to defining module metadata and dependencies, enhancing the efficiency and manageability of PowerShell modules. We explored the key components of a manifest, such as module versioning, authorship details, dependencies, and exported members. By leveraging manifests, PowerShell users can streamline module discovery, ensure version compatibility, and facilitate seamless integration of modules into their workflow. Through practical examples and insights, we equipped you with the knowledge and tools necessary to harness the full potential of PowerShell modules within your development and administration tasks.

# Part 3

Welcome to the sophisticated phase of our scripting journey—Grown-Up Scripting. In this part, we ascend to a higher level of scripting expertise, focusing on advanced techniques and adopting professional-grade practices that distinguish mature scripting endeavors. Chapter 17 initiates a paradigm shift, challenging conventional thinking and encouraging a mindset aligned with the demands of complex scripting scenarios. You'll elevate your scripting skills to a professional level in chapter 18, uncovering principles and practices that differentiate amateur scripts from those meeting industry standards, ensuring reliability, scalability, and maintainability. You'll then enter the realm of source control with chapter 19 by gaining a foundational understanding of Git—a powerful version control system—and discovering its role in enhancing collaboration and tracking changes in your scripts. As we delve into the art of refining and perfecting scripts in chapter 20, you'll learn to meticulously pester your code by testing, probing, and ensuring its resilience in various scenarios. Security takes center stage in chapter 21 as you explore the importance of script signing—a crucial aspect ensuring the integrity and authenticity of your scripts. In conclusion, in chapter 22, you'll explore the process of script publication and understand the steps involved in sharing your scripts with a broader audience. As you progress, you'll refine your scripting skills and adopt a mature and professional approach to script development. Grown-Up Scripting is all about embracing the complexities of advanced techniques, incorporating industry best practices, and ensuring your scripts are functional and exemplary. Let's embark on this journey of script maturity and elevate our scripting prowess together!

# Changing your brain when it comes to scripting

Let's pause our ongoing narrative for a moment. In the previous chapters, our primary focus was creating tools that align with PowerShell's established conventions and practices. While this approach has its merits, there are instances where the most effective way to convey a message is by highlighting its contrast.

> **NOTE** This is our special Bonus Double Chapter; feel free to take your time as you read through this chapter. It's essential to grasp the underlying rationale behind our discussion fully. If certain aspects still need clarification, feel free to engage with the community on PowerShell.org and ask any questions. The concepts explored in this chapter stand as the core pillars of this book; everything else is essentially a means to implement and reinforce these foundational ideas. If you intend to progress to more advanced scripting, as covered in *The PowerShell Scripting & Toolmaking Book* (https://leanpub.com/powershell-scripting-toolmaking), a solid understanding of the principles in this chapter is an absolute necessity.

## 17.1 Example 1

Let's consider a forum post from PowerShell.org, which we've referenced with permission from its original author. The goals were to list the sizes of each user's home folder and show any orphan folders—folders that no longer corresponded to an Active Directory (AD) user. The author posted this code. Note that you need to install the AD module for this to work.

**Listing 17.1    Typical PowerShell**

```
$UserNames = Get-ADUser -Filter * -SearchBase `
"OU=NAME_OF_OU_WITH_USERS3,OU=NAME_OF_OU_WITH_USERS2,
OU=NAME_OF_OU_WITH_USERS1,DC=DOMAIN_NAME,DC=COUNTRY_CODE" |
Select -ExpandProperty samaccountname
$UserRegex = ($UserNames | ForEach{[RegEx]::Escape($_)}) -join "|"
$myArray = (Get-ChildItem -Path "\\file2\Felles\Home\*" -Directory |
Where{$_.Name -notmatch $UserRegex})
#$myArray
foreach ($mapper in $myArray) {
    #Param ($mapper = $(Throw "no folder name specified"))
    # calculate folder size and recurse as needed
    $size = 0
    Foreach ($file in $(ls $mapper -recurse)){
    If (-not ($file.psiscontainer)) {
        $size += $file.length
        }
    }
    # return the value and go back to caller
    echo $size
}
```

## 17.1.1   *The critique*

Now, this isn't meant to beat up on the original author. People learn different things at different times and arrive at their code's condition through various paths. Let's take the code for what it is:

- If asked to solve this problem, we'd write this as two functions, not as one script. One function would sum up folder sizes, which is a useful function in many scenarios. Another would figure out which folders were orphans.
- We'd also take a more PowerShell-native approach, avoiding things such as echo. Instead, we'd aim to output objects because those could be piped to commands that made them into CSV files, HTML reports, and lots more. On most systems, echo should be an alias for Write-Output, which means objects will be written to the pipeline. But using the alias doesn't make that clear, and someone could have used echo as an alias for Write-Host—and then you'd be back to not having objects in the pipeline.
- We'd probably make more use of native PowerShell commands because they tend to run a smidge faster than a script.
- To maximize reuse, we'd try to keep our functions as generic and non-context-specific as possible. This means no hardcoded names or paths.

One thing to remember is that, in Windows, folders *don't* have a size. You must get all the files within that folder instead and add *their* sizes.

### 17.1.2  *Our take*

Here's our first function. We aren't going to explain each line in detail. You can (and should) try the code yourself. Notice that we're explicitly outputting an empty object if a folder doesn't exist.

**Listing 17.2**  `Get-FolderSize`

```
function Get-FolderSize {
    [CmdletBinding()]
    Param(
        [Parameter(Mandatory=$True,
                   ValueFromPipeline=$True,
                   ValueFromPipelineByPropertyName=$True)]
        [string[]]$Path
    )
    BEGIN {}
    PROCESS {
        ForEach ($folder in $path) {
            Write-Verbose "Checking $folder"
            if (Test-Path -Path $folder) {
                Write-Verbose " + Path exists"
                $params = @{'Path'=$folder
                            'Recurse'=$true
                            'File'=$true}
                $measure = Get-ChildItem @params |
                           Measure-Object -Property Length -Sum
                [pscustomobject]@{'Path'=$folder
                                  'Files'=$measure.count
                                  'Bytes'=$measure.sum}
            } else {
                Write-Verbose " - Path does not exist"
                [pscustomobject]@{'Path'=$folder
                                  'Files'=0
                                  'Bytes'=0}
            } #if folder exists
        } #foreach
    } #PROCESS
    END {}
} #function
```

The results of our first function look like this:

```
Path                                              Files   Bytes
----                                              -----   -----
C:\Get-DiskInfo                            35     44101
C:\nope                                             0       0
```

We could pipe that to `Select-Object` to turn the `Bytes` count into another unit, such as megabytes. Still, we feel it's important for our tool to output the lowest-level information possible to maximize its utility. Notice that we didn't test this against home folders per se; we want this to be a generic folder-size-adding-up function. Later, we'll write a controller script to put this function to more specific business use, such as summing up user home folder sizes.

Now, we'll write a second function to deal with orphan folders. This will incorporate our Get-FolderSize function. We assume this function has already been loaded into the PowerShell session. This tool is a bit more task-specific because it has to understand our need to identify orphaned home folders.

**Listing 17.3   Get-UserHomeFolderInfo**

```
function Get-UserHomeFolderInfo {
    [CmdletBinding()]
    Param(
        [Parameter(Mandatory=$True)]
        [string] $HomeRootPath
    )
    BEGIN {}
    PROCESS {
        Write-Verbose "Enumerating $HomeRootPath"
        $params = @{'Path'=$HomeRootPath
                    'Directory'=$True}
        ForEach ($folder in (Get-ChildItem @params)) {           Loops through
            Write-Verbose "Checking $($folder.name)"             each child folder
            $params = @{'Identity'=$folder.name                  in the root
                        'ErrorAction'='SilentlyContinue'}
            $user = Get-ADUser @params            Tests for an AD
            if ($user) {                          user account
                Write-Verbose " + User exists"
                $result = Get-FolderSize -Path $folder.fullname
                [pscustomobject]@{'User'=$folder.name
                                  'Path'=$folder.fullname       Runs our
                                  'Files'=$result.files         Get-FolderSize
                                  'Bytes'=$result.bytes         function
                                  'Status'='OK'}
            } else {
                Write-Verbose " - User does not exist"
                [pscustomobject]@{'User'=$folder.name
                                  'Path'=$folder.fullname
                                  'Files'=0
                                  'Bytes'=0
                                  'Status'="Orphan"}
            } #if User exists
        } #foreach
    } #PROCESS
    END {}
}
```

Here, we're taking a root location that contains home folders, going through them one at a time, and checking to see whether a corresponding AD user exists. If one doesn't, we output a blank object with an Orphan Status property. We could easily use Where-Object to filter for just the orphans so that someone could deal with those. If the User exists, we use Get-FolderSize to get the size information and output the same object. This time, the object is fully populated with an OK status. Either way, writing out the same kind of object ensures consistent output and maximizes the reusability of the information. This code is in the downloadable samples on GitHub broken down by chapter (https://github.com/psjamesp/MOL-Scripting).

### 17.1.3 *Thinking beyond the literal*

The idea here is to take a given task and break it down. In the original forum post, the source data was "all users in AD," which created some challenges regarding finding orphan folders. In our approach, we use the list of folders as the source data and check each against AD. That won't tell us if we have users *without* home folders, but that wasn't a stated problem (and, in most cases, we expect users would bring it up to the help desk if they didn't have a home folder).

We took the one generic portion of the task and wrote it out as its tool: Get-Folder-Size. We ensured it was helpful on its own, accepting pipeline input and such, even though that's not how Get-UserHomeFolderInfo uses it. We incorporated verbose output that will make each function a bit easier to follow and debug, if necessary. And, because we've used functions, each task is tightly scoped and does just one thing, making each function less complex, easier to debug, and easier to understand and maintain.

## 17.2   *Example 2*

Listing 17.4 is an example of a script that will notify a user via email when their password is close to expiring. This is a very long script, so we suggest you download it from GitHub (https://github.com/psjamesp/MOL-Scripting).

Note that you'll need to have the Graph PowerShell module installed (Install-Module Microsoft.Graph) and your application registered in Microsoft Entra ID for this to work.

---

**Listing 17.4   PasswordChangeNotification.ps1**

**Comment help block (but notice it's not very helpful)**

```
<#          This script will connect to Azure AD via Microsoft Graph
and notify users if their password is set to expire in the next 7 days.
It will then send them an email.                                        <──┘
#>
Connect-MgGraph -ClientId 'YOUR_CLINET_ID' -TenantId 'YOUR_TENANT_ID'   <──┐
```

**Connects to Graph API**

```
#Domain's password experation in Days
$PasswordValidDay = get-mgdomain -DomainId PowerShell.org |
 select-object -ExpandProperty PasswordNotificationWindowInDays
```

```
# Check the user's password expiration date
$today = Get-Date                                                       <──┐
$allUsers = get-mguser -All -Property lastPasswordChangeDateTime,mail | <──┐
Where-Object {$_.PasswordPolicies -contains "DisablePasswordExpiration"}
```

**A few lines of code to calculate the date**

**Collects all users into an array**

```
foreach ($user in $allUsers) {                          ◁─┐  Loops
    $passwordExpirationDate = $user.LastPasswordChangeDateTime +  │  through
[System.TimeSpan]::FromDays($PasswordValidDay)               │  the array

    # Define the notification threshold (e.g., 7 days before the password
expires)
    $notificationThreshold = 7

    # Calculate the number of days until password expiration
    $daysUntilExpiration = ($passwordExpirationDate - $today).Days

    if ($daysUntilExpiration -le $notificationThreshold) {   ┌─  Gathers all
        #Send Email using Graph API                    ◁────┤  things needed
        $params = @{                                         │  to send email
            Message         = @{
                Subject       = "Your Password is About to Expire"
                Body          = @{
                    ContentType = 'HTML'Content     = "Your password will
expire on
$passwordExpirationDate. Please update your password."
                }
                ToRecipients  = @(
                    @{
                        EmailAddress = @{
                            Address = $user.mail
                        }
                    }
                )
            }
            SaveToSentItems = $true
        }
        # Send message                                       ┌─  Sends email
        Send-MgUserMail -UserId $from -BodyParameter $params  ◁──┤  via Graph API
    } else {
        Write-Host "Password is not yet expired. Days until expiration
$daysUntilExpiration"
    }

}
```

## 17.2.1 *The walkthrough*

Let's run through this script in major sections, to get you situated with what's happening. We'll repeat a few lines of code inline so that you don't have to keep flipping back and forth. Let's take a closer look at what each step labeled in the preceding code is doing:

1  This script works well, but it's not a tool. First, there is very little help to find on how to use the script.

2  Next, we connect to our Graph API application in Microsoft Entra ID (formerly Azure AD) giving our Client (Application) ID and our Tenant ID:

```
Connect-MgGraph -ClientId 'YOUR_CLINET_ID' -TenantId 'YOUR_TENANT_ID'
```

3  Then, there is a line of code to check the date:

```
$today = Get-Date
```

4  The next block of code checks what the password expiration policy is set for at the domain level. Then, we gather all the users in our directory whose password policy isn't set to "Never Expires":

```
$allUsers = get-mguser -All -Property `
lastPasswordChangeDateTime,mail,passwordProfile | Where-Object
{$_.PasswordPolicies -contains "DisablePasswordExpiration"}
```

5  The next step in the code is to loop through the array. In the big mess of code, we're comparing two dates: today's date minus the last time a user changed their password; and if it's less than our threshold (7 days).

6  Next up is to gather all the information we need to send the user an email that their password is going to expire soon:

```
$params = @{
        Message         = @{
            Subject      = "Your Password is About to Expire"
            Body         = @{
                ContentType = 'HTML'
                Content     = "Your password will expire on
$passwordExpirationDate. Please update your password."
            }
            ToRecipients  = @(
                @{
                    EmailAddress = @{
                        Address = $user.mail
                    }
                }
            )
        }
        SaveToSentItems = $true
}
```

7  Finally, we send the email suing the Graph API:

```
Send-MgUserMail -UserId $from -BodyParameter $params
```

### 17.2.2  *Our take*

This is a good example of what we call a *monolithic script*. It's doing more than one task as part of a larger process, but it's performing all those tasks in a single sequence rather than the tasks being modularized into tools. This kind of script takes a lot of work and can be tough to debug because there's so much going on purely in memory. What we like to do with toolmaking is create smaller, self-contained tools, each representing a boundary. Each tool can be written and tested individually, making coding and debugging much easier.

First, you'll notice that we broke this down into four different functions. `Connect-MyMgGraph`, `Get-PasswordExpirationWindow`, `Check-PasswordExpiration`, and `Send-PasswordExpirationNotification`. Let's look at the first function and break it down. We have two mandatory parameters: the Client ID for the application you made and the Tenant ID for your Microsoft Entra ID (formally Azure AD) tenant. Then, we use the command `Connect-MgGraph` to create the connection to the Graph API:

```
function Connect-MyMgGraph {
    [CmdletBinding()]
    param (
        [Parameter(Mandatory = $true)]
        [string]$ClientId,
        [Parameter(Mandatory = $true)]
        [string]$TenantId
        [Parameter(Mandatory = $true)]
        [string]$from

    )

    # Connect to Microsoft Graph here with the given credentials
    Connect-MgGraph -ClientId $ClientId -TenantId $TenantId -NoWelcome

    Write-Host "Connected to Microsoft Graph"
```

The next function is `Get-PasswordExpirationWindow`. This function is small, but remember, we're trying to break down our code in reusable pieces. It has a single mandatory parameter, and this is the Domain ID. Using the Graph API, it looks to see the organization's password expiration policy:

```
function Get-PasswordExpirationWindow {
    [CmdletBinding()]
    param (
        [Parameter(Mandatory = $true)]
        [string]$DomainId
    )

    $PasswordValidDay = Get-MgDomain -DomainId $DomainId |
Select-Object -ExpandProperty PasswordNotificationWindowInDays
    return $PasswordValidDay
```

The next function is `Check-PasswordExpiration`, which is the bulk of our code. It gathers a list (array) of all users who don't have a password policy of `DisablePasswordExpiration`. Then, we look at the last time the password was set and subtract that from today's date. If it's less than our threshold, we call our last function, `Send-PasswordExpirationNotification`, to email the user that their password is about to expire:

```
function Check-PasswordExpiration {
    [CmdletBinding()]
    param (
        [Parameter(Mandatory = $true)]
        [int]$NotificationThreshold,
```

```
        [Parameter(Mandatory = $true)]
        [string]$DomainId
    )

    $today = Get-Date
    $allUsers = Get-MgUser -All -Property lastPasswordChangeDateTime, `
    mail | Where-Object {$_.PasswordPolicies -contains `
    "DisablePasswordExpiration"}

    foreach ($user in $allUsers) {
        $passwordExpirationDate = $user.LastPasswordChangeDateTime
+[System.TimeSpan]::FromDays((Get-PasswordExpirationWindow -DomainId
$DomainId))

        $daysUntilExpiration = ($passwordExpirationDate - $today).Days

        if ($daysUntilExpiration -le $NotificationThreshold) {
            Send-PasswordExpirationNotification -User $user -ExpirationDate
$passwordExpirationDate
        }
        else {
            Write-Host "Password is not yet expired. Days until expiration:
$daysUntilExpiration"
        }
    }
}
```

Our last function is Send-PasswordExpirationNotification, which uses the Graph
API to send an email letting users know that their password is about to expire:

```
function Send-PasswordExpirationNotification {
    [CmdletBinding()]
    param (
        [Parameter(Mandatory = $true)]
        [PSCustomObject]$User,
        [Parameter(Mandatory = $true)]
        [datetime]$ExpirationDate
    )

    $params = @{
        Message         = @{
            Subject     = "Your Password is About to Expire"
            Body        = @{
                ContentType = 'HTML'
                Content     = "Your password will expire on
$ExpirationDate. Please update your password."
            }
            ToRecipients = @(
                @{
                    EmailAddress = @{
                        Address = $User.mail
                    }
                }
            )
        }
```

```
            SaveToSentItems = $true
        }

    # Send the email using the Graph API
    Send-MgUserMail -UserId $from -BodyParameter $params
}
```

The last two lines of code call our functions. The first calls our `Connect-MyMgGraph`
function to connect to the Graph API:

```
Connect-MyMgGraph -ClientId 'YOUR_CLIENT_ID' -TenantId 'YOUR_TENANT_ID'
```

Finally, we call our `Check-PasswordExpiration` function, and we send it a threshold
of seven days and our domain name:

```
Check-PasswordExpiration -NotificationThreshold 7 -DomainID "Your_Domain"
```

Now, let's take a look at our revised script in the following listing.

Listing 17.5   Revised password expiration code

```
<#
.SYNOPSIS
    Connects to the Microsoft Graph API with the provided client ID and
tenant ID.
.DESCRIPTION
    This function establishes a connection to the Microsoft Graph API using
the provided client ID and tenant ID.
.PARAMETER ClientId
    The client ID for your application.
.PARAMETER TenantId
    The tenant ID associated with your organization.
#>
function Connect-MyMgGraph {
    [CmdletBinding()]
    param (
        [Parameter(Mandatory = $true)]
        [string]$ClientId,
        [Parameter(Mandatory = $true)]
        [string]$TenantId
    )

    # Connect to Microsoft Graph here with the given credentials
    Connect-MgGraph -ClientId $ClientId -TenantId $TenantId -NoWelcome

    Write-Host "Connected to Microsoft Graph"
}

<#
.SYNOPSIS
    Retrieves the password expiration window for a specific domain.
.DESCRIPTION
```

This function retrieves the password expiration window (in days) for a specified domain.
.PARAMETER DomainId
   The ID of the domain for which you want to get the password expiration window.
#>
```
function Get-PasswordExpirationWindow {
    [CmdletBinding()]
    param (
        [Parameter(Mandatory = $true)]
        [string]$DomainId
    )

    $PasswordValidDay = Get-MgDomain -DomainId $DomainId |
Select-Object -ExpandProperty PasswordNotificationWindowInDays
    return $PasswordValidDay
}

<#
.SYNOPSIS
   Checks and notifies users of password expiration.
.DESCRIPTION
   This function checks the password expiration for all users and sends
notifications to those whose passwords are about to expire.
.PARAMETER NotificationThreshold
   The number of days before password expiration to send notifications.
#>
function Check-PasswordExpiration {
    [CmdletBinding()]
    param (
        [Parameter(Mandatory = $true)]
        [int]$NotificationThreshold,
        [Parameter(Mandatory = $true)]
        [string]$DomainId
    )

    $today = Get-Date
    $allUsers = Get-MgUser -All -Property lastPasswordChangeDateTime, mail
| Where-Object {$_.PasswordPolicies -contains "DisablePasswordExpiration"}

    foreach ($user in $allUsers) {
        $passwordExpirationDate = $user.LastPasswordChangeDateTime +
[System.TimeSpan]::FromDays((Get-PasswordExpirationWindow -DomainId
$DomainId))

        $daysUntilExpiration = ($passwordExpirationDate - $today).Days

        if ($daysUntilExpiration -le $NotificationThreshold) {
            Send-PasswordExpirationNotification -User $user -ExpirationDate
$passwordExpirationDate
        }
        else {
            Write-Host "Password is not yet expired. Days until expiration:
$daysUntilExpiration"
        }
```

```
        }
}

<#
.SYNOPSIS
    Sends a password expiration notification email to a user.
.DESCRIPTION
    This function sends an email notification to a user whose password is
about to expire.
.PARAMETER User
    The user object for whom the notification is intended.
.PARAMETER ExpirationDate
    The date on which the user's password will expire.
#>
function Send-PasswordExpirationNotification {
    [CmdletBinding()]
    param (
        [Parameter(Mandatory = $true)]
        [PSCustomObject]$User,
        [Parameter(Mandatory = $true)]
        [datetime]$ExpirationDate
    )

    $params = @{
        Message         = @{
            Subject     = "Your Password is About to Expire"
            Body        = @{
                ContentType = 'HTML'
                Content     = "Your password will expire on
$ExpirationDate. Please update your password."
            }
            ToRecipients = @(
                @{
                    EmailAddress = @{
                        Address = $User.mail
                    }
                }
            )
        }
        SaveToSentItems = $true
    }

    # Send the email using the Graph API
    Send-MgUserMail -UserId $from -BodyParameter $params
}

Connect-MyMgGraph -ClientId 'YOUR_CLIENT_ID' -TenantId 'YOUR_TENANT_ID'
Check-PasswordExpiration -NotificationThreshold 7 -DomainID "Your_Domain"
```

**WARNING**   This exercise was mainly about *how* we'd reorganize things. We
haven't tested this extensively, and we've omitted a few things from the original script due to space considerations in the book. If you decide to finish
this, do so with our blessing, and please share your results with the original
script's author!

## 17.3 Your turn

Let's engage your brain in a "change it to the right way" exercise.

### 17.3.1 Start here

Consider this example (with apologies for the line-wrapping—it's unavoidable and part of the problem we want to illustrate).

**Listing 17.6  Start here**

```
foreach ($domain in (Get-ADForest).domains) {
  Get-ADDomainController -filter * -server $domain |
  sort hostname   |
  foreach {
    Get-CimInstance -ClassName Win32_ComputerSystem -ComputerName
➡ $psitem.Hostname |
    select @{name="DomainController";Expression={$_.PSComputerName}},
➡ Manufacturer, Model,@{Name="TotalPhysicalMemory(GB)"
➡ ;Expression={ "{0:N0}"
-f  ($_.TotalPhysicalMemory / 1Gb) }}
    }
}
```

This isn't *bad* code by any stretch, but it's limited. Let's say that you wanted its output on the screen one day—done! It'll work fine. But tomorrow, you want the output in a CSV file. Oh, and the day after, your boss wants it in an HTML report. What would you change to enable all of those scenarios?

### 17.3.2 Your task

Rewrite the code to conform to native PowerShell patterns and practices we've discussed. You don't need to get fancy and add error handling or anything, although you're free to do so if you want.

### 17.3.3 Our take

Here's how we approached this.

**Listing 17.7  Our solution**

```
function Get-DiskInfo {
 foreach ($domain in (Get-ADForest).domains) {
   $hosts = Get-ADDomainController -filter * -server $domain |
   Sort-Object -Prop hostname
   ForEach ($h in $hosts) {
   $cs = Get-CimInstance -ClassName Win32_ComputerSystem -ComputerName $h
   $props = @{'ComputerName' = $h
              'DomainController' = $h
              'Manufacturer' = $cs.manufacturer
              'Model' = $cs.model
              'TotalPhysicalMemory(GB)'=$cs.totalphysicalmemory / 1GB}
     New-Object -Type PSObject -Prop $props
```

```
    } #foreach $h
  } #foreach $domain
} #function
```

Here are some notes to consider:

- We switched to the ForEach scripting construct because it tends to run a little faster, and we find it easier to read.
- Rather than using Select-Object, we manually constructed an object. We find this easier to read.
- We added both a DomainController property and a ComputerName property. The original code produced DomainController, but we always like to have ComputerName because it lines up better in the pipeline with -ComputerName parameters.
- Most important, we encased the code in a function. This makes it easier to pipe the output to Export-CSV, ConvertTo-HTML, and so on.

Our solution isn't perfect because it's still doing two things: getting computer accounts from AD and disk information. We might write a tool to get domain computer accounts in a proper production environment, perhaps based on some criteria. Then, we'd modify this function to handle only the disk information. If we planned the properties and parameters right, we could use these hypothetical commands like this:

```
Get-CompanyServers | Get-DiskInfo
Get-CompanyServers | Get-DiskInfo | Convertto-html -title "DiskInfo Report"
```

We'll leave it to you to play with this further.

## *Summary*

In this chapter, we embarked on a journey of shifting our mindset toward scripting, embracing advanced techniques and adopting professional-grade practices. We challenged conventional thinking and encouraged a mature approach to scripting.

Throughout this part of the journey, we'll emphasize embracing complexity, incorporating industry best practices, and striving for functional and exemplary scripts. By adopting a mature and professional approach to script development, we aim to elevate our scripting prowess together.

# Professional-grade scripting

We're almost ready to call you a *professional* toolmaker in PowerShell—almost. Before you go around adding "PowerShell Toolmaker" to your résumé, we think you should make certain that you're exhibiting the behaviors and patterns of a true PowerShell pro. With that in mind, this chapter provides essential guidelines and a list of best practices to follow to be recognized as a reliable and skilled professional in the PowerShell world.

## 18.1 Using source control

One hallmark of professional PowerShell scripters is their commitment to ensuring the longevity and maintainability of their code. Source control, discussed in detail in chapter 19, is pivotal in achieving these goals. While some might liken source control to filing taxes, modern tools have greatly streamlined its usage. Integrated seamlessly with platforms such as Visual Studio Code (VS Code), source control is as easy as saving a file and committing changes with a simple keystroke.

Recognize that source control isn't just a chore but a mark of professionalism. Employing source control on your projects offers numerous benefits:

- *Team collaboration*—In team settings, source control helps prevent conflicts by tracking who makes changes and preventing accidental overwrites.
- *Version history*—Revisit previous iterations of your code to correct mistakes or reference past approaches.
- *Backup and recovery*—Source control repositories often become part of an organization's backup strategy, ensuring the safety of your codebase.

- *Code sharing*—Easily share code with others while maintaining control over contributions, which is essential for community-based projects.
- *Issue management*—Leading systems such as Team Foundation Server (TFS), Azure DevOps, and GitHub provide tools to track and discuss problems, and release updates.

Remember, using source control elevates your professional image in the eyes of IT managers and your colleagues.

## 18.2  Code clarity

In the console, shortcuts can save time, but in scripts, readability matters. Avoid using aliases and abbreviated parameter names. We watch PowerShell inventor Jeffrey Snover do demonstrations, and it's all `icm { ps } -com cl2` and stuff, and it looks amazing—and mysterious. Someone must stand with him during demos and explain what he typed. Spell out command and parameter names fully, and embrace tab completion. By doing so, you enhance the readability of your script and minimize typos. Follow this practice right from the start, as it aligns with professional coding.

Again, if it's at the console and just for you, fine—type what you remember and save time. We all do it. But a script is a permanent artifact to be shared with others and checked into source control. It needs to be more readable. *Spell out* every command name, *spell out* every parameter name, and *use* parameter names rather than relying on positional values. Your script will be vastly easier for someone else to read—and, as my coauthor Don Jones often says, in a few months, *you'll* be that "someone else," and Future You will appreciate the effort that Past You put into spelling everything out.

It doesn't even need to take much effort. Are you in front of a computer? Look at the Tab key. It's huge, right? It's almost the size of the Shift key and twice that of any letter key. It's like it *wants* to be pressed. In PowerShell, tab completion is key to spelling things out with less effort. You'll get *everything* spelled out and reduce your bug count because the computer won't ever make a typo for a command or parameter name. Double win!

> **NOTE**  We're not the only ones who make a big deal about this point. If you're using VS Code, you'll be bombarded with red squiggly indicators that something is wrong. That's because the PowerShell extension in VS Code relies on the PowerShell Script Analyzer (PSScriptAnalyzer) tool, which includes rule-checking for aliases. It probably won't detect if you use a positional parameter, but it will recognize if you use `gsv` instead of `Get-Service`. So, write your code the right way from the beginning.

## 18.3  Effective comments

Comments are essential for clarity, but don't overdo it. Provide high-level explanations for complex sections of your script. Inline comments shouldn't merely restate the obvious. Use verbose statements or inline comments to guide readers through your code's logic. Remember, these comments are your way of communicating your thoughts to others. We don't mean this:

```
# Query Win32_ComputerSystem object from WMI
Get-WMIObject –Class Win32_ComputerSystem
```

Gosh, is that what `Get-WmiObject` does? Wow. No, we're not saying you need a line-by-line, blow-by-blow accounting of what your code does, but provide some broad strokes. Here's an example:

```
# see if –NewUser was specified and modify arguments
# We use StartPassword either way
If ($PSBoundParameters.ContainsKey('NewUser')) {
  $args = @{'StartName'=$NewUser
            'StartPassword'=$NewPassword}
} Else {
  $args = @{'StartPassword'=$NewPassword}
  Write-Warning "Not setting a new user name"
}
```

Here, we've used a comment to provide a high-level description of what's happening and why. Comments document *what you were thinking* more than anything else, and that's useful to someone else—and again, that "someone else" will be *you* a few months from now.

We're also broadly okay with using verbose statements instead of some inline comments, for example:

```
Write-Verbose "Closing connection to $computer"
$session | Remove-CimSession
```

Removing a `CimSession` is evident from the command name, so this doesn't warrant an inline comment. But the verbose statement does help document the progression of the script, and here it does so in a way that the verbose output benefits someone *using* the script and someone reading it.

> **NOTE**   So, um, where are this book's inline comments? We've omitted a lot of them because we want to reduce the amount of space we're taking up and to help you focus on the commands. The examples we use in the book aren't, from a practices-and-patterns perspective, the same code we'd deploy in a production environment.

## 18.4   Formatting your code

There is *zero* excuse for mangled-looking code. Unfortunately, listing 18.1 is an all-too-realistic example of what people often post in online forums. Given the line-wrapping in this book, you probably can't read it, but look at the downloadable sample code file, and you'll find it hard to read.

**Listing 18.1    Code that is *not* formatted**

```
function Set-TMServiceLogon {
[CmdletBinding()]
Param(
[Parameter(Mandatory=$True,ValueFromPipelineByPropertyName=$True)]
[string]ServiceName[Parameter(Mandatory=$True,ValueFromPipeline=$True,
ValueFromPipelineByPropertyName=$True)][string[]]$ComputerName,
[Parameter(ValueFromPipelineByPropertyName=$True)]
[string]$NewPassword,[Parameter(ValueFromPipelineByPropertyName=$True)]
[string]$NewUser,
[string]$ErrorLogFilePath
)
BEGIN{}
PROCESS{
    ForEach ($computer in $ComputerName) {
        Do {
     Write-Verbose "Connect to $computer on WS-MAN"
      $protocol = "Wsman"
           Try
{
                $option = New-CimSessionOption -Protocol $protocol
                $session = New-CimSession -SessionOption $option
- ComputerName $Computer -ErrorAction Stop
                If ($PSBoundParameters.ContainsKey('NewUser'))
{
                    $args = @{'StartName'=$NewUser
                          'StartPassword'=$NewPassword}
                }
Else {
                    $args = @{'StartPassword'=$NewPassword}
                    Write-Warning "Not setting a new user name"
                }
                Write-Verbose "Setting $servicename on $computer"
                $params = @{'CimSession'=$session
                  'MethodName'='Change'
        'Query'="SELECT * FROM Win32_Service WHERE Name = '$ServiceName'"
                 'Arguments'=$args}
                $ret = Invoke-CimMethod @params
                switch ($ret.ReturnValue) {
                  0  { $status = "Success" }
                  22 { $status = "Invalid Account" }
                    Default { $status = "Failed: $($ret.ReturnValue)" }
                }
                $props = @{'ComputerName'=$computer;'Status'=$status}
               $obj = New-Object -TypeName PSObject -Property $props
              Write-Output $obj
                Write-Verbose "Closing connection to $computer"
                 $session | Remove-CimSession
    } Catch {
                # change protocol - if we've tried both
                # and logging was specified, log the computer
                Switch ($protocol) {
                'Wsman' { $protocol = 'Dcom' }
                    'Dcom'  {
```

```
                   $protocol = 'Stop'
                        If
($PSBoundParameters.ContainsKey('ErrorLogFilePath')) {
Write-Warning "$computer failed; logged to
$ErrorLogFilePath"
                        $computer | Out-File $ErrorLogFilePath -Append
                          }  }
        }
}
        } Until ($protocol -eq 'Stop')
  } }
END{}
}
```

Go ahead—make sense of that. We dare you. Contrast that to the next listing, which is the same code, doing the same thing.

**Listing 18.2  Code that *is* formatted**

```
function Set-TMServiceLogon {
    [CmdletBinding()]
    Param(
        [Parameter(Mandatory=$True,
                ValueFromPipelineByPropertyName=$True)]
        [string]$ServiceName,
        [Parameter(Mandatory=$True,
                ValueFromPipeline=$True,
                ValueFromPipelineByPropertyName=$True)]
        [string[]]$ComputerName,
        [Parameter(ValueFromPipelineByPropertyName=$True)]
        [string]$NewPassword,
        [Parameter(ValueFromPipelineByPropertyName=$True)]
        [string]$NewUser,
        [string]$ErrorLogFilePath
    )
BEGIN{}                                      Spacing for
                                             readability

PROCESS{
    ForEach ($computer in $ComputerName) {
        Do {
            Write-Verbose "Connect to $computer on WS-MAN"
            $protocol = "Wsman"
            Try {
                $option = New-CimSessionOption -Protocol $protocol
                $session = New-CimSession -SessionOption $option
-ComputerName $Computer -ErrorAction Stop
                If ($PSBoundParameters.ContainsKey('NewUser')) {
                    $args = @{'StartName'= $NewUser              Neatly
                            'StartPassword' = $NewPassword}      structured
                } Else {                                        hash tables
                    $args = @{'StartPassword' = $NewPassword}
                    Write-Warning "Not setting a new user name"
                }
```

```
                        Write-Verbose "Setting $servicename on $computer"
                        $params = @{'CimSession'=$session
                                    'MethodName'='Change'
                                    'Query'="SELECT * FROM Win32_Service WHERE Name
= '$ServiceName'"
                                    'Arguments'=$args}
                        $ret = Invoke-CimMethod @params
                        switch ($ret.ReturnValue) {
                            0 { $status = "Success" }
                            22 { $status = "Invalid Account" }
                            Default { $status = "Failed: $($ret.ReturnValue)" }
                        }
                        $props = @{'ComputerName'=$computer
                                   'Status'=$status}
                        $obj = New-Object -TypeName PSObject -Property $props
                        Write-Output $obj
                        Write-Verbose "Closing connection to $computer"
                        $session | Remove-CimSession
                    } Catch {
                        # change protocol - if we've tried both
                        # and logging was specified, log the computer
                        Switch ($protocol) {
                            'Wsman' { $protocol = 'Dcom' }
                            'Dcom'  {
                                $protocol = 'Stop'
                                If
($PSBoundParameters.ContainsKey('ErrorLogFilePath')) {
Write-Warning "$computer failed; logged to
$ErrorLogFilePath"
                                $computer | Out-File $ErrorLogFilePath -Append
                            } # if logging
                        }
                    } #switch
                } # try/catch
            } Until ($protocol -eq 'Stop')
        } #foreach
    } #PROCESS                    ◁──┐  Comments for
    END{}                            │  closing braces
} #function
```

Outside of this book—where, admittedly, the longer lines still get a little janky—this code is a pleasure to read. You can see where each block of code begins and ends. Look specifically for these things:

- When we close a construct with }, we add a comment indicating what it closes.
- We use blank lines to separate chunks of code to see specific functional units more efficiently.
- We indent four spaces inside each construct.
- Hash tables are constructed with one key-value pair per line, all left-aligned to the same point.

If you're using VS Code (which, again, we suggest you do), it offers a quick-and-easy reformat option that will take care of *all* of this for you! It even tries to format as you type to avoid messiness in the first place. That's the value of a good editor—which costs you zero in the case of VS Code.

> **TIP** Open the command palette in VS Code, and type `Format Document`. Click this, and it will auto-format your document based on best practices. You also can add this line to your settings.json file to enable autoformat on save: `"editor.formatOnSave": true`.

## 18.5 Meaningful variable names

Choose meaningful and descriptive variable names. Avoid Hungarian notation or concise variable names. The clarity in variable names enhances code comprehension and maintainability. Yes, sometimes in this book, we've used `$c` or `$s`, but that's to save horizontal space on the page. A variable that contains a bunch of disk drive objects should be called something like `$drives` (plural helps remind you that it's a collection, not a single object). A username should be in `$username`, not `$un`. The only exception is that variables used to declare parameters should follow parameter-naming conventions, which call for singular nouns: `$ComputerName`, not `$ComputerNames`.

In addition, avoid the Hungarian notation style of variable naming that came with VBScript *back in the 1990s*. Yes, the '90s. Think about that before you create variables called `$strComputer` and `$intCounter`. Those were needed in VBScript because it was a weakly typed, non-object-oriented language; PowerShell has stronger typing and is object oriented. A string is an object of the type `System.String`; there's no need to add `str` to the variable name to remind you of that. Under PowerShell, everything would technically be `$obj` anyway, so the Hungarian style is meaningless and makes you look out of touch with current trends.

## 18.6 Avoiding aliases

While aliases save time in the console, steer clear of them in scripts. Ambiguous aliases can lead to confusion. Instead, use full command names for better readability and understanding. Exceptions are limited to commonly recognized aliases such as `'Where'` instead of `'Where-Object'`. ForEach is less fine because it's easy to confuse it with the language construct `ForEach`; use `ForEach-Object` if you mean to use the command. Avoid hard-to-interpret aliases such as `icm` and `gwmi`; spell out the command names, and forget aliases entirely in a script.

## 18.7 Logic over complexity

Maintain logical structure in your scripts. Avoid nesting complex expressions and using awkward pipelines. Your script's goal is to be a structured, permanent artifact, not a one-liner puzzle. Prioritize readability over cleverness. Here's an example:

```
Gwmi Win32_operatingsystem | select *,@{n='RAM';e={gwmi
win32_computersystem | select -exp totalphysicalmemory} | % { $_ |
Out-File temp.txt -Append ; $_.Reboot() }
```

Please don't run this unless you're feeling brave, but look at how difficult it is to read and follow, with its nested expressions, semicolon-delimited commands, and so on. Again—this is *fine* for the command line as an ad hoc, one-off thing, but not for a script.

We don't automatically avoid all pipeline use in a script; it's one of PowerShell's more powerful features. We'd go about it differently:

```
$os = Get-WmiObject -Class Win32_OperatingSystem
$cs = Get-WmiObject -Class Win32_ComputerSystem
$os | Add-Member -MemberType NoteProperty -Name RAM -Value `
 $cs.TotalPhysicalMemory
$os | Out-File temp.txt -Append
$os.Reboot()
```

Again, we don't recommend running that unless you're brave, but you can see that it's easier to follow. Each line does one thing, building on the previous lines. This isn't the only correct restructure of the original awkward example; there are a dozen ways you could do this, have it accomplish the same thing in the same amount of time, and be more structured and easier to read. The most clever one-liners in PowerShell are often the hardest to unpack and make sense of—don't subject your scripts to that extra mental overhead.

## 18.8   *Providing help*

We get it; documenting is *boring*. Do it anyway. Do you know how upset you get every time you try to look for the help for a command, and it's either anemic or missing? Yeah. Don't be that coder.

Go one better and learn how to use PlatyPS, an open source project used by the PowerShell team to generate external (i.e., not comment-based) help.

## 18.9   *Avoiding Write-Host and Read-Host*

This problem has gotten more confusing as PowerShell has evolved, but the basic maxim still stands: bad things happen every time you use `Write-Host` for output. The moral is that the `-Host` commands are designed to interact with human eyeballs and fingers. In other words, they tie your command to a specific context—human interaction—which is what tools are supposed to avoid. There are, of course, exceptions.

First, if you're writing a controller script that aims to engage tools in a human-interactive context, then the `-Host` commands are obviously fine. They're also fine if you're writing a tool that uses the verb `Show`, one of the official PowerShell verbs. That verb—which you might use in a command like `Show-Menu`—implies human interaction and so, again, implies a specific context.

Second, in PowerShell v5 and later, `Write-Host` in particular, becomes a sort of shortcut to the `Write-Information` channel, alleviating nearly all the context-tying concerns that used to go along with `Write-Host`. We still don't think `Write-Host` is a good idea; if you mean to use the Information stream, use `Write-Information`. Using `Write-Host` makes it clear that you don't know `Write-Information` exists, and you're using `Write-Host` for all the wrong reasons.

> **NOTE** The other counterargument we always get is, "But I need `Write-Host` to show the user what's happening!" On one hand, this is a valid concern. If you have a script or tool that requires some processing time or is running through a complex process, it can be useful to provide feedback. But in that case, take the time to learn how to use the `Write-Progress` cmdlet instead of `Write-Host`.

## 18.10 Sticking with single quotes

In PowerShell, we prefer single quotes for string delimiters unless you require variable or subexpression interpolation such as

```
$message = "The computer name is $ComputerName"
```

or subexpressions such as

```
$message = "Yesterday was $( (Get-Date).AddDays(-1) )"
```

Single quotes provide clarity and prevent unintended variable expansion. If you're not used to using single quotes as string delimiters, this takes some habit-breaking (we can't guarantee that we've followed this rule throughout the book), but it's worth the effort.

## 18.11 Not polluting the global scope

*Do not* jam your own variables into the global scope. It's a horrible practice, it makes debugging scripts vastly more difficult, and, in several situations, it can result in unreliable and inconsistent script execution (as with a host that manages the global scope differently). Modules are free to export variables, which will end up in the global scope, but which PowerShell can manage as part of the module lifecycle. Nothing else should be dumped into the global scope.

## 18.12 Being flexible

We hope it goes without saying, but we will anyway: avoid hardcoding values and references. Don't create a function with a hardcoded value for your Exchange server in your code. Instead, create a nonmandatory parameter, and set a default value. This way, you can easily run your function with the default values, but in the rare situation where you need to specify a different server, you'll also be able to handle that. Don't write a command that looks like this:

```
Function Get-ServerStuff {
$server = 'SRV01'
...
}
```

Sure, you may think you'll never need to specify a different value, but that might change tomorrow. Pros write tools with flexibility in mind:

```
Function Get-ServerStuff {
Param ([string]$ComputerName = 'SRV01')
...
}
```

You have to plan not only for how a user might run your tool today but also for how the tool might change in the future.

## 18.13 *Prioritizing security*

Never hardcode credentials into your script. Use the `[pscredential]` object as a parameter for secure credential handling. Maintain security while providing flexibility for different usage scenarios:

```
Function Get-Diskspace {
[cmdletbinding()]
Param([string]$ComputerName, [pscredential]$Credential)
$PSBoundParameters.Add("classname","win32_logicaldisk")
$PSBoundParameters.Add("filter","drivetype=3")
Get-WmiObject @PSBoundParameters |
Select PSComputerName,DeviceID,Size,Freespace
}
```

The user of this function can run it like this:

```
Get-diskspace -ComputerName SRV01 -credential company\administrator
```

They will be prompted for a password or pass a `credential` object:

```
$cred = get-credential company\administrator
Get-diskspace -ComputerName SRV01 -credential $cred
```

Writing code that uses the `pscredential` object maintains security and flexibility.

## 18.14 *Striving for elegance*

Strive for elegance in your code. Simplify your scripts by avoiding code repetition. Use techniques such as hash table splatting to create cleaner, more readable code. Over time, aim to develop an elegant coding style. As you develop tools, hopefully following the suggestions in this book, try to achieve a level of simplicity or elegance. We think elegant scripts are easier to read and debug, and they often perform better. One concept that can help is to avoid repeating code.

Let's say you're creating code to get system information from Windows Management Instrumentation (WMI) using `Get-CimInstance` based on a variable value. Your initial stab might look like this:

```
Switch ($value) {
"OS" {
    $data = Get-Ciminstance -class win32_operatingsystem
-ComputerName $ComputerName | Select PSComputerName,Version,Caption
}
"CS" {
    $data = Get-Ciminstance -class win32_computersystem
-ComputerName $ComputerName | Select PSComputerName,Model,Manufacturer
}
"CPU" {
    $data = Get-Ciminstance -class win32_processor
-ComputerName $ComputerName | Select PSComputerName,CPUID,Name,MaxClockSpeed
}
"Memory" {
    $data = Get-Ciminstance -class win32_physicalmemory
-ComputerName $ComputerName | Select PSComputerName,Banklabel,Capacity,Speed
}
}
```

This will work fine, but there's a lot of cumbersome copying, pasting, and editing of code. Contrast that with this example:

```
$ComputerName = 'localhost'
$value = "OS"

$cimparams=@{ComputerName=$ComputerName}     ← Uses a hash table
$props = @('PSComputerName')                   with parameters
Switch ($value) {                              for splatting
'OS' {
    $cimparams.Add('classname','win32_operatingsystem')   ← Modifies the
    $props+='Version','Caption'                             parameters
}                                                           on the fly
'CS' {
    $cimparams.Add('classname','win32_computersystem')
    $props+='Model','Manufacturer'
}
'CPU' {
    $cimparams.Add('classname','win32_processor')
    $props+='CPUID','Name','MaxClockSpeed'
}
'Memory' {
    $cimparams.Add('classname','win32_physicalmemory')
    $props+='Banklabel','Capacity','Speed'          Runs
}                                         Get-CimInstance once
}
$data = Get-CimInstance @cimparams | Select-object -Property $props  ←
```

Notice the use of a hash table with parameters for `Get-CimInstance`, which we end up splatting. This is a great technique for simplifying your code. Granted, you need to know about hash tables, splatting, and arrays, but this example feels easier to read and not as heavy handed.

We provide a lot of techniques in this book. You'll have to develop them into an art. Elegant code will come to you over time, as you gain experience and mastery. Picasso's line drawings convey a great deal, with what appears to have been minimal effort, but it took him years to achieve the level of mastery to make that possible. You may be writing your code in crayons today, but, eventually, we want you to create elegant masterpieces.

## Summary

As you progress on your journey to becoming a professional PowerShell scripter, remember that by adopting these professional scripting practices, you'll elevate your PowerShell skills to the next level. These practices make your code more reliable and maintainable, and they help you establish yourself as a respected professional in the PowerShell community.

# An introduction
# to source control
# with Git

One sign of a professional toolmaker is their use of source control. How many of you have a folder on your C: drive in which you keep all of your scripts? Or maybe you have a network drive at your work with all the IT scripts? Because we're in automation and DevOps, properly maintaining our PowerShell projects is critical. For many organizations today, this task falls to *Git*, a source control system first made famous on Linux (it was invented by Linux's inventor, Linus Torvalds). We thought it would be helpful to provide a crash course on Git fundamentals so that you can begin incorporating it into your work. As you might expect, this is a significant topic; you'll need to devote time to learning more than the basics. You may want to look at *Learn Git in a Month of Lunches* by Rick Umali (Manning, 2015, http://mng.bz/mj7P).

## 19.1  Why source control?

Source control is a means of keeping track of what changes have been made to a file, often including a change log or documentation that indicates who made a change and why. Source control also makes knowing the latest or more authoritative version easier. Some systems require you to check out a file to work on it. When you're finished, you can check it in, often with a comment about what you modified and why. While the file is checked out, only you can work with it, which may be fine for smaller teams.

Your organization probably already has a solution for the dev team to use for source control, whether it's Microsoft Team Foundation Services (TFS), GitHub, GitLab, or one of the other dozen source control solutions. Go ahead and use what the rest of your company is using. The last thing you need is yet another source control program to maintain.

## 19.2    *What is Git?*

Many traditional source control systems are centralized. Often, there's a centralized server or database with tightly controlled access. As you can imagine, these types of systems have a fair amount of overhead. Git, on the other hand, was developed as a decentralized source control system. It was developed in the Linux world to help manage source code for the Linux kernel, so it's pretty robust. In the Git paradigm, everyone has their own copies of source files that can be periodically merged and updated.

Git is primarily a command-line tool with only a handful of basic commands you need to get started. As you explore the Git ecosystem, you'll find several graphical frontends and even some PowerShell modules that are essentially wrappers to the Git command. We recommend that you stick with the traditional Git command-line tools. Once you've built up some mastery, feel free to get some GUI tools if that makes you feel better. We also recommend learning from the command line because a wealth of online information almost always uses the command line.

The main reason to use Git is that once you get used to it, it's dead easy. A ton of tools are available to make it even easier. And, because of the way it's built, Git lends itself very well to highly distributed source control. That means you can keep local copies of files to work on, but keep the main copies on a protected server, on a web-based source control service such as GitHub.com, and so on. There are even Git tools available for mobile devices running iOS and Android so that you can take your work with you. Perhaps most importantly, Git has become massively popular in the Power-Shell world, meaning many, many, many community projects—including the source code and documentation for PowerShell Core itself—are hosted in Git (specifically, in the web-based GitHub.com service). Becoming familiar with Git will not only help you with your own projects but also help you contribute to community projects and Power-Shell. If you create your own community projects, hosting them someplace like GitHub will make it easier to recruit other contributors.

### 19.2.1    *Installing Git*

To get started, go to https://git-scm.com/downloads, and download the latest Windows client. Run the setup—you should be able to accept all the defaults. The setup will create an option to launch Git in a Linux-like terminal window, or you can use the traditional Windows console and PowerShell. That's what we usually use.

### 19.2.2    *Git basics*

After the installation is complete, open a PowerShell window. If you had a session open when you installed it, you must restart it to detect the change to your path variable. At a prompt, type the `git` command to get general usage help:

```
PS C:\> git
usage: git [--version] [--help] [-C <path>] [-c name=value]
           [--exec-path[=<path>]] [--html-path] [--man-path] [--info-path]
           [-p | --paginate | --no-pager] [--no-replace-objects] [--bare]
```

```
[--git-dir=<path>]  [--work-tree=<path>]  [--namespace=<name>]
<command> [<args>]
...
```

As we go through the basics, we encourage you go to back and look at more detailed command help. In addition, run `git help tutorial` to open an HTML documentation page. (You should be able to use your web browser.) On that page, you'll also see a link to a user manual that's worth your time.

   We'll use Git as a local source control system with you as the primary user. You'll need to configure a username and email information:

```
git config --global user.email "James@globomantics.com"
git config --global user.name "James Petty"
```

Later, we'll get you started on integrating with GitHub so that you can collaborate with others. If you have GitHub credentials, use them here.

## 19.3  Repository basics

The first thing you need to do is initialize a Git repository. This step essentially tells Git to watch this folder. This can be your module's root directory for your scripting projects. For Git demo purposes, we created a new folder called MyPSTool and changed to that folder:

```
PS C:\> mkdir MyPSTool
    Directory: C:\
Mode                 LastWriteTime         Length Name
----                 -------------         ------ ----
d-----         6/14/2023   3:20 PM                MyPSTool
PS C:\> cd .\MyPSTool
PS C:\MyPSTool>
```

When you run a Git command, you need to be in the repository. We tend to run Git commands from the root.

### 19.3.1  Creating a repository

We want this folder to be managed by Git, so we initialize it as a repository:

```
PS C:\MyPSTool> git init
Initialized empty Git repository in C:/MyPSTool/.git/
PS C:\MyPSTool> Get-ChildItem      -Hidden
    Directory: C:\MyPSTool
Mode                 LastWriteTime         Length Name
----                 -------------         ------ ----
d--h--         6/14/2023   3:26 PM                .git
```

This process creates a hidden directory; we shouldn't ever need to access it or modify anything in it directly. The initialization process also creates the main branch. Later, we'll be able to create additional branches:

```
PS C:\MyPSTool> git status
On branch main
Initial commit
nothing to commit (create/copy files and use "git add" to track)
PS C:\MyPSTool>
```

We'll go ahead and create a few new files and then recheck the status:

```
PS C:\MyPSTool> git status
On branch main
Initial commit
Untracked files:
  (use "git add <file>..." to include in what will be committed)
        file1.ps1
        file2.ps1
nothing added to commit but untracked files present (use "git add" to
track)
```

Git maintains several virtual areas for tracking your work. As you can see, Git tells us we have untracked files. This means they aren't part of the source control system. Let's take care of that oversight.

### 19.3.2  *Staging a change*

The first step is to *stage* the changes by adding the files. We can either add individual files or stage all of them:

```
PS C:\MyPSTool> git add .
```

Let's check the status now:

```
PS C:\MyPSTool> git status
On branch main
Initial commit
Changes to be committed:
  (use "git rm --cached <file>..." to unstage)
        new file:   file1.ps1
        new file:   file2.ps1
```

The files are staged and ready to be committed to the repository. If we modify a staged file, we'll need to re-add it:

```
PS C:\MyPSTool> git status
On branch main
Initial commit
Changes to be committed:
  (use "git rm --cached <file>..." to unstage)
        new file:   file1.ps1
        new file:   file2.ps1
Changes not staged for commit:
  (use "git add <file>..." to update what will be committed)
  (use "git checkout -- <file>..." to discard changes in working directory)
```

```
        modified:   file2.ps1
PS C:\MyPSTool> git add .\file2.ps1
```

Next, let's commit the changes.

### 19.3.3  Committing a change

Committing a change makes it possible to roll back to a given state or undo changes. If it helps, you can think of your git commits as checkpoints, although they're more than that. Now we commit the files, including a message comment:

```
PS C:\MyPSTool> git commit -m 'added basic commands'
[main (root-commit) 038b8f9] added basic commands
 2 files changed, 1 insertion(+)
 create mode 100644 file1.ps1
 create mode 100644 file2.ps1
PS C:\MyPSTool>
```

You have to enter a commit message; it can be as long as needed. We've been known to create a here-string:

```
PS C:\MyPSTool> $m=@"
>> this is a sample longer
>> commit message that can
>> cover more than one line.
>> "@
>>
PS C:\MyPSTool> git commit -m $m.
```

> **NOTE**  See "Using Windows PowerShell 'Here-Strings'" for more about using here-strings (*TechNet*, http://mng.bz/9r4E).

We won't notice any changes to files in the directory—everything is tracked in the hidden .git directory. But we can use Git's log feature to review what has happened:

```
PS C:\MyPSTool> git log
commit 038b8f9ca8b846e9024532e9bda4e272cd24048b
Author: James Petty <James@globomantics.com>
Date:   Wed Jun 14 16:04:11 2023 -0500
    added basic commands
```

The username makes it easy to detect (or blame someone for) changes a specific user makes.

### 19.3.4  Rolling back a change

Let's quickly examine why we're bothering with all this. We created a simple text file and committed it to the repository:

```
PS C:\MyPSTool> set-content -value       'james'      -Path .\data.txt
PS C:\MyPSTool> git add .
PS C:\MyPSTool> git commit -m "Added data.txt"
```

```
[main 9113535] Added data.txt
 1 file changed, 1 insertion(+)
 create mode 100644 data.txt
PS C:\MyPSTool> git log
commit 9113535942d0c35a964deda9e869a0193bb284ad
Author: James Petty <James@globomantics.com>
Date:    Wed Jun 14 16:12:31 2023 -0500
    Added data.txt
commit 038b8f9ca8b846e9024532e9bda4e272cd24048b
Author: James Petty <James@globomantics.com>
Date:    Wed Jun 14 16:04:11 2023 -0500
    added basic commands
PS C:\MyPSTool>
```

Now we'll modify the data.txt file and commit that change:

```
PS C:\MyPSTool> set-content -value "james" -Path .\data.txt
PS C:\MyPSTool> get-content .\data.txt
james
PS C:\MyPSTool> git commit -a -m "set data.txt to james"
[main ee546b7] set data.txt to james
 1 file changed, 1 insertion(+), 1 deletion(-)
PS C:\MyPSTool>
```

This time, we used a shortcut to commit all pending files with -a, skipping the need to run `git -add`.

The log is getting long, so let's get the last three entries:

```
PS C:\MyPSTool> git log -n 3
commit ee546b73819f1ebbc8b7073c79113e0b6adb5c33
Author: James Petty <James@globomantics.com>
Date:    Wed Jun 14 16:15:48 2023 -0500
    set data.txt to james
commit 9113535942d0c35a964deda9e869a0193bb284ad
Author: James Petty <James@globomantics.com>
Date:    Wed Jun 14 16:12:31 2023 -0500
    Added data.txt
commit 038b8f9ca8b846e9024532e9bda4e272cd24048b
Author: James Petty <James@globomantics.com>
Date:    Wed Jun 14 16:04:11 2023 -0500
    added basic commands
PS C:\MyPSTool>
```

The last entered commit is the problem. In this particular situation, we can reset Git like this:

```
PS C:\MyPSTool> git reset --hard head~1
HEAD is now at 9113535 Added data.txt
PS C:\MyPSTool> get-content .\data.txt
don
```

Or suppose some time has passed, and we've made several other commits: in our test repository, we've added new files. Then, we realize we need to roll everything back to this commit:

```
commit 9113535942d0c35a964deda9e869a0193bb284ad
Author: James Petty <James@globomantics.com>
Date:    Wed Jun 14 16:12:31 2023 -0500
    Added data.txt
```

We can use the reset option again, but this time, specify the commit hash number. You don't need the full hash; typically, a short hash of the first seven digits will suffice.

Here's what the repository looks like now:

```
PS C:\MyPSTool> dir
    Directory: C:\MyPSTool
Mode             LastWriteTime        Length Name
----             -------------        ------ ----
-a----     6/14/2023    4:49 PM           13 data.txt
-a----     6/14/2023    3:47 PM           48 file1.ps1
-a----     6/14/2023    3:56 PM           66 file2.ps1
-a----     6/14/2023    4:50 PM            0 foo.txt
-a----     6/14/2023    4:46 PM          786 num.txt
PS C:\MyPSTool> get-content .\data.txt
james
jason
```

Next, we want to roll back to commit 9113535942d0c35a964deda9e869a0193bb284ad using the short hash value:

```
PS C:\MyPSTool> git reset --hard 9113535
HEAD is now at 9113535 Added data.txt
```

Here's what the repository looks like after the change:

```
PS C:\MyPSTool> get-content .\data.txt
don
PS C:\MyPSTool> dir
    Directory: C:\MyPSTool
Mode             LastWriteTime        Length Name
----             -------------        ------ ----
-a----     6/14/2023    5:54 PM            5 data.txt
-a----     6/14/2023    3:47 PM           48 file1.ps1
-a----     6/14/2023    3:56 PM           66 file2.ps1
```

This is a tricky process and not one you want to undertake all the time, but we wanted to demonstrate the value of source control at least.

There are a number of other types of operations you might need to undo as well. Check "Git Basics – Undoing Things" at http://mng.bz/p1AP for some helpful guidance.

### 19.3.5  *Branching and merging*

One of the benefits of Git that can reduce the need to roll back changes is the concept of *branching*. A Git branch is a copy of your files, perhaps from a particular commit. You can work on the files without disturbing your main (production) copies. When you're ready, the changes can be merged into your main branch.

Let's create a branch called dev in the MyPSTool folder:

```
PS C:\MyPSTool> git branch dev
PS C:\MyPSTool> git branch
  dev
* main
```

The asterisk indicates the currently active or checked-out branch. We'll switch to the dev branch and add a file using the PowerShell Set-Content cmdlet:

```
PS C:\MyPSTool> git checkout dev
git : Switched to branch 'dev'
    + CategoryInfo          : NotSpecified: (Switched to branch
'dev':String) [], RemoteException
    + FullyQualifiedErrorId : NativeCommandError
PS C:\MyPSTool> set-content -value '12345' -Path devdata.txt
PS C:\MyPSTool> dir
    Directory: C:\MyPSTool
Mode                 LastWriteTime         Length Name
----                 -------------         ------ ----
-a----         6/14/2023   5:54 PM              5 data.txt
-a----         6/14/2023   6:03 PM              7 devdata.txt
-a----         6/14/2023   3:47 PM             48 file1.ps1
-a----         6/14/2023   3:56 PM             66 file2.ps1
```

PowerShell will detect the branch change as an error; we can ignore it. We've added a file that we can see in the directory. Let's add and commit:

```
PS C:\MyPSTool> git add .
PS C:\MyPSTool> git commit -m "added devdata"
[dev 850ca50] added devdata
 1 file changed, 1 insertion(+)
 create mode 100644 devdata.txt
PS C:\MyPSTool> git status
On branch dev
nothing to commit, working tree clean
```

But watch what happens if we change back to the main branch (we omitted the error message):

```
PS C:\MyPSTool> git checkout       main
PS C:\MyPSTool> dir
    Directory: C:\MyPSTool
Mode                 LastWriteTime         Length Name
----                 -------------         ------ ----
-a----         6/14/2023   5:54 PM              5 data.txt
```

```
-a----        6/14/2023    3:47 PM              48 file1.ps1
-a----        6/14/2023    3:56 PM              66 file2.ps1
```

The file isn't there. If we'd made changes to the files, we wouldn't see those either.

We went ahead and switched back to the dev branch and made a few more changes, and then went back to main. We're curious about the differences between the two branches:

```
PS C:\MyPSTool> git diff dev
diff --git a/data.txt b/data.txt
index f71dff2..910fbb7 100644
--- a/data.txt
+++ b/data.txt
@@ -1,3 +1 @@
 don
-james
-jason
diff --git a/devdata.txt b/devdata.txt
deleted file mode 100644
index e56e15b..0000000
--- a/devdata.txt
+++ /dev/null
@@ -1 +0,0 @@
-12345
```

Don't worry if this doesn't make sense now—checking differences is optional. But now we'll integrate or *merge* the branches:

```
PS C:\MyPSTool> dir
    Directory: C:\MyPSTool
Mode              LastWriteTime         Length Name
----              -------------         ------ ----
-a----        6/14/2023    6:12 PM              5 data.txt
-a----        6/14/2023    3:47 PM             48 file1.ps1
-a----        6/14/2023    3:56 PM             66 file2.ps1
PS C:\MyPSTool> git merge dev
Updating 9113535..b62af84
Fast-forward
 data.txt    | 2 ++
 devdata.txt | 1 +
 2 files changed, 3 insertions(+)
 create mode 100644 devdata.txt
PS C:\MyPSTool> dir
    Directory: C:\MyPSTool
Mode              LastWriteTime         Length Name
----              -------------         ------ ----
-a----        6/14/2023    6:17 PM             18 data.txt
-a----        6/14/2023    6:17 PM              7 devdata.txt
-a----        6/14/2023    3:47 PM             48 file1.ps1
-a----        6/14/2023    3:56 PM             66 file2.ps1
```

We included before and after directory listings so you can see the changes.

Using branches is an ideal way to test and develop new code without worrying about messing up your current version. If you decide to scrap the code or are finished with the branch, you can delete it:

```
PS C:\MyPSTool> git branch -d dev
Deleted branch dev (was b62af84).
```

## 19.4   *Using Git with VS Code*

Once you understand the core Git concepts, such as branches, staging, and committing, you can use Git features in other products, such as Visual Studio Code (VS Code). Git support is integrated into the product, and several third-party Git-related extensions exist. Of course, you must have Git (v2.0.0 or later) installed on your computer for any of this to work.

In VS Code, you can open an entire folder, which is handy when developing a module. If the folder is a Git repository, VS Code will detect that. Figure 19.1 shows our test folder open in VS Code.

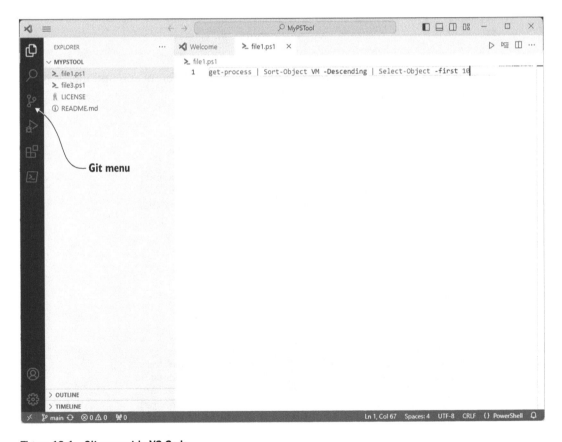

**Figure 19.1   Git support in VS Code**

VS Code detected the current branch. There's also an icon to access Git-related actions. We'll make some changes to files in the repository in the editor.

When changes are detected, VS Code displays a number over the Git icon, indicating the number of files. Click the icon to see the changes, as shown in figure 19.2.

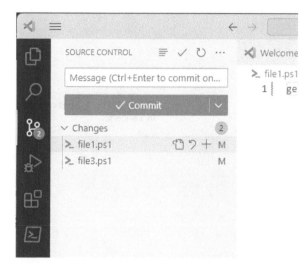

**Figure 19.2   Git changes in VS Code**

In the console, Git shows the changes like this:

```
PS C:\MyPSTool> git status
On branch main
Changes not staged for commit:
  (use "git add <file>..." to update what will be committed)
  (use "git checkout -- <file>..." to discard changes in working directory)
      modified:   file1.ps1
Untracked files:
  (use "git add <file>..." to include in what will be committed)
      file3.ps1
no changes added to commit (use "git add" and/or "git commit -a")
```

But you don't have to use Git from the command line. In VS Code, you can hover the mouse over a file and stage or discard changes on a per-file basis, or you can do the same for all files by hovering over changes. We staged all the changes, as shown in figure 19.3. All that remains is to commit the changes by typing a commit message in the box and clicking the checkmark icon. You can also use the … popup menu to perform other Git actions (see figure 19.4).

You can even check out or create other branches. Access the command palette by pressing the Ctrl-Shift-P shortcut. In the box, type `git`, and VS Code will auto-populate the drop-down list with available commands. Scroll down to the option to create a new branch, and enter a name for the branch. VS Code will create it and automatically

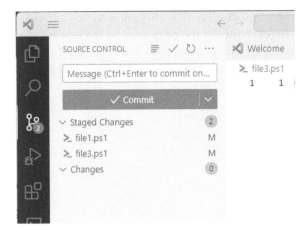

**Figure 19.3   Staged changes in VS Code**

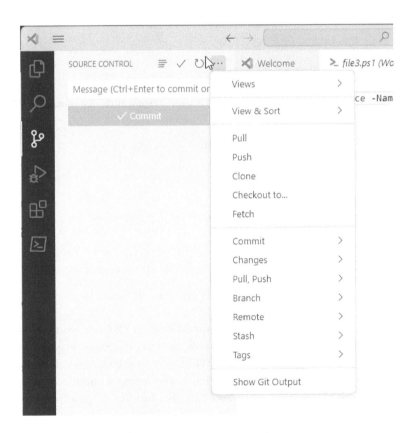

**Figure 19.4   Other Git options**

check it out. You can tell because the lower-left corner will indicate the current branch. When you're ready, click the branch name at the lower left, and in the command palette box, click the name of the branch you want to check out.

VS Code makes it easy to see, undo, and compare changes. We'll let you explore the other Git-related icons in the application.

But VS Code is primarily an editor, not a graphical Git tool, so some operations require the command line. One example is merging. Yes, you can create a new branch, modify, and commit files. But there's no way to merge branches in the version of VS Code that's available as we're working on this book. Fortunately, you can use the integrated terminal to run Git commands (see figure 19.5).

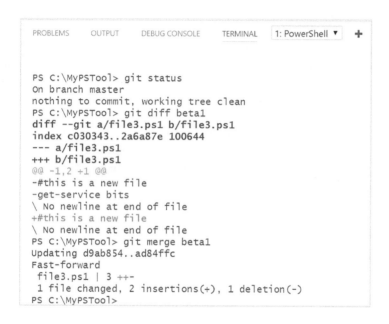

**Figure 19.5   Git commands from the VS Code terminal**

**TIP**   You can learn more about VS Code and source control integration at http://mng.bz/OP5P.

## 19.5   *Integrating with GitHub*

The other cool Git-related tool is GitHub. This is a web-based Git repository hosting service with its own set of features. There are multiple tiers available, and it's up to you to decided what you need. You technically don't have to have Git installed on your computer, but many people do so that they can clone an online repository locally, make changes locally, and push them back to GitHub. This is also how a lot of collaboration is happening today. If you're curious, check out these links:

- https://github.com/psjamesp
- https://github.com/powershellorg
- https://github.com/devops-collective-inc
- https://github.com/powershell

Integrating Git with GitHub, especially when you start cloning other repositories and making changes via pull requests, can be confusing and intimidating. But we wanted to give you some basic exposure to how you can use GitHub with your work.

Suppose that, on GitHub, you want to create a copy of the MyPSTool project you've been working with locally. This is a good place to maintain the main code while you develop and revise locally, and if other people need to work on the project, they can clone their copy of the repository to their desktop.

For the sake of simplicity, we'll use James's GitHub repository (https://github.com/psjamesp), which, as an added benefit, means you can clone the repository and try things yourself. This also means we've modified the username and email in our Git configuration to match James's GitHub account. We're assuming that when you sign up for GitHub (which is free, by the way), you'll use the same names as you do locally or vice versa.

There are two ways to integrate GitHub with a local Git project; which you choose ultimately comes down to where you're starting from. In our case, we already have a local repository that we want to push to GitHub. In GitHub, we'll create a new public repository (see figure 19.6).

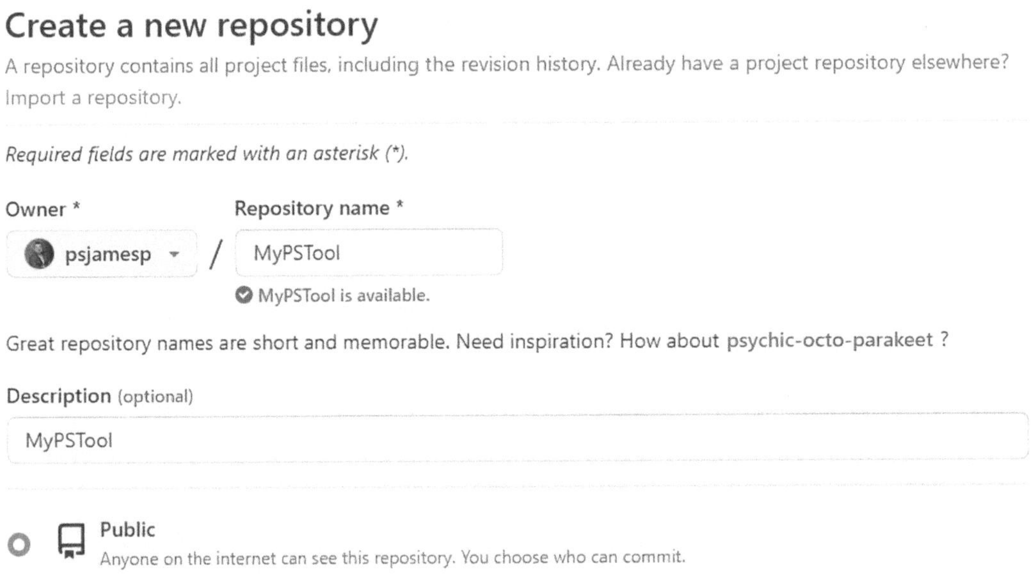

## Create a new repository

A repository contains all project files, including the revision history. Already have a project repository elsewhere? Import a repository.

*Required fields are marked with an asterisk (\*).*

Owner *                    Repository name *

 psjamesp  ▾   /    MyPSTool

                           ✔ MyPSTool is available.

Great repository names are short and memorable. Need inspiration? How about psychic-octo-parakeet ?

Description (optional)

MyPSTool

○  ▭  **Public**
      Anyone on the internet can see this repository. You choose who can commit.

**Figure 19.6   Creating a GitHub repository**

It isn't necessarily required, but we recommend using the same name as your local folder. Feel free to add a description. In this case, you don't need to add a readme file or anything else because you'll be using an existing local repository.

On the next screen, GitHub provides the code you need, depending on your situation. In our case, we want to push an existing repository from the command line. We'll use these commands from the root of the local folder:

```
PS C:\MyPSTool> git remote add origin                   Adds a remote
https://github.com/psjamesp/MyPSTool.git                link to GitHub
PS C:\MyPSTool> git push -u origin main                 Pushes the main
Counting objects: 17, done.                             branch to the remote
Delta compression using up to 2 threads.
Compressing objects: 100% (12/12), done.
Writing objects: 100% (17/17), 1.46 KiB | 0 bytes/s, done.
Total 17 (delta 2), reused 0 (delta 0)
remote: Resolving deltas: 100% (2/2), done.
To https://github.com/psjamesp/MyPSTool.git
 * [new branch]       main -> main
Branch main set up to track remote branch main from origin.
```

You can check the remote configuration like this:

```
PS C:\MyPSTool> git remote
Origin
```

Alternatively, you can have more verbose detail:

```
PS C:\MyPSTool> git remote -v
origin  https://github.com/psjamesp/MyPSTool.git (fetch)
origin  https://github.com/psjamesp/MyPSTool.git (push)
```

In GitHub, you can now see the repository with the most current files from the local folder, as shown in figure 19.7.

You could make changes with the editor in GitHub, but we'll assume you'll make changes locally. Use the local Git commands as you normally would, such as committing files:

```
PS C:\MyPSTool> git commit -m 'new changes'
[main 737445d] new changes
 3 files changed, 9 insertions(+), 1 deletion(-)
 create mode 100644 file4.ps1
```

But now, the next time you check the status, Git tells you that you aren't in synch with the GitHub repository:

```
PS C:\MyPSTool> git status
On branch main
Your branch is ahead of 'origin/main' by 1 commit.
  (use "git push" to publish your local commits)
nothing to commit, working tree clean
```

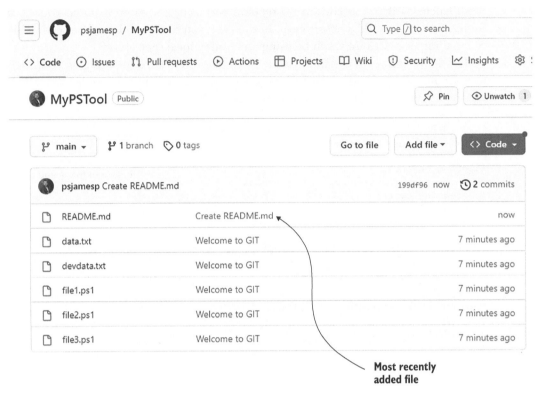

**Figure 19.7   The local repository is now on GitHub.**

It even provides instructions by telling you what to use!

```
PS C:\MyPSTool> git push
Counting objects: 5, done.
Delta compression using up to 2 threads.
Compressing objects: 100% (3/3), done.
Writing objects: 100% (5/5), 600 bytes | 0 bytes/s, done.
Total 5 (delta 0), reused 0 (delta 0)
To https://github.com/psjamesp/MyPSTool.git
   abeeecd..737445d  main -> main
```

Return to the browser and refresh, and you'll see the changes.

If you or a collaborator modify files in GitHub, you must manually check and pull those changes down. Running `git status` won't tell you that remote files have changed:

```
PS C:\MyPSTool> git status
On branch main
Your branch is up-to-date with 'origin/main'.
nothing to commit, working tree clean
```

You'll need to fetch and pull:

```
PS C:\MyPSTool> git fetch
remote: Counting objects: 6, done.
remote: Compressing objects: 100% (5/5), done.
remote: Total 6 (delta 2), reused 0 (delta 0), pack-reused 0
Unpacking objects: 100% (6/6), done.
From https://github.com/psjamesp/MyPSTool
   737445d..01f65d7  main      -> origin/main
```

The `fetch` retrieves remote changes. If you get the prompt, then there are no changes. But if something comes back when you fetch, you need to pull the files from the remote repository:

```
PS C:\MyPSTool> git pull
Updating 737445d..01f65d7
Fast-forward
 data.txt  | 1 -
 file1.ps1 | 2 +-
 2 files changed, 1 insertion(+), 2 deletions(-)
PS C:\MyPSTool>
```

These are the changes we made in GitHub. Once again, the local and remote repositories are in synch.

The other way is to start your project on GitHub first and then clone it locally. Follow the same steps to add a new repository in GitHub; we added one with a readme and license that skips the page with the code commands. Then, click the Clone Or Download button, and copy the link to the clipboard.

In PowerShell, set your location to the parent directory of where you want to create the repository. For our demonstration, we created a GitHub repository for a SharePoint toolset we're planning to build (well, not really). We wanted the local repository to be under C:\scripts, so we made sure we were in that location before running the `git clone` command:

```
PS C:\scripts> git clone https://github.com/psjamesp/sharepointtools.git
Cloning into 'sharepointtools'...
remote: Counting objects: 4, done.
remote: Compressing objects: 100% (3/3), done.
remote: Total 4 (delta 0), reused 0 (delta 0), pack-reused 0
Unpacking objects: 100% (4/4), done.
```

We then changed to the new repository to see the new files:

```
PS C:\scripts> cd .\sharepointtools\
PS C:\scripts\sharepointtools> dir
    Directory: C:\scripts\sharepointtools
Mode            LastWriteTime       Length Name
----            -------------       ------ ----
-a----      6/19/2023   2:59 PM       1088 LICENSE
-a----      6/19/2023   2:59 PM         44 README.md
```

From here on, we used the same steps we showed you.

**TRY IT NOW**   We don't have any exercises for this topic. Using Git is something you have to do on your own. We encourage you to install Git on your test box. Create a folder, and start playing with the Git commands. Experience will be the best teacher. Fortunately, if you run into a problem, a wealth of information and tips are available online.

## Summary

We don't care what source or version control system you use, but we encourage you to use *something*. Git is a good choice because it's widely used, there's an incredible amount of online help and references, and it generally seems to be what all the cool kids are using these days. Git is a technology that's like a foreign language—you won't gain any proficiency unless you use it all the time.

You don't have to do anything with GitHub, but it's a handy collaboration tool, and, if nothing else, a good off-site location. Your company may already have a corporate GitHub account you can use or a private repository server that offers the same functionality.

# Pestering your script

Pester is a powerful tool for automating your testing in PowerShell scripts. As we transition into a DevOps-oriented world, it becomes crucial to ensure the reliability of your scripts. No one wants a broken script running in a production environment. Even if you test your script initially, modifications or unique conditions might arise that require retesting. This chapter will delve into automated unit testing for PowerShell scripts using Pester.

## 20.1 The vision

Here's where we want to get you:

1 You write some code or modify some old code.

2 You check your code into a source control repository.

3 The repository triggers a continuous integration pipeline. Usually incorporating third-party tools, the pipeline builds a virtual machine to test your script. The pipeline copies your script into the virtual machine and runs several automated tests. If the tests fail, you get an email telling you what happened.

4 If the tests pass, your code is deployed to a deployment repository (maybe PowerShellGallery.com or a private repository), making it available for production.

Step 3 in this list, called "The Miracle," is entirely automated. To enable The Miracle, you must contribute an automated testing mechanism to your code. This way, any code revisions can be quickly retested, ensuring its functionality before deployment.

## 20.2   *Problems with manual testing*

We're sure that you've manually tested scripts before—possibly even as you wrote scripts for this book. And that's fine—you should test your code as you go. But there are some problems with manual testing:

- You're lazy. So are we. You're not going to run every possible test every time through, and it will always be the test you didn't run that would have caught the error you just made in your code.
- It's time-consuming. Even if you're not lazy, manual testing takes time and effort that could be better spent elsewhere.
- It doesn't tend to be learned. It's not like you have a huge list of tests you know you need to run; you're probably doing what we do and thinking, "Well, I'll run it with parameters one time and pipe some stuff to it another time, and that's probably good." If you fix a problem, you might test that specific problem right then, but you might or might not retest that specific problem in the future.
- It's manual. You can't achieve The Miracle with manual testing. Remember, PowerShell is all about automation—why should testing be excluded from that?

## 20.3   *Benefits of automated testing*

Automated testing, on the other hand, rocks—mainly because it's *automatic* and *learns*. If you run across a weird condition that broke your code once, you add a test for that condition to your test script, and then you'll never forget to test that weird condition again. Automated tests, therefore, serve as a kind of documented institutional memory. Even if someone else modifies your script, and they don't know about that weird condition, the automated test will have their back and make sure the weird condition gets tested.

Automated testing can even move you to a world of test-driven development (TDD). Let's say you decide to add a new feature to a command. Rather than breaking out and modifying the command's script, you write a few tests to test the proposed new feature. Those tests describe *how* you want the new feature to work, so they serve as a functional specification. The tests will initially fail because you haven't coded up the new feature yet. But then you start coding the new feature and keep coding until all the tests pass. If you did well on the tests, you'll know your feature is working correctly.

## 20.4   *Introducing Pester*

Pester (*PowerShell Tester*) is an open source project bundled with Windows 10 and later (newer versions can be found in the PowerShell Gallery). It's an automated unit-testing framework for PowerShell. In other words, you write your tests in Pester, and Pester runs your tests for you. Pester's basic documentation is in the wiki of its GitHub repository at https://github.com/pester/Pester/wiki.

> **NOTE**  This chapter provides the barest introduction to Pester, intending to whet your appetite. It would be best if you read the docs to discover all the other cool things Pester can do that we don't even mention.

As an interesting side note, Microsoft uses Pester to automate the testing of its own PowerShell resources. All kinds of Pester tests are included in the various open source PowerShell-based components that the PowerShell team has written. These tests number in the thousands! That, if nothing else, should tell you how important and well-regarded Pester is to and by the PowerShell community.

## 20.5   Coding to be tested

To have a successful relationship with Pester, you must start writing commands and scripts that lend themselves to testing. Follow all the advice we've provided in this book. Specifically, focus on making self-contained, single-task tools. Tools that do eight different things will be hard to test because you'll need to test every one of those eight things in all possible combinations and permutations. On the other hand, a tool that does one thing is a lot easier to write tests for.

It would be best if you also recognized that Pester is a *PowerShell* testing framework—not .NET, SQL Server, or anything else. It works best when it only has to deal with PowerShell commands. If you're following our advice—which we'll explore in detail later in this chapter—then you're writing PowerShell commands to wrap any non-PowerShell code you may need to use, meaning, at the end of the day, you're *only* dealing with PowerShell commands. In that scenario, you and Pester will get along fine.

## 20.6   What do you test?

Because this is intended to be a bare-bones introduction to Pester, we'll fudge a few terms that the automated testing industry takes pretty seriously to put them in a better context with PowerShell. Specifically, we'll use the terms *unit testing* and *integration testing* to lay out a couple of scenarios to help you understand what to write tests for.

### 20.6.1   Integration tests

An *integration test* tests the *end state* of your command. If you wrote a command to create an SQL Server database, an integration test would run the command and then check to see whether the database existed. In other words, it tests the final effect of your code on the world at large. An integration test treats your code as a black box, meaning it doesn't necessarily know what's happening *inside* the code. It doesn't test to see whether you instantiated the right .NET classes to connect to SQL Server, and it doesn't test whether the username and password you provided work. It just checks the result. You might use an integration test to verify that your toolset accomplishes a specific task under various situations.

Integration tests are a *good thing*, but they're not the *only thing*.

### 20.6.2   Unit tests

*Unit tests* are more granular, and they're trickier to imagine. They're not concerned with whether your code *accomplishes* anything—they only want to ensure the code *runs*.

For example, you might have a command that can change a service's startup mode and logon password, or it can do just one of those things, depending on which parameters it provides. A unit test will run in all three ways and ensure all the internal logical decisions and code paths run correctly. Whether any particular service is changed or not isn't the concern of the unit test.

Often, you'll write unit tests *and* integration tests. There may be times when you only write unit tests because you're only concerned about your code following the correct paths and logical decisions, and perhaps because *doing something*—which an integration test would require—would damage or negatively affect your environment. This can be a hard concept for folks to grasp. For example, if you wrote a command that reboots a computer, how could you not check to see whether the computer *rebooted?* Well, it depends. If you were calling a command like `Restart-Computer`, you wouldn't need to test *that*—you'd want to test your code that *led up to* `Restart-Computer` being called, which brings us to our next point.

### 20.6.3  *Don't test what isn't yours*

Particularly with unit tests, your goal is to test *your code*. The `Restart-Computer` command *isn't your code*. It's Microsoft's code. If Microsoft's code is broken, that isn't your problem. Your unit test ensures the code you can control works correctly. Let's take that exact scenario and turn it into a Pester example.

## 20.7  *Writing a basic Pester test*

Let's start with the command shown in the following listing. It's deliberately simple so that we can focus on the unit-testing aspect. The command will allow you to either restart or shut down a computer.

> Listing 20.1  A command to test

```
function Set-ComputerState {
    [CmdletBinding()]
    Param(
        [Parameter(Mandatory=$True,
                   ValueFromPipeline=$True,
                   ValueFromPipelineByPropertyName=$True)]
        [string[]]$ComputerName,
        [Parameter(Mandatory=$True)]
        [ValidateSet('Restart','Shutdown')]
        [string]$Action,
        [switch]$Force
    )
    BEGIN {}
    PROCESS {
        ForEach ($comp in $ComputerName) {
            $params = @{'ComputerName' = $comp}
            # force?
            if ($force) {
                $params.Add('Force',$true)
            }
```

```
                    # which action?
                    If ($Action -eq 'Restart') {
                        Write-Verbose "Restarting $comp (Force: $force)"
                        Restart-Computer @params
                    } else {
                        Write-Verbose "Stopping $comp (Force: $force)"
                        Stop-Computer @params
                    }
                }
            } #PROCESS
            END {}
}
```

**READ IT NOW**   Take some time to read through this command and develop an expectation for what it does and how it works. You may think of other, and even better, ways to accomplish its task. We've gone this route to help illustrate Pester testing well.

When it comes to unit testing, we know right away two things we won't be testing: whether `Restart-Computer` or `Stop-Computer` work, even though those are the only two things that are *doing* anything! Remember, if we were writing an integration test, that would matter. The difference is that unit tests don't care about the result; they care about whether *our code runs correctly*. We won't unit test them because those two commands aren't our code.

---

### Inside or outside?

Another way to think about unit and integration tests is like this: *How much of your code does the test know about?*

With an integration test, your code is a black box, as we suggested earlier. The test doesn't know how you accomplished a restart or a shutdown; it only cares whether it occurred. The integration test *doesn't know anything* about the contents of your command; it isn't going to try to make sure every possible code path is tested, every possible parameter is used, and so on.

With a unit test, your code is an open book. The test doesn't care about the result of running your code—it only cares about whether *all* of your code ran. Was every parameter used in some way? Did every code path execute? Was every logical decision run in every possible combination? It's about the *code*, not the *result*.

Again, both kinds of tests are essential, but we're focused on unit tests for now.

---

### 20.7.1   Creating a fixture

We'll start by loading the Pester module and asking it to create a new test fixture for us:

```
PS C:> Import-Module Pester
PS C:> Mkdir example
PS C:> New-Fixture –Path example –Name Set-ComputerState
```

**Installing and updating Pester**

We're assuming that the Pester module is available on your system; on Windows 10 or later, it will be available by default. If you don't have the module, install it first from the PowerShell Gallery by running `Install-Module Pester`.

If you're running Windows 10 or later, the shipping version of the Pester module is outdated. Unfortunately, updating the module from the PowerShell Gallery is problematic. You can't uninstall the shipping version (at least, not easily), and you may have problems getting the latest version. See the blog post "Power-Shell Package-Management and PowerShellGet Module Changes in Windows 10 Version 1511, 1607, and 1703" from Microsoft MVP Mike Robbins (August 3, 2017, http://mng .bz/40c7) for more details. As a last resort, you should be able to install the latest version of the Pester module and have it run side by side with the shipping version with this command:

```
Install-module pester -Repository psgallery -force –SkipPublisherCheck
```

This new *fixture* is a couple of blank files: one for our code (Set-ComputerState.ps1) and one for our tests (Set-ComputerState.Tests.ps1). Think of the fixture as a skeleton. We'll open both in Visual Studio Code (VS Code). We'll paste our function into Set-ComputerState.ps1 as a starting point, replacing the empty `Set-ComputerState` function already there.

> **TRY IT NOW**    Follow along with us, set up your fixture, and paste listing 20.1 into the code script.

The test script—which you should create on your own by running the previous commands, so we won't provide a copy as a downloadable sample—should look like this:

```
BeforeAll {
    . $PSCommandPath.Replace('.Tests.ps1', '.ps1')
}

Describe "Set-ComputerState" {
    It "Returns expected output" {
        Set-ComputerState | Should -Be "YOUR_EXPECTED_VALUE"
    }
}
```

Aside from the first three commands at the top, which link this test code to the code script, there are two sections:

- The `Describe` block is designed to contain a set of tests. These all execute within the same scope. Scoping in Pester is both complex and powerful, and as you get into more complex tests, you'll often define multiple `Describe` blocks. For now, we'll stick with this one.

- The It block represents a single test, which our code will either pass or fail. A Describe block often contains many It blocks, each testing a specific, discrete condition.

### 20.7.2 Writing the first test

Let's modify the provided It block to test something:

```
Describe "Set-ComputerState" {
    It "accepts one computer name" {
        Set-ComputerState -ComputerName SERVER1 -Action restart |
        Should Be $true
    }
}
```

This is the basic model for an It block: you run something and then tell Pester what the result should have been. However, what we've written here won't work because our Set-ComputerState function never outputs anything to the pipeline. Therefore, it isn't piping anything to Should, so it Should not look at a $true value as we've implied. This brings us to a heck of a problem—when we have a function that doesn't produce any output, and we're not attempting to test if it does anything, how do we test the dang thing?

Our dilemma, stated more specifically, is that we need to see *how many times* Restart-Computer *is called without calling* Restart-Computer. Tricky. The answer to that trick is a key element of Pester: the mock.

### 20.7.3 Creating a mock

In testing, you'll often want to have some commands that *seem* to run but *don't* run. For example, you might need Import-CSV to import a specific CSV file, but you don't want to create the file. Or, in our case, we want Restart-Computer to *seem* to run so we can figure out if our code tried to run it, but we don't want to restart a computer. This is where Pester's mocking comes into play. It creates a fake replacement for an existing command, and that fake can do whatever you like:

```
Describe "Set-ComputerState" {
    BeforeAll {
        Mock Restart-Computer { return 1}
        Mock Stop-Computer { return 1}
    }

    It "accepts one computer name" {
        Set-ComputerState -computerName Localhost -action Restart |
        Should -Be 1
    }
}
```

Our fake version of Restart-Computer will now output 1. It won't restart any computers—just output 1. So, if it's called once, the result of Set-ComputerState should be 1.

We've told Pester as much with our `It` block. Let's try running this simple test to see whether it works. From our example folder, which contains our test script, we have to run `Invoke-Pester`:

```
Describing Set-ComputerState
 [+] accepts one computer name 678ms
Tests completed in 678ms
Passed: 1 Failed: 0 Skipped: 0 Pending: 0 Inconclusive: 0
```

> **TRY IT NOW**   The results are better in full color, so see if you can get similar output by copying what we've done so far.

The `[+]` tells us that our single test passed.

### 20.7.4  Adding more tests

Let's add a few more tests:

```
Describe "Set-ComputerState" {
    Mock Restart-Computer { return 1 }
    Mock Stop-Computer { return 1 }
    It "accepts and restarts one computer name" {
        Set-ComputerState -ComputerName SERVER1 -Action Restart |
        Should -Be 1
    }
    It "accepts and restarts many names" {
        $names = @('SERVER1','SERVER2','SERVER3')
        $result = Set-ComputerState -ComputerName $names -Action Restart    ◁─── Saves the results
        $result.Count | Should -Be 3      ◁───                                    to a variable
    }                                          Tests the
    It "accepts and restarts from the pipeline" {   result count
        $names = @('SERVER1','SERVER2','SERVER3')
        $result = $names | Set-ComputerState -Action Restart
        $result.count | Should -Be 3
    }
}
```

We took a different approach on the second two tests. Remember, each time our mocked `Restart-Computer` runs, it outputs `1`. That means running it three times doesn't output `3`; it outputs three `1`s. We capture that collection of integers into `$result`. Then, on a new line, we pipe `$result.Count` to `Should`, checking whether the array contains three items. This tells us that our mocked command was called three times. Here are the results:

```
Describing Set-ComputerState
 [+] accepts and restarts one computer named 252ms
 [+] accepts and restarts many names 374ms
 [+] accepts and restarts from the pipeline 332ms
Tests completed in 959ms
Passed: 3 Failed: 0 Skipped: 0 Pending: 0 Inconclusive: 0
```

Perfect! But there's a slightly better way to construct these tests. When you mock a command in Pester, behind the scenes, it automatically tracks how many times the mock was used. Because our only goal is to count the number of times our fake command was run, we could let Pester do all the work for us. We'll do this by using the `Should -Invoke` command:

```
Describe "Set-ComputerState" {
    Mock Restart-Computer { return 1 }
    Mock Stop-Computer { return 1 }
    It "accepts and restarts one computer name" {
        Set-ComputerState -ComputerName SERVER1 -Action Restart
        Should -Invoke Restart-Computer -Exactly 1          ⊲───┐ Tests how many
    }                                                            times the mock
    It "accepts and restarts many names" {                       was called
        $names = @('SERVER1','SERVER2','SERVER3')
        Set-ComputerState -ComputerName $names -Action Restart
        Should -Invoke Restart-Computer -Exactly 3
    }
    It "accepts and restarts from the pipeline" {
        $names = @('SERVER1','SERVER2','SERVER3')
        $names | Set-ComputerState -Action Restart
        Should -Invoke Restart-Computer -Exactly 3
    }
}
```

Let's try it:

```
Describing Set-ComputerState
 [+] accepts and restarts one computer named 740ms
 [-] accepts and restarts many names 144ms
   Expected Restart-Computer to be called 3 times exactly but was called 4
times
   18:          Should -Invoke Restart-Computer -Exactly 3
   at <ScriptBlock>, \\vmware-host\Shared Folders\Documents\example\Set-
ComputerState.Tests.ps1: line 18
 [-] accepts and restarts from the pipeline 409ms
   Expected Restart-Computer to be called 3 times exactly but was called 7
times
   24:          Should -Invoke Restart-Computer -Exactly 3
   at <ScriptBlock>, \\vmware-host\Shared Folders\Documents\example\Set-
ComputerState.Tests.ps1: line 24
Tests completed in 1.29s
Passed: 1 Failed: 2 Skipped: 0 Pending: 0 Inconclusive: 0
```

That's not good. Looking at the failure output, it appears as if the counter doesn't reset for each `It` block by default. We have to modify the command so that it knows we want to count for each `It` block rather than adding up everything that happened in the parent `Describe` block:

```
Describe "Set-ComputerState" {
    Mock Restart-Computer { return 1 }
```

```
    Mock Stop-Computer { return 1 }
    It "accepts and restarts one computer name" {
        Set-ComputerState -ComputerName SERVER1 -Action Restart
        Should -Invoke Restart-Computer -Exactly 1 -Scope It        ◄───────┐
    }                                                                      Tracks asserted
    It "accepts and restarts many names" {                                mocks in the
        $names = @('SERVER1','SERVER2','SERVER3')                          It scope
        Set-ComputerState -ComputerName $names -Action Restart
        Should -Invoke Restart-Computer -Exactly 3 -Scope It
    }
    It "accepts and restarts from the pipeline" {
        $names = @('SERVER1','SERVER2','SERVER3')
        $names | Set-ComputerState -Action Restart
        Should -Invoke Restart-Computer -Exactly 3 -Scope It
    }
}
```

And now, let's try it again:

```
Describing Set-ComputerState
  [+] accepts and restarts one computer name 430ms
  [+] accepts and restarts many names 335ms
  [+] accepts and restarts from the pipeline 283ms
Tests completed in 1.05s
Passed: 3 Failed: 0 Skipped: 0 Pending: 0 Inconclusive: 0
```

That's exactly what we were looking for.

### 20.7.5 *Code coverage*

If one of the goals of unit testing is to ensure that all of your code runs, then you
need to know whether you've hit that goal. Pester can help. Running `Invoke-Pester`
`-Code-Coverage ./Set-ComputerState.ps1` will generate a *code-coverage report* for that
script, like this one:

```
Describing Set-ComputerState
  [+] accepts and restarts one computer name 1.64s
  [+] accepts and restarts many names 68ms
  [+] accepts and restarts from the pipeline 1.55s
Tests completed in 3.26s
Passed: 3 Failed: 0 Skipped: 0 Pending: 0 Inconclusive: 0
Code coverage report:
Covered 70.00 % of 10 analyzed commands in 1 file.
Missed commands:
File                    Function          Line Command
----                    --------          ---- -------
Set-ComputerState.ps1 Set-ComputerState   24 $params.Add('Force',$true)
Set-ComputerState.ps1 Set-ComputerState   32 Write-Verbose "Stopping $comp
(Force: $force)"
Set-ComputerState.ps1 Set-ComputerState   33 Stop-Computer @params
```

This helps you understand what's missing. Getting 100% code coverage means *every line of code ran*; it doesn't necessarily mean you're finished testing because sometimes you need to test different variations with that same code. But code coverage does help you spot code paths you may have missed. In our case, we can see that we've never run the code that accounts for our –Force parameter, and we've never run a test where we try to stop a computer, rather than restart it. Let's add some more tests:

```
Describe "Set-ComputerState" {
    Mock Restart-Computer { return 1 }
    Mock Stop-Computer { return 1 }
    It "accepts and restarts one computer name" {
        Set-ComputerState -ComputerName SERVER1 -Action Restart
        Should -Invoke Restart-Computer -Exactly 1 -Scope It
    }
    It "accepts and restarts many names" {
        $names = @('SERVER1','SERVER2','SERVER3')
        Set-ComputerState -ComputerName $names -Action Restart
        Should -Invoke Restart-Computer -Exactly 3 -Scope It
    }
    It "accepts and restarts from the pipeline" {
        $names = @('SERVER1','SERVER2','SERVER3')
        $names | Set-ComputerState -Action Restart
        Should -Invoke Restart-Computer -Exactly 3 -Scope It          Additional
    }                                                                  tests
    It "accepts and force-restarts one computer name" {
        Set-ComputerState -ComputerName SERVER1 -Action Restart -Force
        Should -Invoke Restart-Computer -Exactly 1 -Scope It
    }
    It "accepts and shuts down one computer name" {                   Additional
        Set-ComputerState -ComputerName SERVER1 -Action Shutdown       tests
        Should -Invoke Stop-Computer -Exactly 1 -Scope It
    }
}
```

And let's run that:

```
Describing Set-ComputerState
  [+] accepts and restarts one computer name 552ms
  [+] accepts and restarts many names 64ms
  [+] accepts and restarts from the pipeline 86ms
  [+] accepts and force-restarts one computer name 277ms
  [+] accepts and shuts down one computer name 115ms
Tests completed in 1.1s
Passed: 5 Failed: 0 Skipped: 0 Pending: 0 Inconclusive: 0
Code coverage report:
Covered 100.00 % of 10 analyzed commands in 1 file.
```

We now have more confidence that we're testing all of our code paths and that our code is responding how we want it to.

## Summary

To close out this chapter, the following listing includes our completed test script, for your reference.

**Listing 20.2    Completed Pester test**

```
$here = Split-Path -Parent $MyInvocation.MyCommand.Path
$sut = (Split-Path -Leaf $MyInvocation.MyCommand.Path) `
➥  -replace '\.Tests\.', '.'
. "$here\$sut"
Describe "Set-ComputerState" {
    Mock Restart-Computer { return 1 }
    Mock Stop-Computer { return 1 }
    It "accepts and restarts one computer name" {
        Set-ComputerState -ComputerName SERVER1 -Action Restart
        Should -Invoke Restart-Computer -Exactly 1 -Scope It
    }
    It "accepts and restarts many names" {
        $names = @('SERVER1','SERVER2','SERVER3')
        Set-ComputerState -ComputerName $names -Action Restart
        Should -Invoke Restart-Computer -Exactly 3 -Scope It
    }
    It "accepts and restarts from the pipeline" {
        $names = @('SERVER1','SERVER2','SERVER3')
        $names | Set-ComputerState -Action Restart
        Should -Invoke Restart-Computer -Exactly 3 -Scope It
    }
    It "accepts and force-restarts one computer name" {
        Set-ComputerState -ComputerName SERVER1 -Action Restart -Force
        Should -Invoke Restart-Computer -Exactly 1 -Scope It
    }
    It "accepts and shuts down one computer name" {
        Set-ComputerState -ComputerName SERVER1 -Action Shutdown
        Should -Invoke Stop-Computer -Exactly 1 -Scope It
    }
}
```

Of course, this may not be a *complete* test. We haven't added any integration tests, for example, and we haven't tested to ensure that only values such as Restart and Shutdown are accepted for the –Action parameter. This test could certainly grow to be more complex—and we invite you to expand it to further explore how Pester can help automate your testing. You can jump on all this by reading the help topic about_pester.

# Signing your script

In the world of highly effective PowerShell toolmakers, script signing is a habit that can't be overlooked. While some might find it daunting or unnecessary, we firmly believe in its importance, which is why this chapter exists. Whether you anticipate your scripts staying within your organization or not, script signing, coupled with source control, should be a part of your toolkit.

## 21.1 The significance of script signing

Why should you invest your time and effort in script signing? At its core, a signed script serves two crucial purposes. First, it authenticates the identity of the script's author. Now, this doesn't necessarily guarantee the script's safety or quality, but if the script is signed, you can at least trace it back to its creator. Second, signing ensures script integrity, verifying if the code has been tampered with since it was signed. Protecting your code is paramount, especially when it leaves the confines of your organization. Let's say you receive a script from Sally or download one from a blog. How confident are you that every line of code is precisely as Sally intended? If she has signed the file, you can be certain that every character is a true reflection of Sally's work. Should any malicious code be discovered, you can hold Sally accountable.

Internally, accidental modifications can happen. An innocent intern or an unwitting boss might inadvertently alter your script. Without code signing, you may only realize something is amiss when your script produces less-than-optimal results. With signed scripts, PowerShell acts as your guardian, instantly notifying you of any problems and allowing you to investigate promptly. PowerShell lives up to its name as a powerful tool. A small piece of code can wreak havoc. Protect your code and, in turn, yourself, by embracing script signing.

## 21.2   *A word about certificates*

Before delving into script signing, you'll need a certificate. Certificates are vital in identity verification, acting as digital ID cards. Commercial certificate authorities (CAs) are responsible for certifying identities by embedding the certificate holder's identity within the certificate. Certificates revolve around trust. If you trust the CA, you can trust the certificate it issues.

Code signing is a significant responsibility for CAs because code has the potential to cause considerable harm. Obtaining a Class 3 code-signing certificate from a commercial CA typically requires rigorous identity verification processes and is often granted to organizations rather than individuals. However, organizations can set up their internal public key infrastructure (PKI), run their own CA, and establish the rules for certificate issuance. If your code stays within your organization, this is a cost-effective alternative to purchasing a commercial code-signing certificate.

In cases where you are the sole user and maintainer of your code on your personal computer, you can create a self-signed certificate. While convenient for development, self-signed certificates should be replaced with real certificates when deploying code to others, even within your organization.

> **Certificates, trust, and necessary effort**
>
> It's no secret that managing certificates can be a hassle. They expire, necessitating renewal, and setting up an internal PKI is a complex task. However, as IT professionals, this is part of our core competency, and we must be proficient in managing this security aspect.
>
> The traditional CA model faces competition from innovative approaches such as notarization, which allows the creation of self-signed certificates with the oversight of trusted individuals. While beyond the scope of this chapter, it's worth exploring this decentralized trust system as an alternative to centralized CA trust models.

Once you have a certificate, you can install it and begin using it—which we'll cover briefly. Because this isn't a chapter on PKI, we'll refresh your memory that certificates consist of *key pairs*. In particular, yours will have a *private key* that you should keep incredibly safe and secure, even password-protecting it within the Windows certificate store so that it can't be used without your permission. The private key is used to generate script *signatures*. A signature is a copy of your script (or, more commonly, a hash, which is still unique to the script but takes up less room) that is encrypted using the private key and bundled along with information about your certificate (but not the private key).

Anyone else who trusts the source of your certificate can then decrypt that signature, using the *public key* side of the key pair. Their ability to decrypt it using your public key means they can confirm your identity because only your closely held private key could have encrypted the script in the first place. They can then compare the previously encrypted script to the clear-text version; if the two match, they know the code is exactly as you wanted it to be.

## 21.3  Configure your script signing policy

To make script signing effective, you need to configure your environment to require signed scripts. Signing a script alone is insufficient if PowerShell isn't instructed to enforce this requirement. In an elevated PowerShell session, execute the following command:

```
Set-Executionpolicy AllSigned -force
```

The –Force parameter will suppress the confirmation prompt. It would be best if you only did this once on any machine where you'll be running scripts. Presumably, this is your desktop or a centralized management server. You only want to rarely have to run an interactive script on a remote server, so you can leave those execution policies set to Restricted, which is the default.

Even if you use *Invoke-Command* to run a local script on a remote server, Power-Shell is running the *contents* of the command remotely. You should probably verify the script locally before running it remotely. We'll show you that in a few minutes.

You can also use Group Policy to configure script-execution policies if you're in an Active Directory (AD) domain. Note that these policies aren't security boundaries but rather are like the covers on launch switches for nuclear missiles. We covered all of this in much greater detail in chapter 7.

## 21.4  Code-signing basics

Delving into the basics of certificates and PKI is beyond the scope of this chapter, but here's a simplified explanation. A certificate is a cryptographic means of verifying your identity. When you sign a script in PowerShell, your certificate's identity information is included in the script's signature block, confirming you as the script's author. Additionally, PowerShell computes a hash value based on the script's content and embeds it in the script's signature. If any modification, no matter how minor, is made to the file, the signature breaks, and PowerShell reports the script as changed.

### 21.4.1  Acquiring a code-signing certificate

Not all certificates can be used for script signing; they must be Class 3 code-signing certificates that support Microsoft's Authenticode extension.

> **NOTE**  *Class 3* is a term that VeriSign used back in the day; it's rare to see it now. Most people just call them code-signing certificates.

A CA trusted by your computer must also issue the certificate. Suppose you intend to distribute signed tools outside of your organization. In that case, you'll most likely need a certificate from a third-party vendor such as VeriSign or DigiCert because anyone downloading your code will trust them to have issued your certificate. But we expect that most of you have an AD domain, ideally with a certificate infrastructure (Active Directory Certificate Services [AD CS]). With this, you can quickly go through the web-based interface to request a code-signing certificate under your organization's policies. You can then configure Group Policy so that domain members will trust your certificate (this will usually be in place if the PKI was set up correctly). The details are beyond the scope of this book, but if you get stuck, we're confident the residents of the forums at PowerShell.org can help.

> **NOTE** To summarize, step 1 is to find a CA—either commercial or external. Remember that code-signing certificates aren't cheap, and a cheap one wouldn't be worth the digital ink it's made of. Certificates are usually issued only to organizations such as companies, not to individuals, and when obtained commercially, they typically have a reasonably extensive identity verification process.

Another option for testing purposes, or if you intend that your PowerShell scripts and tools will never leave your desktop, is to use a self-signed certificate. In years past, this meant mastering the arcane command-line utility makecert.exe. But the PowerShell PKI module, which you should get when you install the Remote Server Administration Tools, includes a command that makes this easier. If you want to try out code signing, run a command like this:

```
PS Cert:\> New-SelfSignedCertificate -type CodeSigningCert -Subject
"CN=James Petty" -CertStoreLocation Cert:\CurrentUser\My\ -testroot
    PSParentPath: Microsoft.PowerShell.Security\Certificate::CurrentUser\My

Thumbprint                                Subject        EnhancedKeyUsageList
----------                                -------        --------------------
F33E9122D73BE220117339E9647F0037F3F875A6  CN=James Petty    Code Signing
```

Naturally, insert your own name in the CN= part. Because this is a self-signed certificate, include the -TestRoot parameter. You'll still get a certificate you can use, but PowerShell will give you an "unknown error" message because it can't verify the certificate chain. That is, your computer doesn't *trust itself* as a source of certificates.

We've told PowerShell to store the certificate for the current user. This is easy enough to verify with the -codesigningcert parameter on Get-ChildItem. We'll use the dir alias:

```
PS C:\> dir Cert:\CurrentUser\My\ -CodeSigningCert
    PSParentPath: Microsoft.PowerShell.Security\Certificate::CurrentUser\My
Thumbprint                                Subject
----------                                -------
F33E9122D73BE220117339E9647F0037F3F875A6CN=James Petty
```

You can have multiple code-signing certificates installed, but you can only sign with a single one. If you have multiple certificates installed, you'll need to use PowerShell and filter for the exact one.

> **TIP** In the certificate world, a certificate's *thumbprint* is its official, unique name. You'll see many references to it, and now you know how to find it.

### 21.4.2   *Trusting self-signed certificates*

Before using a self-signed certificate, you may need to take a few additional steps outside of PowerShell. At a prompt, run this command to open the certificate management snap-in:

```
Certmgr.msc
```

Navigate to where you stored the certificate, as shown in figure 21.1. You'll see that CertReq Test Root issues it. The problem you'll run into is that the certificate for this root isn't completely trusted. Why would it be? Again, you can't use your crayon-made, self-signed driver's license because nobody but you trusts it; it's the same situation with a self-signed certificate. You can install that root certificate by dragging and dropping it from the Intermediate Certification Authority container to Trusted Root Certification Authority, as indicated in figure 21.2.

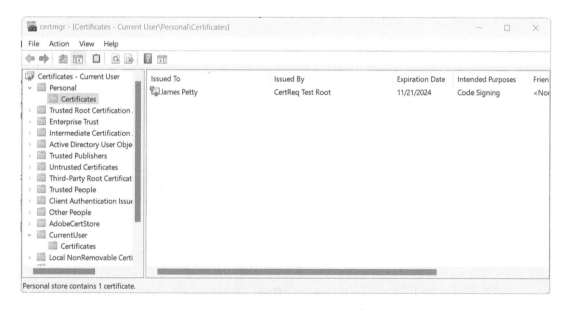

**Figure 21.1   Selecting the self-signed certificate**

You'll be prompted with a warning dialog box. Go ahead and install the certificate. Now you won't get PowerShell error messages about an untrusted root when you use a certificate that was created by your own computer.

> **NOTE**   This procedure won't compromise your computer; it will just make it trust the certificates that it produced. Certificates produced elsewhere will still need to be trusted in the usual fashion.

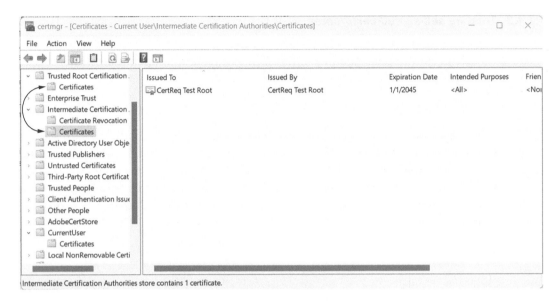

Figure 21.2   **Moving the self-signed root certificate**

### 21.4.3  Signing your scripts

To sign a PowerShell script, you need a reference to the certificate. We find it easy to save the code-signing certificate to a variable:

```
PS C:\> $cert = dir Cert:\CurrentUser\My\ -CodeSigningCert
```

You may want to add this type of line to your PowerShell profile script so that it's always available. In our scripts directory, we have an extremely simple PowerShell script:

```
PS C:\scripts> get-content psvm.ps1
get-process | sort vm -desc | select -first 5
```

The cmdlet we'll use is called Set-AuthenticodeSignature. That is a lot to type and a good reason to use tab completion. But because you're likely to be signing scripts interactively, we suggest creating an alias in your PowerShell profile:

```
Set-Alias -Name sign -Value Set-AuthenticodeSignature
```

We'll use this alias if for no other reason than to keep our examples short:

```
PS C:\scripts> sign .\psvm.ps1 -Certificate $cert
    Directory: C:\scripts
SignerCertificate                          Status            Path
-----------------                          ------            ----
9D16AF2573AC6C01A33752CA5135F3700A6FE9CFCN Valid             psvm.ps1
```

Here's what the file looks like now:

```
PS C:\scripts> get-content .\psvm.ps1
get-process | sort vm -desc | select -first 5
# SIG # Begin signature block
# MIIFWAYJKoZIhvcNAQcCoIIFSTCCBUUCAQExCzAJBgUrDgMCGgUAMGkGCisGAQQB
# gjcCAQSgWzBZMDQGCisGAQQBgjcCAR4wJgIDAQAABBAfzDtgWUsITrck0sYpfvNR
# AgEAAgEAAgEAAgEAAgEAMCEwCQYFKw4DAhoFAAQWlS7aTI+/TUJU7Izf4mzM8b1
# HmWgggL6MIIC9jCCAd6gAwIBAgIQYcqwRS2cF6ZKK2DMJNsC6DANBgkqhkiG9w0B
# AQsFADATMREwDwYDVQQDDAhBcnQgRGVjbzAeFw0xNzA2MTkxNDQ5NDNaFw0xODA2
# MTkxNTA5NDZaMBMxETAPBgNVBAMMCEFydCBEZWNvMIIBIjANBgkqhkiG9w0BAQEF
# AAOCAQ8AMIIBCgKCAQEAotwzL7nKq3uG1oZ/uMAwSELAeVaoIqFHr+zW1hWwW+UG
# h/dftEaGsAmETjPnYRkABkGLqloiXXhmLQjY+QKtn51cue78B85mrSF5dqrfuuK6
# XIVm7rjvMGwqyU6mpCs2RA3c+eObqgQZMJeOd/U9BnawlUijTcYGXptxc7M7ewWp
# oVGSm2C385hB09pZJ5UpmonW81iZZ+nkoos1oMC2jdhdETR2JC/cfpjU1sP406Et
# s2gR5jIiZuBBzTMgAlU4IRU38gXiS8q2UA3oyysyd2/+svRgDx/SrO+HV5ZmEqiF
# epsY8DpaWn86MLYn+rjPSLgPbW6SNkwvHg58trEsIwIDAQABo0YwRDAOBgNVHQ8B
# Af8EBAMCB4AwEwYDVR01BAwwCgYIKwYBBQUHAwMwHQYDVR0OBBYEFH1ccCLNFjh0
# ZqYdX2NvAASUku2PMA0GCSqGSIb3DQEBCwUAA4IBAQCXxfRfgI4KbsvXk0HKVI65
# fJ4CAXDJaZyx2WtuaH4HF1WjhPMh9JjupA2244p/vH1FWERZ5llwR9AcwA8kK8EM
# 6aPD5Nu0MGis7gFvzK1K/dnxmgv+7ICS9j92GM4qIa8bcfIwBTTPehQKaJS2Q+bg
# cm3eipPI4nxPPhSXLdg3FcglNfwU3aqQznHfmWj5cVgiqtMbe/CBh9hDcCFeW+y1
# X6aAY1q+ADrMjILnhOETFpIn3eHmdHiC/q0PpKGJzn+uhwLncaVnahRaSXhIbApc
# /9VqkPEg4kJFYVbewIeOjPWB+2IVtdtgag9X9HwTTP4nEIQ7KEz4jKMM9hPGacnV
# MYIByDCCAcQCAQEwJzATMREwDwYDVQQDDAhBcnQgRGVjbwIQYcqwRS2cF6ZKK2DM
# JNsC6DAJBgUrDgMCGgUAoHgwGAYKKwYBBAGCNwIBDDEKMAigAoAAoQKAADAZBgkq
# hkiG9w0BCQMxDAYKKwYBBAGCNwIBBDAcBgorBgEEAYI3AgELMQ4wDAYKKwYBBAGC
# NwIBFTAjBgkqhkiG9w0BCQQxFgQUsoYetaVPGXeBkFV4ddJTInDikFwwDQYJKoZI
# hvcNAQEBBQAEggEARmE9VVlQ+HMYTFnOQ+lJGLvOcm7RKi5+pEVFhxTwoahbu6Zb
# oZLEB6zUKx2RxLWkO1+FWiOJWGAAARPnNWCCxBKqAnedtqPNc0UVQ0J5gxuVzfO6
# J5Q+3Uu7YbrbgeErC/hYOMmu9hY8a7H7ttxD0p0qHscV7R1kOSxrUGehU3+KLKFU
# heKQlOL26DVGdk3KRayZTGzpDXHavkGAtcjcyiQPSPyRdmFcagdZ4VzrKzTT4m1w
# i+uHap5xQ80EQBxfgHZT3yXKRA1tl9Mgnmi9XNcUro25i0tiKZTjkZe0voPJ7MX1
# ePgJFLinSiRvIvzoqpOgN51CfQ/yWWdCsH+v4w==
# SIG # End signature block
```

You shouldn't need to mess with the signature block unless you want to completely delete it. That's the only way to unsign a file.

You can also easily sign an entire directory full of scripts:

```
PS C:\scripts> dir *.ps1 | sign -Certificate $cert -WhatIf
What if: Performing the operation "Set-AuthenticodeSignature" on target
"C:\scripts\DirReport.ps1".
What if: Performing the operation "Set-AuthenticodeSignature" on target
"C:\scripts\psvm.ps1".
What if: Performing the operation "Set-AuthenticodeSignature" on target
"C:\scripts\lastdayofwork.ps1".
What if: Performing the operation "Set-AuthenticodeSignature" on target
"C:\scripts\newhire.ps1".
```

You can sign .ps1, .psm1, and .ps1xml files.

**TIP**   Note that you can't sign .psd1 files, which are a manifest for a script module. If you allow the execution of unsigned scripts on your system, then, in theory, a piece of malware could find a .psd1 file and modify it to load a malicious script when you loaded your otherwise all-signed module! It's a risk, but to be fair, that same piece of malware could attack you in a few dozen other ways too. Be aware of the possibility so you can be extra cautious when the situation calls for it.

### 21.4.4   *Testing script signatures*

Use `Get-AuthenticodeSignature` to test a script's signature:

```
PS C:\scripts> Get-AuthenticodeSignature .\psvm.ps1
    Directory: C:\scripts
SignerCertificate                          Status                Path
-----------------                          ------                ----
9D16AF2573AC6C01A33752CA5135F3700A6FE9CF   Valid                 psvm.ps1
```

The output from `Get-AuthenticodeSignature` is another type of object. The object properties are self-explanatory:

```
PS C:\scripts> Get-AuthenticodeSignature .\psvm.ps1 | select *
SignerCertificate       : [Subject]
                            CN=James Petty
                          [Issuer]
                            CN=CertReq Test Root, OU=For Test Purposes Only
                          [Serial Number]
                            5B0A36A612E5A78F400FEE5F02F930BB
                          [Not Before]
                            6/19/2017 10:07:53 AM
                          [Not After]
                            6/19/2018 10:27:53 AM
                          [Thumbprint]
                            9D16AF2573AC6C01A33752CA5135F3700A6FE9CF
TimeStamperCertificate  :
Status                  : Valid
StatusMessage           : Signature verified
Path                    : C:\scripts\psvm.ps1
SignatureType           : Authenticode
IsOSBinary              : False
```

If you didn't follow our suggestion to install the self-signed root certificate, you'll see an "unknown error" status. That's okay, but you won't be able to run the script.

If you have an `AllSigned` execution policy, you can still run the script:

```
PS C:\scripts> set-executionpolicy allsigned -force
PS C:\scripts> .\psvm.ps1
Do you want to run software from this untrusted publisher?
File C:\scripts\psvm.ps1 is published by CN=James Petty and is not trusted
on
your system. Only run scripts from trusted publishers.
[V] Never run  [D] Do not run  [R] Run once  [A] Always run  [?] Help
```

```
(default is "D"): a
Handles  NPM(K)    PM(K)      WS(K)     CPU(s)     Id  SI ProcessName
-------  ------    -----      -----     ------     --  -- -----------
   1179      80    73368        472       9.31    376   2 SearchUI
    873      44    67712      43888     579.25    472   0 svchost
   3395     194    97616      27868     446.81   1116   0 svchost
    948      29    56096      22904       2.19   4920   2 powershell
    876      37    99696      47176       4.33   6080   0 powershell
```

The first time we run the script, we're prompted about trusting the certificate. We'll tell PowerShell always to trust it, and, from then on, we can run the script with no prompts.

Now we'll make a slight change to the script, but without re-signing it, and attempt to run it:

```
PS C:\scripts> .\psvm.ps1
File C:\scripts\psvm.ps1 cannot be loaded. The contents of file
C:\scripts\psvm.ps1 might have been changed by an unauthorized user or
process, because the hash of the file does not match the hash stored in the
digital signature.
The script cannot run on the specified system. For more information, run
Get-Help about_Signing..
    + CategoryInfo          : SecurityError: (:) [], PSSecurityException
    + FullyQualifiedErrorId : UnauthorizedAccess
```

We get a rather severe error message, and the script isn't executed. We want that! If we didn't make any changes, we want to investigate and figure out what changed. When ready, we can re-sign the script and be ready to go.

## Summary

Implementing script signing isn't that difficult, especially if you have an AD PKI (which ends up being easier and cheaper than a commercial CA) or another brand of PKI internally. You can probably even configure your scripting editor to sign scripts for you—many of them offer an option to do that when you save the file. If nothing else, it's a snap to sign all of your scripts at once. As we've explained before, implementing digital signatures or requiring their use isn't a security boundary. However, it adds a critical safety check to ensure that the script you, or someone else, are about to run is *exactly* the script you wrote.

# Publishing your script

We hope that as you progress through this book, or shortly after that, you'll develop a fantastic, well-crafted PowerShell tool that solves an immediate problem. It would be even more rewarding if it leads to a substantial raise for you. However, beyond personal gains, we hope you'll consider sharing your creation with the broader PowerShell community. In recent years, this has become conveniently achievable through the PowerShell Gallery, which hosts thousands of modules and scripts.

## 22.1  The importance of publishing

Publishing your script offers several benefits. First, it's a generous act, contributing positively to the broader PowerShell community. We want to express our gratitude in advance for your willingness to do so. Moreover, it's an excellent means to share your tools with colleagues or yourself. You can publish your current version to the Power-Shell Gallery (often called PSGallery) and install or update it as needed. If you have a new version, you can also effortlessly publish it. The beauty is that your older versions remain accessible, allowing you to test or reference them when necessary.

## 22.2  Exploring the PowerShell Gallery

The PowerShell Gallery is a free website maintained by Microsoft and accessible at www.powershellgallery.com. Although you can interact with it directly, you're more likely to use a set of PowerShell cmdlets such as `Find-Module` and `Install-Module` for most interactions. Microsoft has implemented stringent checks during script uploads to ensure adherence to best practices. They also employ the PowerShell Script Analyzer commands to scrutinize your code. Initial rejection is possible if your code fails specific tests. To ensure a smooth experience, consider using Visual

Studio Code (VS Code) for development, as it can help you pass these tests. It's crucial to remember that Microsoft can't guarantee the effectiveness of a module, so you run anything you download at your own risk. This underscores the importance of maintaining a robust testing environment.

## 22.3 Other publishing options

While we emphasize PowerShell Gallery's accessibility, note that it's essentially a specialized type of website functioning as a NuGet-based repository. NuGet-based repositories have long been recognized as reliable publication and distribution mechanisms. Anyone can establish a NuGet-based repository, and your organization may have one. While we won't delve into the intricacies of setting up and managing such servers in this book, publishing them from PowerShell should closely mirror what we've discussed for the PowerShell Gallery.

## 22.4 Before you publish

Before you publish, we assume your project is complete, tested, and properly documented. This means it includes at least comment-based help. Your project reflects you, so you want to make the best impression possible. But there are a few other preliminary things to check off first.

### 22.4.1 Are you reinventing the wheel?

Although there's no rule against publishing something that already exists, it's worth double-checking. Is there already a module that offers the same functionality as yours? How is yours different? Use `Find-Module` to see what existing modules may compete with yours.

Suppose you have a module with some Active Directory (AD)–related commands. You can run

```
find-module *activedirectory* | Select Version,Name,Author, `
 Description,PublishedDate
```

or search by tags

```
find-module -tag ad,activedirectory
```

You can also use your web browser by visiting www.powershellgallery.com and searching (see figure 22.1). You can even refine your search-specific types and categories on the website.

You can also search for modules that are operating-system-specific or cross-platform. The tags can quickly determine this. For example, let's look at the DBATools module (see figure 22.2). If we expand the Package Details section, we can see the tags for Mac and Linux. DBATools can be run on PowerShell installed on any of these operating systems.

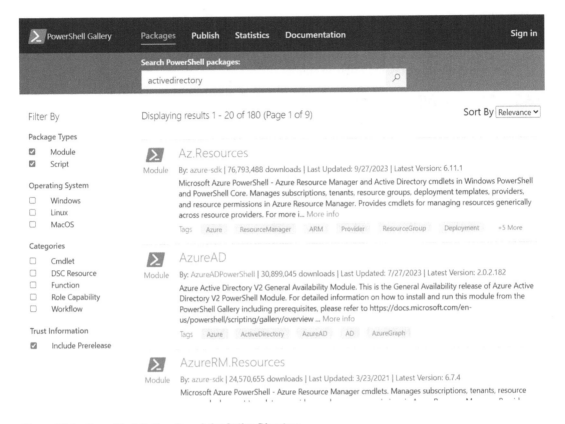

**Figure 22.1    PowerShell Gallery Search for Active Directory**

**Figure 22.2    Shows DBATools with Mac and Linux tags**

## 22.4.2  *Updating your manifest*

You'll need a proper manifest, as generated by `New-ModuleManifest`. In it, make sure you configure these settings:

- `ModuleVersion`—The accepted standard is known as *semantic versioning*. Technically, your value should be in the format *a.b.c.*, such as 1.0.0. But you can get by with something like 1.0.
- `Author`—This will most likely be your name. Try to use the same value on all of your projects so people can identify what belongs to you. Don't use "Don Jones"

on one and "Donald Jones" on another. Pick one and live with it. The only way to change it is to publish a new version.

- `Description`—This is a biggie. You need to provide complete information about why your module exists, what problems it solves, and how it's different from related projects.
- `PrivateData`—This is another biggie because Microsoft will pull values from the manifest to populate metadata for your project in the gallery:
  - `Tags`—You should enter at least one tag. You can enter as many as make sense, separated by commas. Take a look at existing modules to get a sense for what tags people are using.
  - `LicenseUri`—Ideally, your project is also in a publicly accessible source control system such as GitHub. Insert the address to your license file here, which of course you have.
  - `ProjectUri`—This can be the URL to your GitHub repository or wherever your project lives online. Some people like to be able to check your source code. Or, in the case of GitHub, use the Issues feature to report bugs or ask questions.

We assume you've already set the expected values for things such as `RootModule`, `Guid`, and `FunctionsToExport`.

### 22.4.3 *Getting an API key*

Before publishing to the PowerShell Gallery, you must be a registered user with an API key. On the PowerShell Gallery website (www.PowerShellGallery.com), click the Register link, and follow the instructions. (Websites change, so we won't bother with screenshots.) At some point in the process, you'll get an API key. You can always find your key by logging in and clicking your name to view your profile. You should see the Credentials section. Click the Show Key link to see everything. Assuming you have a secure computer, you might consider putting your API key into a password manager or key vault and using the PowerShell Secrets Module to retrieve it. You also can copy the value and, in your PowerShell profile, create a variable:

```
$PSGalleryKey = 2XXXX7bd-771d-9999-8XXa-da41XXXX1abc
```

However, we prefer the first option. This will come in handy when it comes time to publish your module.

## 22.5 *Ready, set, publish*

When you publish a module to the PowerShell Gallery, the `Publish-Module` cmdlet will create a NuGet package from your module folder. The person who installs the module will, in essence, get a copy of your folder. Remember when your Mom told you to clean your room because company was coming over? This is like that. Deleting temporary, scratch, or redundant files from your directory takes a few minutes. If you're using Git, the hidden .git directory will be ignored. If you need to retain files for development that aren't part of the final project, you can create a separate, clean directory with just the module files.

If you have a well-constructed manifest, you should be able to run a command like this:

```
Publish-Module -path c:\scripts\MyTools -repository PSGallery
  -nugetapikey $psgallerykey
```

In this example, we use the saved API key we set earlier. If you didn't complete your manifest as we suggested, you should run the command and specify additional parameters such as -Tags and -FormatVersion.

Unfortunately, you can't publish your module without pushing it to the PowerShell Gallery. We'd love to have an option to publish or save the package locally so we could verify its contents before sharing it with the world. The best you can do is save the module from the PowerShell Gallery and look at the downloaded files. If you don't like something, update your module, increase the version number, and republish.

### 22.5.1 *Managing revisions*

At some point, you may improve your module or fix bugs. You can republish your module to the PowerShell Gallery using the same steps. The most important task to remember is to update the version number in your module manifest. Users can get the most recent version when they run Update-Module.

Once your module is published, there's no way to manage it through PowerShell—you'll have to use the PowerShell Gallery web page. To do so, follow these steps:

1 Sign in to your account.
2 Click your account name link.
3 Click Manage My Items.
4 Select a module from the list.
5 Scroll down the page until you see the Version History section. You can't delete anything, but you can hide a version. Click a link under Listed. All versions probably say Yes.
6 Uncheck the box on the next page to disable showing this particular version in search results.
7 Click Save.

Now, nobody will be able to see this version with Find-Module.

On the module page, you'll also see an Edit Module link. You can modify a few things, such as the module description and summary, which appear in Additional Metadata when you use Find-Module. These are the same items you can configure in your module manifest, which is a better place to make those changes.

## 22.6 Publishing scripts

Your module should have all the functions and tools you need. How you might use them will be done with a controller script. The controller script automates the process so that instead of typing a specific sequence of actions using commands from your published module, you only need to run the script. You might want to share your controller scripts. Microsoft recently provided an online repository for scripts, which might be an option.

### 22.6.1 Using the Microsoft script repository

You can find scripts with the `Find-Script` cmdlet. You can run it without parameters or search for something in a script name:

```
PS C:\> find-script *weather*
Version    Name              Repository   Description
-------    ----              ----------   -----------
1.0        Get-Weather       PSGallery    Shows Weather information....
```

With our example you may see a warning message or two, which appears to be related to a problem with a script in the repository and not anything you've done wrong locally or in running `Find-Script`.

If you see a script you like, you can save it to a folder so you can inspect it:

```
PS C:\> save-script get-weather -path c:\dltemp
```

You can now look at the file—in our case, c:\dltemp\get-weather.ps1—and decide what to do with it. If you like it, you can copy it to your scripts directory, or you can take advantage of a PowerShell feature and install it:

```
PS C:\> install-script get-weather
PATH Environment Variable Change
Your system has not been configured with a default script installation path
yet, which means you can only run a script by specifying the full path to
the script file. This action places the script into the folder 'C:\Program
Files\PowerShell\Scripts', and adds that folder to your PATH
environment variable. Do you want to add the script installation path
'C:\Program Files\PowerShell\Scripts' to the PATH environment
variable?
[Y] Yes  [N] No  [S] Suspend  [?] Help (default is "Y"): y
```

As you can read from the prompt, installed scripts go into a specific directory, which is added to the path:

```
PS C:\> get-command get-weather
CommandType     Name                Version Source
-----------     ----                ------- ------
ExternalScript Get-Weather.ps1              C:\Program·Files\WindowsPowerShell\...
PS C:\> get-command get-weather | Select path
Path
```

```
----
C:\Program Files\WindowsPowerShell\Scripts\Get-Weather.ps1
```

As an added benefit, you don't need to specify the full path to the script file. You can type the name of the script, and it will run:

```
PS C:\> get-weather "Austin"
Weather report: Austin
     \   /      Sunny
      .-.       100-102 °F
   ? (   ) ?    ? 0 mph
      `-'       9 mi
     /   \      0.0 in
```

Like modules, you can also update and uninstall scripts. Even better, you can publish your own scripts. As with modules, the whole world will see your code, so make sure it's clean, well-documented, and includes all the other things we've talked about that you should be doing as a professional toolmaker.

### 22.6.2  *Creating ScriptFileInfo*

Before you can publish a script, you need to create a special type of header that includes all the necessary metadata such as tags, versioning, and requirements. You do this with the New-ScriptFileInfo cmdlet. You can either append your script code to this file or move the comment block to your script file. We'll demonstrate by publishing one of Jeff Hicks's scripts that checks for module updates in the PowerShell Gallery:

```
PS C:\> New-ScriptFileInfo -Path C:\Work\PSReleaseTools.ps1 -Version 1.0.0
-Author 'Jeff Hicks' -Description 'Check for module updates from the
PowerShell gallery and create a comparison object' -Copyright 2017 -Tags
PowerShellget,Module,PSGallery
```

The filename must have a .ps1 file extension. Here's the result—the headings should be self-explanatory and are similar to what you'd use in a module manifest:

```
<#PSScriptInfo
.VERSION 1.0.0
.GUID 7da2acc6-30d8-4cc9-a3d9-ba645fceebb2
.AUTHOR Jeff Hicks
.COMPANYNAME
.COPYRIGHT 2023
.TAGS PowerShellget Module PSGallery
.LICENSEURI
.PROJECTURI
.ICONURI
.EXTERNALMODULEDEPENDENCIES
.REQUIREDSCRIPTS
.EXTERNALSCRIPTDEPENDENCIES
.RELEASENOTES
#>
<#
```

```
.DESCRIPTION
 Check for module updates from the PowerShell Gallery and create a
comparison object
#>
Param()
```

Take everything except the `Param()` line and move it to the beginning of the script file. We'll clean it up a bit and verify that we haven't messed up anything:

```
PS C:\> Test-ScriptFileInfo -Path C:\scripts\Check-ModuleUpdate.ps1 |
 select *
Name                      : Check-ModuleUpdate
Version                   : 1.0.0
Guid                      : 7da2acc6-30d8-4cc9-a3d9-ba645fceebb2
Path                      : C:\scripts\Check-ModuleUpdate.ps1
ScriptBase                : C:\scripts
Description               : Check for module updates from the PowerShell
                            Gallery and create a comparison object
Author                    : Jeff Hicks
CompanyName               :
Copyright                 : 2023
Tags                      : {PowerShellget, Module, PSGallery}
ReleaseNotes              : {This code is described at
http://jdhitsolutions.com/blog/powershell/5…}
RequiredModules           :
ExternalModuleDependencies :
RequiredScripts           :
ExternalScriptDependencies :
LicenseUri                :
ProjectUri                : https://gist.github.com/jdhitsolutions/8a49...
IconUri                   :
DefinedCommands           :
DefinedFunctions          :
DefinedWorkflows          :
```

We didn't get any errors, so we'll assume we're good. Once you have something like this, it's simple to keep as a snippet or file that you can copy, paste, and modify as necessary. Just be sure to generate a new GUID, using the `New-Guid` cmdlet, for each new script you intend to publish.

### 22.6.3   Publishing the script

Publishing a script to the PowerShell Gallery also requires the API key. Once you've updated the script file with the necessary metadata, you can easily publish it:

```
Publish-Script -Path C:\scripts\Check-ModuleUpdate.ps1 -NuGetApiKey
 $psgallerykey -Repository PSGallery
```

In less than a minute, the script will be available for download and installation:

```
PS C:\> find-script check-moduleupdate
WARNING: Unable to resolve package source ''.
```

```
WARNING: Cannot bind argument to parameter 'Path' because it is an empty
string.
Version  Name                  Repository  Description
-------  ----                  ----------  -----------
1.0.0    Check-ModuleUpdate    PSGallery   Check for module updates from ...
```

You may see a different version, depending on changes Jeff makes and republishes.

### 22.6.4 *Managing published scripts*

As is true for published modules, there are no commands in PowerShell for managing a published script. If you need to change the script, do so, and then edit the script file-info header with a new version. You should be able to run `Publish-Script` as you did before.

For modules, you can also use the Manage My Items page on the PowerShell Gallery website, as we showed you earlier. Scroll down the list until you find the script. You'll see that it has a Script type. As with modules, you can't delete published items but can hide previous versions. Follow the same steps as described earlier.

## *Summary*

There's no requirement that you publish or share your modules and scripts, but this is a relatively painless process to make your beautiful code available to everyone who needs it. In the long run, we think Microsoft will offer more guidance and tools for IT pros to set up internal repositories, which makes sense. In the meantime, you can become familiar with the process by publishing to the PowerShell Gallery.

*Part 4*

Welcome to the pinnacle of our scripting exploration—Advanced Techniques. In this concluding part, we get into the intricacies of advanced scripting, pushing the boundaries of our skills to new heights and exploring the most advanced and best techniques that define mastery in the scripting domain.

When we embark on chapter 23, we tackle the inevitable challenges of bugs head-on. You'll learn advanced techniques for bug identification, diagnosis, and resolution, honing your skills to create functional and resilient scripts in the face of complexities. In chapter 24, you'll elevate the presentation of your script outputs and explore advanced methods to enhance your script results' visual appeal and usability, ensuring your audience receives clear and compelling information. You'll unravel the full potential of the.NET Framework in chapter 25 while discovering advanced scripting techniques that use the capabilities of the .NET Framework and expanding the horizons of what your scripts can achieve. Next, we'll dive into sophisticated data storage practices in chapter 26, and explore alternatives beyond Microsoft Excel as we delve into advanced methods for storing and managing data, providing scalable solutions for your scripting endeavors. Finally, in chapter 27, we'll reflect on the endless possibilities and continuous evolution in the scripting landscape. Scripting is an ever-evolving journey, and this chapter serves as an inspiration to embrace the dynamic nature of the scripting realm. As we navigate through these chapters, you'll not only master advanced techniques but also gain insights into the limitless potential of scripting. The chapters in Advanced Techniques are the culmination of our scripting expedition, equipping you with the skills to overcome challenges, present your scripts with finesse, harness the power of the .NET

Framework, explore innovative data storage methods, and embrace the perpetual growth inherent in scripting. Let's embark on this final stretch of our journey, where the pursuit of mastery is never truly at an end.

# Squashing bugs

No comprehensive scripting guide is complete without addressing the critical topic of debugging. To put it bluntly, debugging can be frustrating. But don't worry—we're here to offer valuable insights and practical tips to make debugging more manageable.

## 23.1 The three kinds of bugs

In the world of scripting, bugs generally fall into three categories: syntax, results, and logic bugs. Results bugs, a relatively new category, has emerged to help address specific scenarios that often perplex scriptwriters. These bug families, in ascending order of complexity, are as follows:

- *Syntax bugs*—You typed something wrong. Perhaps you typed *ForEach* instead of *Foreach Object*, for example, or you forgot to close a { (curly bracket). PowerShell will try to alert you to many syntax bugs by using a little red squiggly underline thing. But there's a more insidious class of syntax bugs that PowerShell can't help with: mistyping a variable name in a script—for example, *$CompuerName* instead of *$ComputerName*—will create undesired results, but PowerShell won't be able to help by default. If you're using Visual Studio Code (VS Code), you may see a red squiggle under the variable until you use it somewhere else in your script.
- *Results bugs*—A command produces something you don't expect. For example, if you expect `Test-Connection SERVER1` to return `$True` when SERVER1 is online, you'll be disappointed when it doesn't, and the code which made that assumption might not work as you expected.

- *Logic bugs*—These are the trickiest to resolve because they don't result in obvious errors. Logic bugs occur when your script's commands execute without error, but there's a problem in how your code is structured or written. We'll dedicate most of this chapter to help you conquer logic bugs.

---

**An almost-fourth category: The PowerShell "gotcha"**

A unique situation could be considered a blend of syntax and results bugs. Consider the following command:

```
Get-CimInstance –ClassName Win32_OperatingSystem |
Select-Object –Prop PSHostName,Version,BuildNumber
```

This command runs without errors, but it produces output with one blank column. The peculiar part is the `PSHostName` property requested with `Select-Object`. The Common Information Model (CIM) class we've retrieved doesn't have a `PSHostName` property. PowerShell, however, can create new properties on the fly, which can be useful in many situations. In this case, it has created a new property named `PSHostName` without any content. You won't get the expected results if you later rely on `PSHostName` having values. For now, let's classify this as a results bug and refer you to section 23.3.

---

## 23.2 Dealing with syntax bugs

The simplest way to handle syntax bugs is to never make a typo and pay attention to PowerShell's red squiggly underlines, highlighting potential problems. Additionally, you can enhance your script's reliability by adding `Set-StrictMode –Version 2.0` at the script's beginning. This command modifies PowerShell's behavior in the following ways:

- You're supposed to call PowerShell functions using a specific syntax. For example, a function with three input parameters could be called by running `My-Function 1 2 3`, passing the values `1`, `2`, and `3` to the parameters in order. Newcomers sometimes use a method-style syntax like `My-Function(1,2,3)`, which passes a single array of three elements to the first parameter. Strict mode disallows that and will throw an error. You can avoid the problem by always using named parameters when calling a function, as in `My-Function –Param 1 –OtherParam 2 –ThirdParam 3`.
- Referring to nonexistent properties of objects typically returns a `$null` value; in strict mode, doing so produces an error. This will *not* solve the `Select-Object` gotcha we described in the sidebar earlier—that condition is, as we noted, a specific *feature* of the command.
- Referring to a variable that hasn't been assigned a value in the current scope will usually cause PowerShell to go up the scope tree to try and find the variable. For example, referring to `$ErrorActionPreference` in a script works because the global scope, rather than your local scope, contains that predefined variable. In strict mode, this behavior changes. Referring to variables that haven't yet been

assigned a value in the current scope will produce an error. This helps avoid "I mistyped the variable name—argh!" syntax errors.

We recommend using strict mode in all of your scripts. We don't do so in all of our sample and demo code, but that's because they aren't production-ready files.

> **Using the latest version**
>
> You might have noticed that the `-Version` parameter for `Set-StrictMode` also offers a `"Latest"` option. While using `"Latest"` seems convenient, it's essential to consider the potential consequences. Currently, 2.0 is the latest documented version, making it a safer choice. You can be confident that your code will work as expected with version 2.0. If Microsoft introduces a 3.0 option, you may want to revisit your code, as significant changes to PowerShell could accompany it.

## 23.3   Dealing with results bugs

To tackle results bugs, follow the scripting process we've advocated throughout this book. Always begin by running individual commands directly in the console before incorporating them into your scripts. This way, you can observe the output and establish reliable expectations based on concrete evidence. Although this may seem overly simple, scriptwriters often overlook it in their haste to create code.

## 23.4   Dealing with logic bugs

Now, let's delve into the most challenging category: logic bugs. We've uncovered a straightforward rule that simplifies the process of identifying and fixing logic bugs: logic errors occur when a property or variable contains something different from what you assumed. To illustrate this concept, consider the script in listing 23.1, which contains a function that's supposed to get disk information using the `Get-CimInstance` command.

> **TRY IT NOW**   Go ahead and grab this script from the downloadable code samples at http://mng.bz/rjgE and run it. It won't hurt anything, but it also won't work correctly. If you've run into this problem yourself at some point, the reason will be apparent, but we'll use this as an example of the procedure we follow to debug problems like this. We also aren't annotating the code because we want you to follow the debug process.

**Listing 23.1   A buggy script for you to consider**

```
function Get-DiskInfo {
    [CmdletBinding()]
    Param(
        [Parameter(Mandatory=$True,
                    ValueFromPipeline=$True)]
        [string[]]$ComputerName
    )
```

```
    BEGIN {
        Set-StrictMode -Version 2.0
    }
    PROCESS {
        ForEach ($comp in $ComputerName) {
            $params = @{'ComputerName' = $comp
                        'ClassName' = 'Win32_LogicalDisk'}
            $disks = Get-CimInstance @params
            ForEach ($disk in $disks) {
                $props = @{'ComputerName' = $comp
                           'Size' = $disk.size
                           'DriveType' = $disk.drivetype}
                if ($disk.drivetype -eq 'fixed') {
                    $props.Add('FreeSpace',$disk.FreeSpace)
                } else {
                    $props.Add('FreeSpace','N/A')
                }
                New-Object -TypeName PSObject -Property $props
            } #foreach disk
        } #foreach computer
    } #PROCESS
    END {}
}
Get-DiskInfo -ComputerName localhost
```

The problem with this script, as with all logic bugs, is that we have either a variable or a property that contains something *other* than what we thought it did. In this particular example, which is deliberately simple, this is a results-style bug. We wouldn't be in this pickle if we'd bothered to run the command at the console and see what it produced. But in some scripts, you're populating variables and properties with values that you've calculated or constructed, so it's more complex than running a command to see what it produces. For this example, we'll treat this as a pure logic bug and follow the procedure for figuring those out.

Suppose the core problem is a property or a variable not containing what you expect. In that case, the fix is to determine which property or variable the code contains and determine what the property or variable contains. We're going to cover several distinct methods for doing this.

**NOTE** With the advent of VS Code and PowerShell support therein, we've changed our debugging approach. We don't use Write-Debug anymore, nor, in most interactive debugging cases like this, do we use Set-PSBreakpoint as much. Those are still useful, and in more advanced books such as *The PowerShell Scripting & Toolmaking Book* (https://leanpub.com/powershell-scripting-tool-making), we get into their intricacies. However, we now rely on VS Code's features to begin debugging.

### 23.4.1  Setting breakpoints

A *breakpoint* lets you run a script to a specific place; the script will pause when it encounters the breakpoint. That pause lets you examine the script, check the contents of variables and properties, execute the script line by line, or resume normal execution. Breakpoints are your core debugging tool, and they're tremendously useful.

We like to set a breakpoint just after we've set a variable's contents or before we're about to rely on the contents of a variable or a property. Figure 23.1 shows our script in VS Code; we've moved to line 17 and pressed F9 to toggle a breakpoint. It displays as a red dot just to the left of the line number.

```powershell
10        }
11        PROCESS {
12            ForEach ($comp in $ComputerName) {
13                $params = @{'ComputerName' = $comp
14                            'ClassName' = 'Win32_LogicalDisk'}
15                $disks = Get-CimInstance @params
16                ForEach ($disk in $disks) {
17                    $props = @{'ComputerName' = $comp
18                                'Size' = $disk.size
19                                'DriveType' = $disk.drivetype}
20                    if ($disk.drivetype -eq 'fixed') {
21                        $props.Add('FreeSpace',$disk.FreeSpace)
22                    } else {
23                        $props.Add('FreeSpace','N/A')
24                    }
25                    New-Object -TypeName PSObject -Property $props
26                } #foreach disk
27            } #foreach computer
28        } #PROCESS
29        END {}
30    }
31    Get-DiskInfo -ComputerName localhost
32
```

**Figure 23.1  Setting a breakpoint in VS Code**

With the breakpoint set, we can press F5 to run the script and begin debugging. Figure 23.2 shows what happens when execution reaches line 17: a Debug pane opens on the left side of the VS Code window, and the PowerShell terminal pane indicates that we've hit a breakpoint. The script is paused, and line 17 is highlighted.

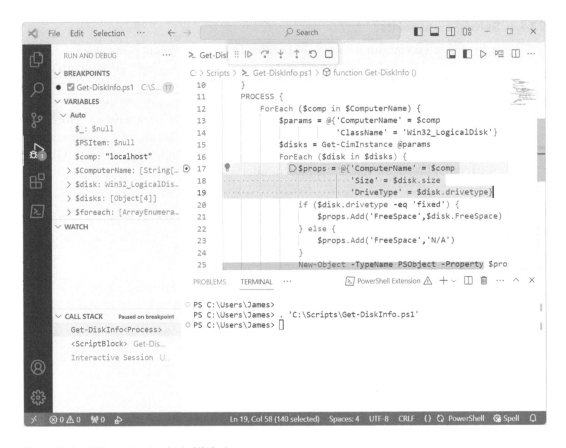

**Figure 23.2   Hitting a breakpoint in VS Code**

While the breakpoint is active, we can use that Terminal pane to examine things. For example, we'll run `$disk` to see what that variable currently contains. Figure 23.3 shows the result.

Sharp-eyed readers will have spotted the problem: the `DriveType` property contains 3, but our code clearly expected it to contain a string value such as `'fixed'`. Let's pretend for a moment that you're not sharp-eyed—we have another debugging trick up our sleeves.

> **TRY IT NOW**   This next bit is cooler to watch in person than in a book. We suggest you get VS Code up and running, make sure the PowerShell extension is active, and start a new file. Please save the file with a .ps1 filename extension (so VS Code knows it's PowerShell), and paste in the contents of listing 23.1. Set a breakpoint on line 17 as we've done and run the script.

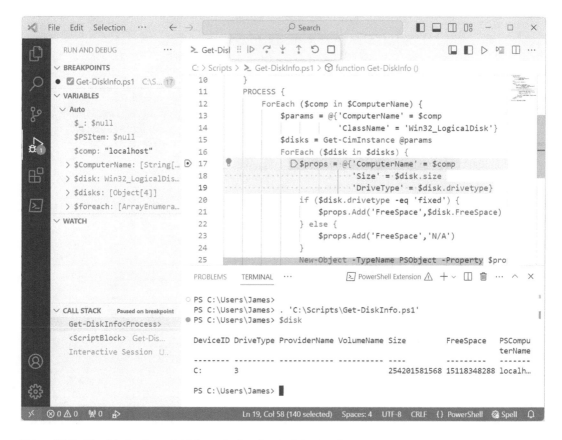

**Figure 23.3  Checking out a variable's contents when in debug mode**

At line 17, the script is about to enter an `If` construct, where it will make a logical decision. These decisions are often where logic bugs manifest themselves. The script will decide whether it will create a `FreeSpace` property containing an actual free space value or insert `'N/A'` as that value. Press F11, the Step Into command; as shown in figure 23.4, and the script will advance one line and pause again. You're about to execute the logic construct.

Press F11 once more. The script jumps to line 23—you can visually observe the logic's outcome. That means `$disk.drivetype` doesn't contain `'fixed'`. You expected it to—and so you've found the bug's exact location. At this point, you can press Shift-F5 to stop debugging so that you can begin fixing the problem.

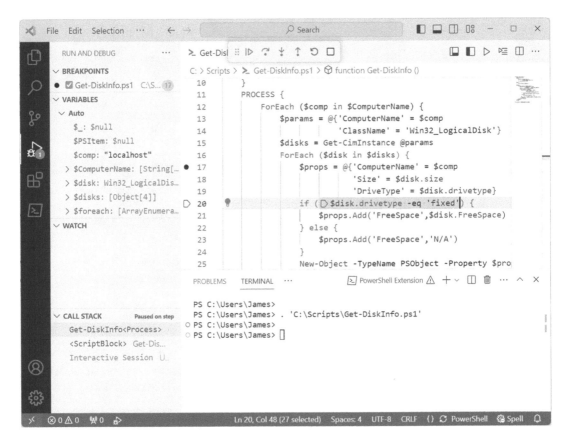

**Figure 23.4   Stepping into the next line of code during debugging**

### It's all about the expectations

We've skipped a somewhat valuable lesson—or saved it for this specific point. Debugging is all about finding where your assumptions and expectations differ from reality. The implication is that you *have* expectations. In other words, you must have an idea of what your script will do. Debugging will let you observe whether it does those things.

These are your expectations. When it comes time to debug, you're merely comparing reality to those expectations; where they differ, you've found your bug.

If you don't have an expectation for what the script will do each step of the way, and if you don't have an expectation for what each variable and property will contain, then you can't debug.

### 23.4.2  *Setting watches*

Because "what the variables and properties contain" is such a crucial part of debugging, VS Code offers a feature called *watches* that focuses specifically on that part. In VS Code, you can select Remove All Breakpoints from the Debug menu to give yourself a clean slate. The Debug pane is still open, though—press Ctrl-Shift-D if you accidentally closed it. Under the WATCH section, click the + icon (it won't be visible until you move your cursor over the WATCH section header). In the text box that appears, type $disk, and press Enter. It would be best if you had something that looks like figure 23.5.

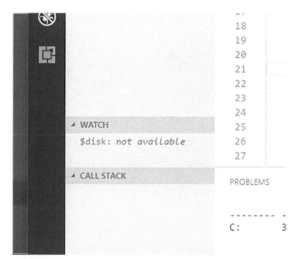

**Figure 23.5   Adding a watch for** $disk

We see that the variable is currently 'unavailable', which makes sense because the script isn't running. We'll re-enable the breakpoint on line 17, which is just after $disk is defined in the ForEach loop, and then run the script.

### 23.4.3  *So much more*

VS Code uses PowerShell's PSBreakpoint commands to provide these debugging features. There's more to explore beyond what we've covered in this chapter. Please read the help documentation for VS Code to learn about the additional capabilities it offers for debugging. While the techniques we've introduced are fundamental, they provide a solid foundation for squashing bugs in your scripts.

But you *knew* it was a `Win32_LogicalDisk`. The subsequent *use* of the `$disk` variable is to check the `Size` and `DriveType` properties on line 17, as shown in figure 23.6. Double-click the watch to edit it. Add `.drivetype` to the end of `$disk`; as figure 23.7 shows, on our system, we see that `DriveType` is 3.

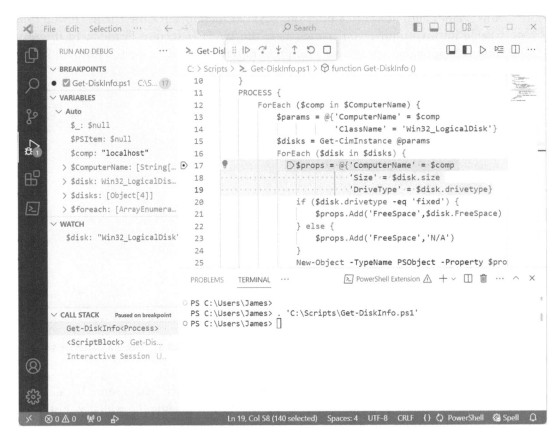

**Figure 23.6   Watching `$disk` reveals what's in the variable at this moment.**

The benefit of these watches is that you can press F5 again to run the script until it re-encounters the line 17 breakpoint. On our computer, we'd see `DriveType` change to 5—you'll likely have something different, based on your computer's configuration. And rather than having to type out `$disk.drivetype` every time, you can quickly refer to the watches and see what all of your variables are doing.

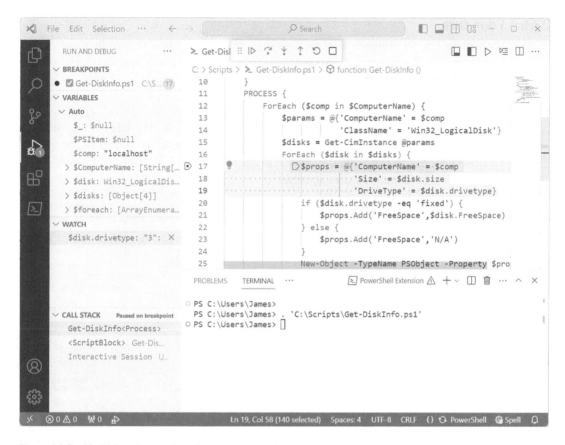

**Figure 23.7  Modifying the watch to focus on a specific property**

### 23.4.4 Don't be lazy

After all that, you may be thinking, "That's a lot of work." What's even more work is trying to spot a problem by reading the code or making random guesses about what might be wrong. And we've seen real people do exactly that. Take the time to learn the process and your editor's debugging features. It may take forever, but it's still a faster process than debugging by chance.

Oh, and make sure you make only one change at a time. Don't change five things at once because you won't know which change solves your problem and you'll risk introducing more bugs. Change one thing, then test. If it solves your bug, great. If not, change your code back, and try something else. In addition, be prepared that you might have multiple bugs but not see all of them until the first one or two are fixed.

## 23.5   *Your turn*

With these few techniques, believe it or not, you're equipped to handle most of the logic bugs you'll write into a PowerShell script. But don't take our word for it—use your new debugging skills.

### 23.5.1   *Start here*

Listing 23.2 is a buggy script. That's right, it *won't run* as is. We know that—it's the whole point of this exercise. We don't want you to run the script—for now, get it into VS Code, where you can look at it. Save it as a file with a .ps1 filename extension, or VS Code's PowerShell magic won't activate.

---

**Listing 23.2   A buggy script that awaits your debugging skills**

```
Function Get-DiskCheck {
    [cmdletbinding(DefaultParameterSetName = "name")]
    Param(
        [Parameter(Position = 0, Mandatory,
            HelpMessage = "Enter a computer name to check",
            ParameterSetName = "name",
            ValueFromPipeline)]
        [Alias("cn")]
        [ValidateNotNullorEmpty()]
        [string[]]$ComputerName,
        [Parameter(Mandatory,
            HelpMessage = "Enter the path to a text file of the computer
names",
            ParameterSetName = "file"
        )]
        [ValidateScript( {
                if (Test-Path $_) {
                    $True
                }
                else {
                    Throw "Cannot validate path $_"
                }
            })]
        [ValidatePattern("\.txt$")]
        [string]$Path,
        [ValidateRange(10, 50)]
        [int]$Threshhold = 25,
        [ValidateSet("C:", "D:", "E:", "F:")]
        [string]$Drive = "C:",
        [switch]$Test
    )
    Begin {
        Write-Verbose "[BEGIN  ] Starting: $($MyInvocation.Mycommand)"
        $cimParam = @{
            Classname    = "Win32_LogicalDisk"
            Filter       = "DeviceID='$Drive'"
            Computername = $Null
            ErrorAction  = "Stop"
        }
```

```
        } #begin
    Process {
        if ($PSCmdlet.ParameterSetName = 'name') {
            $names = $Computernme
        }
        else {
            #get list of names and trim off any extra spaces
            Write-Verbose "[PROCESS] Importing names from $path"
            $names = Get-Content -Path $path | Where {$_ -match "\w+"} |
    foreach {$_.Trim()}
        }
        if ($test) {
            Write-Verbose "[PROCESS] Testing connectivity"
            #ignore errors for offline computers
            $names = $names | Where {Test-WSMan $_ -ErrorAction
    SilentlyContinue}
        }
        foreach ($computer in $names) {
            $cimParam.ComputerName = $Computer
            Write-Verbose "[PROCESS] Querying $($computer.toUpper())"
            Try {
                $data = Get-Ciminstance @cimParam
                #write custom results to the pipeline
                $data | Select ComputerName,
                DeviceID, Size, Freespace,
                @{Name = "PctFree"; Expression =
    {[math]:Round(($_.freespace / $_.size) * 100, 2)}},
                @{Name = "OK"; Expression = {
                        [int]$p = ($_.freespace / $_.size) * 100
                        if ($p -ge $Threshhold) {
                            $True
                        }
                        else {
                            $false
                        }
                    }
                }, @{Name = "Date"; Expression = {(Get-Date)}}
            }
            Catch {
                Write-Warning "[$($computer.toUpper())] Failed.
    $($_.Exception.message)"
            }
        } #foreach computer
    } #process
    End {
        Write-Verbose "[END    ] Ending: $($MyInvocation.Mycommand)"
    } #end
}
```

### 23.5.2  *Your task*

Begin by *reading* the script. What will it do? What will each variable contain along the way? What will the various properties contain? You may spot several bugs in your

read-through—we've included both logic and syntax bugs for your debugging pleasure. Don't assume you've found all the bugs by reading the script.

Once you're finished with the read-through, *debug* the script. Use the techniques
introduced in this chapter and see whether you can produce a flawless version that
runs perfectly.

### 23.5.3 *Our take*

This chapter is much more about the procedure than the code, but to ensure you
found everything, the following listing shows the corrected script. Looking for a fun
bonus exercise? We didn't annotate the listing; instead, try using Compare-Object to
compare listings 23.2 and 23.3, or compare your corrected script to either one of
those to see what changed between them.

**Listing 23.3   Buggy script, completely debugged**

```
Function Get-DiskCheck {
    [cmdletbinding(DefaultParameterSetName = "name")]
    Param(
        [Parameter(Position = 0, Mandatory,
            HelpMessage = "Enter a computer name to check",
            ParameterSetName = "name",
            ValueFromPipeline)]
        [Alias("cn")]
        [ValidateNotNullorEmpty()]
        [string[]]$ComputerName,
        [Parameter(Mandatory,
            HelpMessage = "Enter the path to a text file of the computer
names",
            ParameterSetName = "file"
        )]
        [ValidateScript( {
                if (Test-Path $_) {
                    $True
                }
                else {
                    Throw "Cannot validate path $_"
                }
            })]
        [ValidatePattern("\.txt$")]
        [string]$Path,
        [ValidateRange(10, 50)]
        [int]$Threshhold = 25,
        [ValidateSet("C:", "D:", "E:", "F:")]
        [string]$Drive = "C:",
        [switch]$Test
    )
    Begin {
        Write-Verbose "[BEGIN  ] Starting: $($MyInvocation.Mycommand)"
        $cimParam = @{
            Classname       = "Win32_LogicalDisk"
            Filter          = "DeviceID='$Drive'"
```

```
                ComputerName = $Null
                ErrorAction  = "Stop"
            }
        } #begin
        Process {
            if ($PSCmdlet.ParameterSetName -eq 'name') {
                $names = $ComputerName
            }
            else {
                #get list of names and trim off any extra spaces
                Write-Verbose "[PROCESS] Importing names from $path"
                $names = Get-Content -Path $path | Where {$_ -match "\w+"} |
    foreach {$_.Trim()}
            }
            if ($test) {
                Write-Verbose "[PROCESS] Testing connectivity"
                #ignore errors for offline computers
                $names = $names | Where {Test-WSMan $_ -ErrorAction
    SilentlyContinue}
            }
            foreach ($computer in $names) {
                $cimParam.ComputerName = $Computer
                Write-Verbose "[PROCESS] Querying $($computer.toUpper())"
                Try {
                    $data = Get-Ciminstance @cimParam
                    #write custom results to the pipeline
                    $data | Select PSComputerName,
                    DeviceID, Size, Freespace,
                    @{Name = "PctFree"; Expression =
    {[math]::Round(($_.freespace / $_.size) * 100, 2)}},
                    @{Name = "OK"; Expression = {
                            [int]$p = ($_.freespace / $_.size) * 100
                            if ($p -ge $Threshhold) {
                                $True
                            }
                            else {
                                $false
                            }
                        }
                    }, @{Name = "Date"; Expression = {(Get-Date)}}
                }
                Catch {
                    Write-Warning "[$($computer.toUpper())] Failed.
    $($_.Exception.message)"
                }
            } #foreach computer
        } #process
        End {
            Write-Verbose "[END    ] Ending: $($MyInvocation.Mycommand)"
        } #end
    }
```

## Summary

By the end of this chapter, you gained valuable insights into debugging PowerShell scripts, which is an essential skill for any scriptwriter. We covered the three main types of bugs: syntax, results, and logic bugs, with a focus on addressing logic bugs, which are often the most challenging to resolve. By using techniques like setting breakpoints and watches in your preferred integrated development environment, such as Visual Studio Code (VS Code), you can efficiently identify and fix bugs in your scripts. Remember, debugging is all about comparing your expectations with reality, and with practice, you'll become adept at squashing bugs in your PowerShell scripts. Now, put your newfound debugging skills to the test by tackling the buggy script provided in this chapter and see how well you can debug it using the techniques you learned.

# Enhancing script output presentation

Throughout this book, our guiding principle has been to help you create tools that excel in doing one thing and one thing only. These tools remain agnostic to the origins of their input as long as it can be seamlessly channeled to a parameter. Similarly, tools don't concern themselves with the destination or purpose of their output. Consequently, they don't focus on creating beautifully formatted output. You can rely on the built-in `Format-` cmdlets or `Select-Object` to enhance the aesthetics or cater to management preferences. However, in this chapter, we'll delve into two advanced techniques for elevating the visual appeal of your output and surpassing the capabilities of `Format-` commands.

## 24.1 Our starting point

We'll start with the following code, which we copied from the end of chapter 17.

**Listing 24.1 Starting point for this chapter**

```
function Get-DiskInfo {
 foreach ($domain in (Get-ADForest).domains) {
   $hosts = Get-ADDomainController -filter * -server $domain |
   Sort-Object -Prop hostname
   ForEach ($h in $hosts) {
    $cs = Get-CimInstance -ClassName Win32_ComputerSystem `
                        # -ComputerName $h
    $props = @{'ComputerName' = $h
              'DomainController' = $h
              'Manufacturer' = $cs.manufacturer
              'Model' = $cs.model
              'TotalPhysicalMemory(GB)'=$cs.totalphysicalmemory / 1GB
              }
```

```
    New-Object -Type PSObject -Prop $props
  } #foreach $h
 } #foreach $domain
} #function
Export-ModuleMember -function Get-DiskInfo
```

Save this as a new module named Test.psm1, which means it's in a folder also named Test under the Documents/PowerShell/Modules folder. Thus, the complete filename is Documents/PowerShell/Modules/Test/Test.psm1. Got all that?

As is, the output isn't fantastic looking. The code has five properties, which exceeds the property count of four that lets PowerShell create a table by default. That means the output is, by default, returned as a list:

```
PS C:\> get-diskinfo
DomainController        : SRV1
ComputerName            : SRV1
Model                   : Virtual Machine
Manufacturer            : Microsoft Corporation
TotalPhysicalMemory(GB) : 31.5475044250488
```

We don't like it. Maybe you want a table or specific default properties. But you know not to build any formatting *into* the command itself because that would break the excellent rules those two great PowerShell guys laid down in their scripting book, right?

## 24.2 Creating a default view

Instead, let's take advantage of the formatting system built into PowerShell. The goal is to have your command output always display as a table without using any additional commands to make that happen (e.g., piping to `Format-Table`). You'll create a *default view*, which PowerShell's formatting subsystem will use automatically to render the command output. You'll only change the *visual representation* of the command's output—you won't modify the actual output objects in any way.

### 24.2.1 Exploring Microsoft's views

Nearly every native core command you run in PowerShell has a default view defined already. Run `cd $pshome` in PowerShell to switch to PowerShell's home folder, and then run `Dir`. You'll see several files with a. format.ps1xml filename extension. These are the ones we're after because they're where Microsoft defines the default views for the shell's core commands.

> **Lies and mysteries**
>
> Hopefully, you're aware that these default views can make it seem like PowerShell is lying sometimes. For example, running `Get-EventLog system -newest 10` displays a neatly formatted table (try it!), but some of the column names are different from the underlying property names. When looking at a predefined list or table, the headers are defined in the view and *don't necessarily represent the underlying objects*. When you run

Get-Process, the numbers you see are calculated by the default view; the underlying data is in bytes, not kilobytes, megabytes, or whatever. Views are visual, and you have to be careful about relying on them as descriptors of the actual data in play.

You can do the same sort of lying when you create views. Don't want the table header to be ComputerName? No problem—you can have it show up as Mandolin if you want. This will create no end of confusion for anyone using your command because they might try to run something like Get-Whatever | Select-Object mandolin, only to get a blank column as the output because there's no actual "mandolin" property. This continues a fine tradition of PowerShell being a little sneaky.

We should also point out that we're about to mess with XML files with *no* formal definition or *document type declaration (DTD)*. This is allegedly because Microsoft wants the freedom to tinker with this system in the future (although it never has in 15+ years); if Microsoft doesn't document the file formats, you can't complain if they change on you one day (or so goes the theory). Frankly, we've seen the formatting subsystem's code (PowerShell is open source now, remember!), and we'd be more willing to believe that the company is a little embarrassed by it all and doesn't want to document it because it brings up painful memories. What documentation does exist is at http://mng.bz/QBX0, and good luck with that—it's terse.

We document this stuff more thoroughly in *PowerShell in Depth*, if you're interested (Manning, 2014; http://mng.bz/xjzq). This chapter will serve more as a tutorial than a comprehensive look at what you can accomplish.

The file to open—in Notepad, Visual Studio Code (VS Code), or your favorite editor, as you prefer—is dotnettypes.format.ps1xml. There are other format files, but this biggie contains the views for most of the core object types PowerShell works with. Let's walk through a bit of it, because you'll be copying from it. It starts like this:

```
<?xml version="1.0" encoding="utf-8" ?>
<!-- ********************************************************************
These sample files contain formatting information used by the Windows
PowerShell engine. Do not edit or change the contents of this file
directly. Please see the PowerShell documentation or type
Get-Help Update-FormatData for more information.
Copyright (c) Microsoft Corporation. All rights reserved.
THIS SAMPLE CODE AND INFORMATION IS PROVIDED "AS IS" WITHOUT WARRANTY
OF ANY KIND,WHETHER EXPRESSED OR IMPLIED, INCLUDING BUT NOT LIMITED TO
THE IMPLIED WARRANTIES OF MERCHANTABILITY AND/OR FITNESS FOR A PARTICULAR
PURPOSE. IF THIS CODE AND INFORMATION IS MODIFIED, THE ENTIRE RISK OF USE
OR RESULTS IN CONNECTION WITH THE USE OF THIS CODE AND INFORMATION
REMAINS WITH THE USER.
******************************************************************** -->
<Configuration>
<ViewDefinitions>
```

The first line and last two lines are essential for making your file. Start up a new file in VS Code right now, and copy and paste those three lines at the top of the new file.

Save the new file in the same folder as your .psm1 file (assuming you're following along with us). Name it TestViews.format.ps1xml. Saving it will cue VS Code to provide the correct syntax coloring for XML, which is what this is. Go ahead and finish the file by closing those two opening tags:

```
<?xml version="1.0" encoding="utf-8" ?>
<Configuration>
<ViewDefinitions>
</ViewDefinitions>
</Configuration>
```

Everything in XML comes in paired sets of *tags*, and each pair needs to be nested within another pair. The opening `<?xml ?>` bit isn't a tag; it's a document definition, so there's only one of those.

Everything else in the file consists of `<View></View>` sections. Each of these is a *view*, as the tag name implies, and defines a single way of displaying a single kind of object. Here's one as an example:

```
<View>
<Name>System.CodeDom.Compiler.CompilerError</Name>          ←⎤    Name of the view
<ViewSelectedBy>                                             ←⎤    Optional selection
<TypeName>System.CodeDom.Compiler.CompilerError</TypeName>    ⎦    criteria
</ViewSelectedBy>
<ListControl>                      ←——— View type
<ListEntries>
<ListEntry>
<ListItems>                        ←——— List definition
<ListItem>
<PropertyName>ErrorText</PropertyName>
</ListItem>
<ListItem>
<PropertyName>Line</PropertyName>
</ListItem>
<ListItem>
<PropertyName>Column</PropertyName>
</ListItem>
<ListItem>
<PropertyName>ErrorNumber</PropertyName>
</ListItem>
<ListItem>
<PropertyName>LineSource</PropertyName>
</ListItem>
</ListItems>
</ListEntry>
</ListEntries>
</ListControl>
</View>
```

Let's break this down:

- The view has a name. These are often object-type names, but that's not required. Frankly, the idea of views having a name you could refer to never played out. The idea was that a single object type could have multiple view options and that by using the `Format-` commands, you could tell PowerShell which one to use. But there's no way to list them all, and the idea never went anywhere.

- A particular object type name selects the view. This is important! Right now, the command is producing objects of the type `System.PSCustomObject`. That's a commonly used type, and it's not unique to this command—which is a problem. You can only make a view if your command produces an object having a unique type. You'll have to fix this in your command.
- This example shows a list-type view as opposed to a table-type view.
- The list view consists of list entries, and each entry includes a list item. In this example, they specify the property names to display in the list.

**TRY IT NOW** Scroll through the file and examine some of the other types of views and other elements—besides property names—that they include. Notice that table controls, in particular, are more complex, including an entire section just for the column headers, followed by sections for what those columns will contain.

### 24.2.2 Adding a custom type name to output objects

You know you need to modify the code. The following listing shows that change.

**Listing 24.2 Adding a custom type name to an object**

```
function Get-DiskInfo {
 foreach ($domain in (Get-ADForest).domains) {
   $hosts = Get-ADDomainController -filter * -server $domain |
   Sort-Object -Prop hostname
   ForEach ($h in $hosts) {
    $cs = Get-CimInstance -ClassName Win32_ComputerSystem -ComputerName $h
    $props = @{'ComputerName' = $h
               'DomainController' = $h
               'Manufacturer' = $cs.manufacturer
               'Model' = $cs.model
               'TotalPhysicalMemory(GB)'=$cs.totalphysicalmemory / 1GB
               }
     $obj = New-Object -Type PSObject -Prop $props          ◄——┐ Saves the
     $obj.psobject.typenames.insert(0,'Toolmaking.DiskInfo') ◄—  object to
     Write-Output $obj                                           a variable
   } #foreach $h                              Inserts a new
  } #foreach $domain                          type name
} #function
Export-ModuleMember -function Get-DiskInfo
```

This isn't a major change: you saved the output object into a variable, `$obj`, rather than immediately emitting it to the pipeline. You then insert a type name, `Toolmaking` `.DiskInfo`, and place the object into the pipeline. The new type name will replace the original generic type name.

### Selecting a type name

.NET Framework's type-naming conventions are designed to make each type name universally unique. You wouldn't want to add a custom type name such as "System .DiskInfo" because, for all you know, it either already exists or could exist in the future. `System` is considered a *namespace*, and it's "owned" by Microsoft. Everything starting with `System.` is under Microsoft control, and you shouldn't intrude into the company's playground.

We essentially defined a new `Toolmaking` namespace, under which we have free reign to create whatever we want—and you should do the same, perhaps using a form of your organization's name as the top-level namespace. If you work in IT operations and are specifically on the Storage team, maybe you'd select `MyCompany .ITOps.Storage.DiskInfo` as your custom type name in this example. The idea is to create a hierarchy that allows individual groups to have complete control over their own namespace without fear of overlapping each other.

### 24.2.3  Creating a new view file

The next listing shows the start of the new view file. Notice that we found a table view we like the look of to use as a starting point.

Listing 24.3  **Starting a new view file**

```xml
<?xml version="1.0" encoding="utf-8" ?>
<Configuration>
<ViewDefinitions>
<View>
<Name>System.Reflection.Assembly</Name>
<ViewSelectedBy>
<TypeName>System.Reflection.Assembly</TypeName>
</ViewSelectedBy>
<TableControl>                          ◁──── Table definition
<TableHeaders>
<TableColumnHeader>                      ◁┐ Defines table
<Label>GAC</Label>                        │ headers
<Width>6</Width>
</TableColumnHeader>
<TableColumnHeader>
<Label>Version</Label>
<Width>14</Width>
</TableColumnHeader>
<TableColumnHeader/>                     ◁─┘ Singleton tag
</TableHeaders>
<TableRowEntries>                        ◁─┐ Corresponding values
<TableRowEntry>
<TableColumnItems>
<TableColumnItem>
<PropertyName>GlobalAssemblyCache</PropertyName>
</TableColumnItem>
<TableColumnItem>
<PropertyName>ImageRuntimeVersion</PropertyName>
```

```
</TableColumnItem>
<TableColumnItem>
<PropertyName>Location</PropertyName>
</TableColumnItem>
</TableColumnItems>
</TableRowEntry>
</TableRowEntries>
</TableControl>
</View>
</ViewDefinitions>
</Configuration>
```

You have some work to do, like adding the custom type name and arranging the table the way you like. But we want to call your attention to this line in particular:

```
<TableColumnHeader/>
```

This is a sneaky XML thing that Microsoft often uses, and it will mess you up. Remember how we said that XML elements come in pairs? Well, that's not always true. This *singleton* tag both opens and closes itself—that's what the slash at the end means. It's exactly the same as

```
<TableColumnHeader>
</TableColumnHeader>
```

Go count the number of table column headers in the file right now. It would help if you came up with three. The number of table column entries *must* match! If they don't, the view won't load into the shell. Those singleton tags, however, can be super easy to miss when you're copying and pasting, resulting in a broken formatting file, so, watch for them. They mean, "I want a column here, but I don't want to specify anything for the header—just use the underlying property name and figure out the width on your own, thanks." Here's the finalized file.

**Listing 24.4  Final view file**

```
<?xml version="1.0" encoding="utf-8" ?>
<Configuration>
<ViewDefinitions>
<View>
<Name>DiskInfo</Name>                        ←⌐ View name
<ViewSelectedBy>
<TypeName>Toolmaking.DiskInfo</TypeName>     ←⌐ Uses the custom
</ViewSelectedBy>                                 type name
<TableControl>
<TableHeaders>                               ←⌐ Table headers
<TableColumnHeader>
<Label>Host</Label>
<Width>16</Width>
</TableColumnHeader>
<TableColumnHeader>
<Label>DC</Label>
```

```
<Width>16</Width>
</TableColumnHeader>
<TableColumnHeader>
<Label>Model</Label>
</TableColumnHeader>
<TableColumnHeader>                        ┐ Forces this
<Label>RAM</Label>                         │ column to
<Alignment>Right</Alignment>    ◁──┘ align right
</TableColumnHeader>
</TableHeaders>
<TableRowEntries>                  ┐ Table values
<TableRowEntry>                 ◁──┘
<TableColumnItems>
<TableColumnItem>
<PropertyName>ComputerName</PropertyName>
</TableColumnItem>
<TableColumnItem>
<PropertyName>DomainController</PropertyName>
</TableColumnItem>
<TableColumnItem>
<PropertyName>Model</PropertyName>
</TableColumnItem>
<TableColumnItem>
<PropertyName>TotalPhysicalMemory(GB)</PropertyName>
</TableColumnItem>
</TableColumnItems>
</TableRowEntry>
</TableRowEntries>
</TableControl>
</View>
</ViewDefinitions>
</Configuration>
```

We've made liberal use of carriage returns to complete the sections and make them easier to perceive, but there's still some unintentional word-wrapping in the book. We suggest opening the XML file in a text editor or VS Code to review it. Here are some notes to consider:

- You provide a name (which must only be unique *for each type name*; it's fine if there's a view with this same name *for another type*) and the custom type name.
- You can ensure the same number of column headers and entries by not using those annoying singleton tags.
- You specify a right alignment for the numeric RAM column.
- The column headers don't match the underlying property names. That's because the property names are too darn long—there's no way you can make a great-looking display with those long names.

The big takeaway here is that we *didn't* do a good job of designing the tool. Look at that property—TotalPhysicalMemory(GB)—and you'll see it isn't very pleasant. We only did that so the default output of the tool would *look nice*, and we shouldn't have cared. We've made an awkward-looking, difficult-to-refer-to property that will be difficult to type *forever*.

Let's change the code. Listing 24.5 includes the new code, and listing 24.6 shows the revised view file to go with it. This was designed explicitly to illustrate why worrying about appearance from inside a tool is a bad idea and the importance of fixing mistakes like these when you realize you've made them.

**Listing 24.5   Revised tool code**

```
function Get-DiskInfo {
 foreach ($domain in (Get-ADForest).domains) {
   $hosts = Get-ADDomainController -filter * -server $domain |
   Sort-Object -Prop hostname
   ForEach ($h in $hosts) {
    $cs = Get-CimInstance -ClassName Win32_ComputerSystem -ComputerName $h
    $props = @{'ComputerName' = $h
               'DomainController' = $h
               'Manufacturer' = $cs.manufacturer
               'Model' = $cs.model
               'TotalPhysicalMemory'=$cs.totalphysicalmemory / 1GB
               }
    $obj = New-Object -Type PSObject -Prop $props
    $obj.psobject.typenames.insert(0,'Toolmaking.DiskInfo')
    Write-Output $obj
   } #foreach $h
  } #foreach $domain
} #function
Export-ModuleMember -function Get-DiskInfo
```

**Listing 24.6   Revised view**

```
<?xml version="1.0" encoding="utf-8" ?>
<Configuration>
<ViewDefinitions>
<View>
<Name>DiskInfo</Name>
<ViewSelectedBy>
<TypeName>Toolmaking.DiskInfo</TypeName>
</ViewSelectedBy>
<TableControl>
<TableHeaders>
<TableColumnHeader>
<Label>Host</Label>
<Width>16</Width>
</TableColumnHeader>
<TableColumnHeader>
<Label>DC</Label>
<Width>16</Width>
</TableColumnHeader>
<TableColumnHeader>
<Label>Model</Label>
</TableColumnHeader>
<TableColumnHeader>
<Label>RAM</Label>
<Alignment>Right</Alignment>
```

```
</TableColumnHeader>
</TableHeaders>
<TableRowEntries>
<TableRowEntry>
<TableColumnItems>
<TableColumnItem>
<PropertyName>ComputerName</PropertyName>
</TableColumnItem>
<TableColumnItem>
<PropertyName>DomainController</PropertyName>
</TableColumnItem>
<TableColumnItem>
<PropertyName>Model</PropertyName>
</TableColumnItem>
<TableColumnItem>
<PropertyName>TotalPhysicalMemory</PropertyName>
</TableColumnItem>
</TableColumnItems>
</TableRowEntry>
</TableRowEntries>
</TableControl>
</View>
</ViewDefinitions>
</Configuration>
```

That feels much better!

### 24.2.4  *Adding the view file to a module*

You've already saved the view file in the same folder as your module's .psm1 file. But that won't magically tell PowerShell to *use* the view file. Instead, you need to create a module manifest, just as you've done previously, and save it as Test.psd1 (because Test is the module's name). When creating the manifest, you need to specify the format view. Or, if you've already created a manifest, you can add the format view to it. Let's take the latter approach so you can see how it's done. Run this command:

```
new-modulemanifest -Path test.psd1 -RootModule test.psm1
```

This creates the .psd1 file but doesn't specify the view. Open it, and edit it as shown in the following listing.

Listing 24.7  **Completed module manifest**

```
#
# Module manifest for module 'test'
#
# Generated by: User
#
# Generated on: 09/24/2023
#
@{
# Script module or binary module file associated with this manifest.
RootModule = 'test.psm1'
```

```
# Version number of this module.
ModuleVersion = '1.0'
# Supported PSEditions
# CompatiblePSEditions = @()
# ID used to uniquely identify this module
GUID = 'e2baeaab-4dc7-4eda-a8a8-ad38298e3af0'
# Author of this module
Author = 'User'
# Company or vendor of this module
CompanyName = 'Unknown'
# Copyright statement for this module
Copyright = '(c) 2023 User. All rights reserved.'
# Description of the functionality provided by this module
# Description = ''
# Minimum version of the PowerShell engine required by this module
# PowerShellVersion = ''
# Name of the PowerShell host required by this module
# PowerShellHostName = ''
# Minimum version of the PowerShell host required by this module
# PowerShellHostVersion = ''
# Minimum version of Microsoft .NET Framework required by this module. This
prerequisite is valid for the PowerShell Desktop edition only.
# DotNetFrameworkVersion = ''
# Minimum version of the common language runtime (CLR) required by this
module. This prerequisite is valid for the PowerShell Desktop edition only.
# CLRVersion = ''
# Processor architecture (None, X86, Amd64) required by this module
# ProcessorArchitecture = ''
# Modules that must be imported into the global environment prior to
importing this module
# RequiredModules = @()
# Assemblies that must be loaded prior to importing this module
# RequiredAssemblies = @()
# Script files (.ps1) that are run in the caller's environment prior to
importing this module.
# ScriptsToProcess = @()
# Type files (.ps1xml) to be loaded when importing this module
# TypesToProcess = @()
# Format files (.ps1xml) to be loaded when importing this module
FormatsToProcess = @('./TestView.format.ps1xml')
# Modules to import as nested modules of the module specified in
RootModule/ModuleToProcess
# NestedModules = @()
# Functions to export from this module, for best performance, do not use
wildcards and do not delete the entry, use an empty array if there are no
functions to export.
FunctionsToExport = '*'
# Cmdlets to export from this module, for best performance, do not use
wildcards and do not delete the entry, use an empty array if there are no
cmdlets to export.
CmdletsToExport = '*'
# Variables to export from this module
VariablesToExport = '*'
# Aliases to export from this module, for best performance, do not use
wildcards and do not delete the entry, use an empty array if there are no
```

```
aliases to export.
AliasesToExport = '*'
# DSC resources to export from this module
# DscResourcesToExport = @()
# List of all modules packaged with this module
# ModuleList = @()
# List of all files packaged with this module
# FileList = @()
# Private data to pass to the module specified in
RootModule/ModuleToProcess. This may also contain a PSData hashtable with
additional module metadata used by PowerShell.
PrivateData = @{
    PSData = @{
        # Tags applied to this module. These help with module discovery in
online galleries.
        # Tags = @()
        # A URL to the license for this module.
        # LicenseUri = ''
        # A URL to the main website for this project.
        # ProjectUri = ''
        # A URL to an icon representing this module.
        # IconUri = ''
        # ReleaseNotes of this module
        # ReleaseNotes = ''
    } # End of PSData hashtable
} # End of PrivateData hashtable
# HelpInfo URI of this module
# HelpInfoURI = ''
# Default prefix for commands exported from this module. Override the
default prefix using Import-Module -Prefix.
# DefaultCommandPrefix = ''
}
```

If you're having trouble spotting it, this is all we changed:

```
# Format files (.ps1xml) to be loaded when importing this module
FormatsToProcess = @('./TestView.format.ps1xml')
```

We uncommented the `FormatsToProcess` line and added the `TestView.format.ps1xml` file, which—based on this—is in the same folder as the .psd1 and .psm1 files. With everything in place, you should be able to run the command and see the new view as its default output:

```
PS C:\> get-diskinfo
Host            DC              Model                        RAM
----            --              -----                        ---
SRV1            SERV            Virtual Machine    1.99906539916992
```

## 24.3  *Your turn*

We want to give you a chance to run through this independently. We'll provide you with a tool and then ask you to make a custom view for it.

### 24.3.1 *Start here*

The next listing shows a PowerShell tool. This should work fine (and should look familiar because we used it earlier); you need to create a custom view for it. That also means saving it as a module.

**Listing 24.8** `Starting-point script`

```
function Get-MachineInfo {
    [CmdletBinding()]
    Param(
        [Parameter(ValueFromPipeline=$True,
                   Mandatory=$True)]
        [Alias('CN','MachineName','Name')]
        [string[]]$ComputerName
    )
 BEGIN {}
 PROCESS {
    foreach ($computer in $ComputerName) {

        $session = New-CimSession -ComputerName $computer `
                                  -SessionOption $option
        # Query data
        $os_params = @{'ClassName'='Win32_OperatingSystem'
                       'CimSession'=$session}
        $os = Get-CimInstance @os_params
        $cs_params = @{'ClassName'='Win32_ComputerSystem'
                       'CimSession'=$session}
        $cs = Get-CimInstance @cs_params
        $sysdrive = $os.SystemDrive
        $drive_params = @{'ClassName'='Win32_LogicalDisk'
                          'Filter'="DeviceId='$sysdrive'"
                          'CimSession'=$session}
        $drive = Get-CimInstance @drive_params
        $proc_params = @{'ClassName'='Win32_Processor'
                         'CimSession'=$session}
        $proc = Get-CimInstance @proc_params |
                Select-Object -first 1
        # Close session
        $session | Remove-CimSession
        # Output data
        $props = @{'ComputerName'=$computer
                   'OSVersion'=$os.version
                   'SPVersion'=$os.servicepackmajorversion
                   'OSBuild'=$os.buildnumber
                   'Manufacturer'=$cs.manufacturer
                   'Model'=$cs.model
                   'Procs'=$cs.numberofprocessors
                   'Cores'=$cs.numberoflogicalprocessors
                   'RAM'=($cs.totalphysicalmemory / 1GB)
                   'Arch'=$proc.addresswidth
                   'SysDriveFreeSpace'=$drive.freespace}
        $obj = New-Object -TypeName PSObject -Property $props
        Write-Output $obj
```

```
        } #foreach
    } #PROCESS
    END {}
    } #function
```

### 24.3.2   *Your task*

We want your custom view to include five columns: ComputerName, OSVersion, Model, Cores, and RAM. Use the original property names for all columns rather than making up different column headers.

### 24.3.3   *Our take*

The following listing shows our modified tool—we needed to add the custom type name.

**Listing 24.9   Modified .psm1 file**

```
function Get-MachineInfo {
    [CmdletBinding()]
    Param(
        [Parameter(ValueFromPipeline=$True,
                   Mandatory=$True)]
        [Alias('CN','MachineName','Name')]
        [string[]]$ComputerName
    )
 BEGIN {}
 PROCESS {
    foreach ($computer in $ComputerName) {

        # Connect session
        $session = New-CimSession -ComputerName $computer `
                                  -SessionOption $option
        # Query data
        $os_params = @{'ClassName'='Win32_OperatingSystem'
                       'CimSession'=$session}
        $os = Get-CimInstance @os_params
        $cs_params = @{'ClassName'='Win32_ComputerSystem'
                       'CimSession'=$session}
        $cs = Get-CimInstance @cs_params
        $sysdrive = $os.SystemDrive
        $drive_params = @{'ClassName'='Win32_LogicalDisk'
                          'Filter'="DeviceId='$sysdrive'"
                          'CimSession'=$session}
        $drive = Get-CimInstance @drive_params
        $proc_params = @{'ClassName'='Win32_Processor'
                         'CimSession'=$session}
        $proc = Get-CimInstance @proc_params |
                Select-Object -first 1
        # Close session
        $session | Remove-CimSession
        # Output data
        $props = @{'ComputerName'=$computer
                   'OSVersion'=$os.version
                   'SPVersion'=$os.servicepackmajorversion
```

```
                        'OSBuild'=$os.buildnumber
                        'Manufacturer'=$cs.manufacturer
                        'Model'=$cs.model
                        'Procs'=$cs.numberofprocessors
                        'Cores'=$cs.numberoflogicalprocessors
                        'RAM'=($cs.totalphysicalmemory / 1GB)
                        'Arch'=$proc.addresswidth
                        'SysDriveFreeSpace'=$drive.freespace}
            $obj = New-Object -TypeName PSObject -Property $props
            $obj.psobject.typenames.insert('Toolmaking.MachineInfo')    ◄───┐
            Write-Output $obj                                                │
        } #foreach                                           Inserts the custom
    } #PROCESS                                                    type name │
} #PROCESS
END {}
} #function
```

Listing 24.10 shows our view file. Because we wanted to use property names as column headers, we could have resorted to the singleton tag trick for most of these (we wanted the Cores and RAM columns right-aligned, so we needed the full tags). But those singletons have messed us up so often that we felt better about making each column header a full tag pair.

> **Listing 24.10   Our new .format.ps1xml file**

```xml
<?xml version="1.0" encoding="utf-8" ?>
<Configuration>
<ViewDefinitions>
<View>
<Name>MachineInfo</Name>
<ViewSelectedBy>
<TypeName>Toolmaking.MachineInfo</TypeName>
</ViewSelectedBy>
<TableControl>
<TableHeaders>
<TableColumnHeader>
<Label>ComputerName</Label>
</TableColumnHeader>
<TableColumnHeader>
<Label>OSVersion</Label>
</TableColumnHeader>
<TableColumnHeader>
<Label>Model</Label>
</TableColumnHeader>
<TableColumnHeader>
<Label>Cores</Label>
<Alignment>Right</Alignment>
</TableColumnHeader>
<TableColumnHeader>
<Label>RAM</Label>
<Alignment>Right</Alignment>
</TableColumnHeader>
</TableHeaders>
<TableRowEntries>
```

```
<TableRowEntry>
<TableColumnItems>
<TableColumnItem>
<PropertyName>ComputerName</PropertyName>
</TableColumnItem>
<TableColumnItem>
<PropertyName>OSVersion</PropertyName>
</TableColumnItem>
<TableColumnItem>
<PropertyName>Model</PropertyName>
</TableColumnItem>
<TableColumnItem>
<PropertyName>Cores</PropertyName>
</TableColumnItem>
<TableColumnItem>
<PropertyName>RAM</PropertyName>
</TableColumnItem>
</TableColumnItems>
</TableRowEntry>
</TableRowEntries>
</TableControl>
</View>
</ViewDefinitions>
</Configuration>
```

The following listing shows our manifest file for the module.

Listing 24.11   Our new .psd1 file

```
#
# Module manifest for module 'test'
#
# Generated by: User
#
# Generated on: 09/24/2023
#
@{
# Script module or binary module file associated with this manifest.
RootModule = 'test.psm1'
# Version number of this module.
ModuleVersion = '1.0'
# Supported PSEditions
# CompatiblePSEditions = @()
# ID used to uniquely identify this module
GUID = 'e2baeaab-4dc7-4eda-a8a8-ad38298e3af0'
# Author of this module
Author = 'User'
# Company or vendor of this module
CompanyName = 'Unknown'
# Copyright statement for this module
Copyright = '(c) 2023 User. All rights reserved.'
# Description of the functionality provided by this module
# Description = ''
# Minimum version of the PowerShell engine required by this module
```

```
# PowerShellVersion = ''
# Name of the PowerShell host required by this module
# PowerShellHostName = ''
# Minimum version of the PowerShell host required by this module
# PowerShellHostVersion = ''
# Minimum version of Microsoft .NET Framework required by this module. This
prerequisite is valid for the PowerShell Desktop edition only.
# DotNetFrameworkVersion = ''
# Minimum version of the common language runtime (CLR) required by this
module. This prerequisite is valid for the PowerShell Desktop edition only.
# CLRVersion = ''
# Processor architecture (None, X86, Amd64) required by this module
# ProcessorArchitecture = ''
# Modules that must be imported into the global environment prior to
importing this module
# RequiredModules = @()
# Assemblies that must be loaded prior to importing this module
# RequiredAssemblies = @()
# Script files (.ps1) that are run in the caller's environment prior to
importing this module.
# ScriptsToProcess = @()
# Type files (.ps1xml) to be loaded when importing this module
# TypesToProcess = @()
# Format files (.ps1xml) to be loaded when importing this module
FormatsToProcess = @('./TestView.format.ps1xml')
# Modules to import as nested modules of the module specified in
RootModule/ModuleToProcess
# NestedModules = @()
# Functions to export from this module, for best performance, do not use
wildcards and do not delete the entry, use an empty array if there are no
functions to export.
FunctionsToExport = '*'
# Cmdlets to export from this module, for best performance, do not use
wildcards and do not delete the entry, use an empty array if there are no
cmdlets to export.
CmdletsToExport = '*'
# Variables to export from this module
VariablesToExport = '*'
# Aliases to export from this module, for best performance, do not use
wildcards and do not delete the entry, use an empty array if there are no
aliases to export.
AliasesToExport = '*'
# DSC resources to export from this module
# DscResourcesToExport = @()
# List of all modules packaged with this module
# ModuleList = @()
# List of all files packaged with this module
# FileList = @()
# Private data to pass to the module specified in
RootModule/ModuleToProcess. This may also contain a PSData hashtable with
additional module metadata used by PowerShell.
PrivateData = @{
    PSData = @{
        # Tags applied to this module. These help with module discovery in
online galleries.
```

```
        # Tags = @()
        # A URL to the license for this module.
        # LicenseUri = ''
        # A URL to the main website for this project.
        # ProjectUri = ''
        # A URL to an icon representing this module.
        # IconUri = ''
        # ReleaseNotes of this module
        # ReleaseNotes = ''
    } # End of PSData hashtable
} # End of PrivateData hashtable
# HelpInfo URI of this module
# HelpInfoURI = ''
# Default prefix for commands exported from this module. Override the
default prefix using Import-Module -Prefix.
# DefaultCommandPrefix = ''
}
```

## Summary

This chapter focused on enhancing the presentation of script output in PowerShell. The guiding principle remains to create tools that excel at their specific tasks without concerning themselves with input origins or output destinations. The chapter introduced advanced techniques for improving the visual appeal of output beyond the capabilities of built-in `Format-` cmdlets.

The chapter began with a code snippet from a previous chapter, illustrating the need for better output presentation. It then explored creating a default view using PowerShell's formatting system, leveraging existing view definitions for native core commands. The process involved understanding and modifying XML-based format files to define custom views.

Key concepts covered include the following:

- Exploring default views for native PowerShell commands
- Modifying format files to define custom views for specific object types
- Creating a module manifest to specify the format view for a custom PowerShell module
- Demonstrating the process through a hands-on exercise involving a PowerShell script for retrieving machine information

Overall, the chapter provided valuable insights into improving the visual representation of script output in PowerShell, empowering you to create more polished and professional tools.

# Wrapping up
# the .NET Framework

As you begin exploring the possibilities of what PowerShell can achieve, you'll inevitably encounter situations where there's no prebuilt cmdlet to perform your desired task. In many instances, you may find that the extensive .NET Framework, or possibly an external command, an old component object model (COM) object, or something else, can address your needs. Can you use raw .NET components in your scripts? The answer isn't a straightforward no, but it's also not a definitive yes.

## 25.1  Why PowerShell exists

To understand this better, let's reflect on why PowerShell exists in the first place. Microsoft Windows, as an operating system, offers an abundance of tools designed to facilitate automation. It's inherent to the nature of computers. The challenge with Windows has always been that these automation capabilities are tailored for professional software developers and may not be user-friendly for administrators without extensive programming expertise or those pressed for time.

You could automate Windows effectively if you were well-versed in C++, C#, and other first-class Windows programming languages. However, you face difficulties if you lack this knowledge or the time to delve into these lower-level languages or their APIs.

PowerShell didn't come into being to introduce new automation capabilities to Windows. Instead, it aimed to provide an administrator-friendly means of using what already existed. When you run a PowerShell cmdlet such as `Get-Process`, you're not executing brand-new code invented by someone at Microsoft. Inside that cmdlet, you'll find fundamental .NET Framework references coded in C#. In essence, a C# developer acted as a translator for you. You run a PowerShell cmdlet, and it's translated into the C# and .NET Framework understood by Windows.

In essence, PowerShell is a translator—a wrapper. PowerShell cmdlets wrap around .NET Framework, Common Information Model (CIM), COM, and other Windows APIs. This approach delivers a more consistent user experience: cmdlet names follow a uniform naming convention, accept input via parameters, and so on. You don't need to be familiar with the thousands of Windows APIs or the half-dozen languages required to access them. PowerShell translates for you, all thanks to the work of the developers who crafted PowerShell's cmdlets.

So, is using raw .NET Framework components in your scripts permissible? In their raw form, no. However, performing a developer's work by creating your wrappers for that .NET functionality is acceptable. Instead of integrating arbitrary C#-like .NET code into your script, you'll craft your cmdlets to make .NET appear as a typical PowerShell command. This is what we'll explore in this chapter.

**NOTE**   This topic has become less frequent because Microsoft has diligently created numerous cmdlets. In the past, we often used domain name server (DNS) as an example, but today, we have an array of DNS-specific PowerShell cmdlets. Please bear with us if our example may appear somewhat light or not entirely real-world. We aim to impart the process and pattern of building custom PowerShell cmdlets, which remains as relevant as ever.

### 25.1.1   A crash course in .Net

If you're going to use .NET, you have to know some of the terminology; otherwise, the documentation makes no sense:

- A *type* is a definition of a software thing. You see this word in PowerShell all the time—whenever you run Get-Member, for example, you see the *type name* of whatever you piped to Get-Member.

- A *class* is a kind of type. A class is a definition for a piece of functioning software. The class describes how to interact with the software, but it's just a definition. For example, System.Diagnostics.Process is the type name for a class that describes running processes on Windows.

- An *instance* is a concrete implementation of a class. For example, the Local Security Authority Subsystem Service (LSASS) process is represented by an instance of System.Diagnostics.Process. In most cases, you need to have an *instance* of a class to interact with it. For example, you can't terminate a process unless you have a specific one to terminate.

- Some classes are *abstract*, meaning you don't need a concrete instance to interact. For example, the Math class in .NET is abstract, so you don't have to *instantiate* the class to calculate tangents and cosines.

- Classes consist of *members*. These are the things that make up the definition of the class, and they are where Get-Member takes its name. There are some common kinds of members:
  - *Properties* describe whatever the class represents, like a process name or a service status. Sometimes, properties are read-only; other times, you can change

them. For example, you might be able to change a service name, but you can't modify the `Status` property to change whether the service is running.

- *Methods* take actions. A method might terminate a process or start a service. Sometimes, methods take *arguments*, which are like command parameters. Restarting a computer might let you specify a forced restart or a power-off, for example.

- *Events* are triggered when something happens to an instance, such as a service completing its startup. Although PowerShell isn't great at event-driven coding, you can sort of subscribe to an event, allowing you to execute code when the event occurs.

The first big question people ask about working with .NET is, "How do I find the bit of .NET that will do what I need?" This is like asking, "Who in the government can make such and such happen?" We don't know. We use Google a lot. Look, .NET is huge—vastly huge. You may think it's a huge distance down the road to your grocery store, but that's peanuts compared to .NET. And half the stuff Microsoft sells *adds* to .NET. So, yeah, use Google.

Once you think you've found the bit of .NET you want, you'll usually find its documentation on Microsoft's website, generally by following a Google query for the class name. For example, plug in `System.Diagnostics.Process`, and you'll find a page like http://mng.bz/G9PN. Those pages are version-specific, so you have to make sure you're selecting (from the drop-down at the top of the page) the right .NET Framework version. In addition, that URL will probably cease to exist the minute this book hits paper—Microsoft is like that. That's why we Google.

## 25.2 Exploring a class

PowerShell's versatility shines in its ability to function as an immediate window for .NET, enabling you to experiment with .NET code in real time. Let's delve into some practical examples.

For instance, you can use the `Math` class from .NET for mathematical operations:

```
[Math]::Abs(-5)
```

**TRY IT NOW** Go ahead and try this on your workstation.

This example uses the `Math` class from .NET, which consists entirely of static members:

- The `[]` (square brackets) are PowerShell's convention for identifying types. By putting a type name in these brackets, you're telling PowerShell to look up the corresponding type—in this case, a class—in .NET. This is exactly the same as declaring a variable as a `[string]`—in that case, you're referring to the `System.String` class.

- The `::` (double colons) refer to static members of a class. These are always used with a `[classname]` because you're not instantiating the class. In other words, you wouldn't use double colons with an instance stored in a variable (as in, $myobject::method).

- Abs() is a static method of the Math class, which we looked up in Microsoft Developer Network (MSDN). It returns the absolute value of whatever input you provide.

Let's do something a little more complex—and a little more fun: making your computer talk to you (thanks to Mark Minasi for this suggestion). Make sure your audio is turned on and turned up to 11 for this one, and follow along.

We Googled ".NET speech synthesis" and found ourselves at http://mng.bz/z0yZ. The System.Speech.Synthesis *namespace* is documented there. In other words, System.Speech.Synthesis isn't the name of a type (meaning it isn't the name of a class). Instead, it's the top-level portion of the name of several types (including classes). The top part of the documentation page lists the classes that fall under this namespace. Other types include *enumerations*, which are structures that define various allowable input arguments (and assign easier-to-remember names, rather than numbers, to those arguments). The remarks toward the end of the page provide some basic overviews of how to use the classes in this namespace.

The remarks seem to indicate System.Speech.Synthesis.SpeechSynthesizer is the class we want to play with, so we'll click through to http://mng.bz/0lPz, the documentation page for that.

**NOTE**  Microsoft sometimes reorganizes its documentation, so if these URLs don't work, don't panic! Google for the class name, and you'll get to wherever the docs are at the time.

Of particular interest is that none of the methods—remember, methods do things, and we want to do something, so we're looking at methods—are static. We can tell because none of them have the little *S* icon that Microsoft uses to denote static members. Lacking any static methods, we'll need to instantiate the class to create a concrete instance providing access to methods. Instantiating a class requires us to use a special method called a *constructor*, which constructs the instance. Many classes have many constructors, often accepting input arguments to tell the new instance how to build itself. In this case, the class is only listed with one constructor, and it has no input arguments, so this should be easy:

```
PS C:\> $talk = new-object system.speech.synthesis.speechsynthesizer
new-object : Cannot find type
[system.speech.synthesis.speechsynthesizer]: verify that the
assembly containing this type is loaded.
At line:1 char:9
+ $talk = new-object system.speech.synthesis.speechsynthesizer
+         ~~~~~~~~~~~~~~~~~~~~~~~~~~~~~~~~~~~~~~~~~~~~~~~~~~~~~
    + CategoryInfo          : InvalidType: (:) [New-Object], PSArgum
   entException
    + FullyQualifiedErrorId : TypeNotFound,Microsoft.PowerShell.Comm
   ands.NewObjectCommand
```

Well, crud—that's not so easy. We're guessing that PowerShell probably doesn't load the `Speech` portion of the `System` namespace automatically. Why would it? We probably must manually load that assembly to get that part of .NET into memory. The top of the documentation says that the assembly is System.Speech.dll:

```
PS C:\> Add-Type -AssemblyName System.Speech
PS C:\> $talk = new-object system.speech.synthesis.speechsynthesizer
```

It's important to specify the –`AssemblyName` parameter and to omit the .dll filename extension. This should work for any core part of .NET that's part of the Global Assembly Cache (GAC); .NET knows how to find the correct physical file. And, as you can see, we now have a `$talk` variable with our `SpeechSynthesizer` instance. Let's make it talk.

The docs list a few `Speak()` methods, each of which accepts a different type of input argument. These are called *overloads*. In .NET, you can have multiple methods with the same name, as long as each one accepts a unique combination of input arguments. It looks like one overload accepts a string, so we should be able to run this:

```
PS C:\> $talk.speak('PowerShell to the rescue!')
```

Huzzah! It worked! From here, we can start playing around with other methods and properties of the instance to see what they do.

## 25.3 Making a wrapper

We're not finished. Remember, this .NET stuff is ugly—we want to make it PowerShell pretty. So, let's write a wrapper. Check out the following listing, which includes a call to the new function so we can test it.

**Listing 25.1   Wrapper for the speech synthesizer**

```
function Invoke-Speech {
    [CmdletBinding()]
    Param(
        [Parameter(Mandatory=$true,                    Command that takes
                    ValueFromPipeline=$true)]          pipeline input
        [string[]]$Text
    )
    BEGIN {                                             Loads the
        Add-Type -AssemblyName System.Speech           assembly once
        $speech = New-Object -TypeName
System.Speech.Synthesis.SpeechSynthesizer
    }
    PROCESS {
        foreach ($phrase in $text) {
            $speech.speak($phrase)
        }
    }
    END {}
}
"One","Two","Three" | Invoke-Speech
```

We want to call out a few items:

- We've tried to stick with native PowerShell patterns as much as possible. The function accepts pipeline input, for example, and we use that technique in the test call.
- In pipeline mode, there's no reason to repeatedly add the assembly and instantiate the synthesizer, so that's done in a Begin block.
- When $speech goes out of scope, the synthesizer will cease to exist automatically, so removing the object in the End block is unnecessary. Similarly, we don't feel the need to unload the assembly (it's not hurting anything or taking up memory), so we don't do so.

This isn't ideal, though. In playing with the speech object, we noticed that it has a Speak() method for *synchronous* speech—meaning the script will pause while the speech happens—and a SpeakAsync() method, which will fire off the speaking and allow the script to continue. We can see uses for both models, so we'd like to include those as options for someone using our wrapper command. Here's the new code.

**Listing 25.2   Adding SpeakAsync() support**

```
function Invoke-Speech {
    [CmdletBinding()]
    Param(
        [Parameter(Mandatory=$true,
                   ValueFromPipeline=$true)]            Adds a new
        [string[]]$Text,                        ◁──┐   parameter
        [switch]$Asynchronous
    )
    BEGIN {
        Add-Type -AssemblyName System.Speech
        $speech = New-Object -TypeName
    System.Speech.Synthesis.SpeechSynthesizer
    }
    PROCESS {
        foreach ($phrase in $text) {                    Invokes SpeakAsync() if a
            if ($Asynchronous) {              ◁──┐      new parameter is used
                $speech.SpeakAsync($phrase)
            } else {                                    Otherwise, uses the
                $speech.speak($phrase)        ◁──┐      Speak() method
            }
        }
    }
    END {}
}
1..10 | Invoke-Speech -Asynchronous
Write-Host "This appears"
```

"This appears" will be displayed before any of the . . . uh . . . other output:

```
This appears
IsCompleted
```

```
----------
    False
    False
    False
    False
    False
    False
    False
    False
    False
    False
```

Well, that's awkward looking. Going back and reading the docs, it appears that Speak-Async() returns an object indicating whether the speech is completed. We don't care about that, so we need to suppress it. Here's our final attempt.

**Listing 25.3  Suppressing the SpeakAsync() output**

```
function Invoke-Speech {
    [CmdletBinding()]
    Param(
        [Parameter(Mandatory=$true,
                    ValueFromPipeline=$true)]
        [string[]]$Text,
        [switch]$Asynchronous
    )
    BEGIN {
        Add-Type -AssemblyName System.Speech
        $speech = New-Object -TypeName
å System.Speech.Synthesis.SpeechSynthesizer
    }
    PROCESS {
        foreach ($phrase in $text) {
            if ($Asynchronous) {
                $null = $speech.SpeakAsync($phrase)    ⟵─┤  $null to the left to
            } else {                                        suppress the output
                $speech.speak($phrase)
            }
        }
    }
    END {}
}
1..10 | Invoke-Speech -Asynchronous
Write-Host "This appears"
```

**TRY IT NOW**  Seriously, give this a run. It's fun. Then, check out http://mng .bz/YRa7, which is a more complex version of our wrapper that you'll love playing with. Bravo Zulu!

Wrapping this small amount of code may seem like a waste of time, but it isn't—it's an investment. Here are a few of the things you gain:

- Nobody else on your team will need to research this object again—they can use your simple, PowerShell-compliant command. We'd obviously add help to this to make it even more PowerShell-native.
- If you start getting into unit testing with Pester, you *can't* mock .NET stuff—but because you've written a wrapper, you *could* mock calls to `Invoke-Speech`, if needed.
- Documentation—if you take the time to produce at least comment-based help—is built-in rather than requiring a Google search and MSDN spelunking.

## 25.4  *A more practical example*

Here's a more practical example, which you might use in a controller script. Let's say you want to provide a graphical input box for your script. We used to do this in VBScript, and the functionality is still available in the Visual Basic part of the .NET Framework. First you need to add the assembly:

```
Add-Type -AssemblyName "microsoft.visualbasic"
```

The `[microsoft.visualbasic.interaction]` class has a static method called `InputBox()` that takes three arguments, in this order: a prompt, a title, and a default choice. Run this code to create the input box shown in figure 25.1:

```
[microsoft.visualbasic.interaction]::inputbox ("Enter a server name",
"PSServer Management",$null)
```

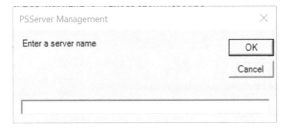

**Figure 25.1  An input box**

The user enters a value and clicks OK, and the value is written to the pipeline. You would need to add error handling and validation in case they entered nothing or clicked Cancel. If you wanted to use this often, you could create a function around it. For example, we've written a short one in the following listing.

**Listing 25.4  Quick and easy `InputBox` wrapper**

```
function Invoke-InputBox {
  [CmdletBinding()]
  Param(
    [Parameter(Mandatory=$True)]
    [string]$Prompt,
    [Parameter(Mandatory=$True)]
```

```
    [string]$Title,
    [Parameter()]
    [string]$Default = ''
)
Add-Type -Assembly Microsoft.VisualBasic
[microsoft.visualbasic.interaction]::inputbox($prompt,$title,$default)
} #function
```

This illustrates how small a wrapper can be, how easy it is to create, and how much easier wrappers can make it for someone else to use .NET.

## 25.5 Your turn

This is such an important task that we'd like you to give it a try.

### 25.5.1 Start here

The System.Net.Dns class has a static method named GetHostByAddress(). It's designed to look up a hostname, given its IP address. Go on—look it up online, and experiment with it in the shell.

### 25.5.2 Your task

Write a Get-DnsHostByAddress wrapper function. It should accept one or more IP addresses, and, for each one, emit an object containing the IP address and the corresponding hostname. If no hostname is available, it should return a null for the hostname.

### 25.5.3 Our take

Playing with this on the command line, we discovered that the method returns an object with three properties: HostName, which is great; Aliases, which could be fun; and AddressList, which looks to be an array. We decided to keep this simple and focus only on HostName in our wrapper, as shown in the following listing.

**Listing 25.5 Our wrapper for looking up DNS hostnames**

```
function Get-DnsHostByAddress {
    [CmdletBinding()]
    Param(
        [Parameter(Mandatory=$true,
                   ValueFromPipeline=$true)]
        [string[]]$Address
    )
    BEGIN {}
    PROCESS {
        ForEach ($Addr in $Address) {
            $props = @{'Address'=$addr}
            Try {
                $result = [System.Net.Dns]::GetHostByAddress($addr)
                $props.Add('HostName',$result.HostName)
            } Catch {
                $props.Add('HostName',$null)
            }
```

```
           New-Object -TypeName PSObject -Property $props
        } #foreach
      } #PROCESS
    END {}
} #function
Get-DnsHostByAddress -Address '204.79.197.200','192.168.254.254',
 '35.166.24.88'
```

There are a few things we'd like you to notice:

- We made sure to test both a legitimate IP address (hi, Bing.com!) as well as a bad one because we have different output in each situation.
- In normal command error handling, we'd have to specify an -ErrorAction to ensure a trappable exception. .NET methods don't work that way—when they fail, they always produce a trappable exception, so our Try block works perfectly.
- You might prefer to use Unknown or some value other than $null for failed hosts. We like $null, so we used that.
- We started a hash table for our eventual output object's properties right up front. Then, depending on the outcome of the query, we added a HostName property. We like this technique—it lets us dynamically construct our output a piece at a time and then push it all out into the pipeline as an object when finished.

## Summary

This chapter provided an insightful exploration into the integration of PowerShell with the .NET Framework. It began by discussing the raison d'être of PowerShell, which is to provide a user-friendly interface for leveraging existing automation capabilities within Windows. PowerShell achieves this by acting as a translator or wrapper around various Windows APIs, including the .NET Framework, COM, and CIM.

The chapter then delved into the fundamentals of .NET, introducing key concepts such as types, classes, instances, and members. It emphasized the vastness of the .NET ecosystem and the importance of leveraging online resources, like Microsoft's documentation, to navigate it effectively.

Next, the chapter demonstrated how PowerShell can interact with .NET classes in real time, allowing you to perform tasks such as mathematical operations and text-to-speech synthesis. It illustrated the process of utilizing .NET classes within PowerShell scripts and emphasized the benefits of creating PowerShell wrappers for .NET functionality to enhance usability and maintainability.

We concluded with practical examples of creating PowerShell wrappers for .NET functionality, including a wrapper for speech synthesis and an input box function. We encouraged you to experiment with integrating .NET functionality into PowerShell scripts and provided a hands-on exercise to reinforce learning.

Overall, chapter 25 served as a valuable guide for harnessing the power of the .NET Framework within PowerShell scripts, empowering you to extend PowerShell's capabilities and streamline automation tasks effectively.

# Storing data—not in Excel!

26

PowerShell offers the capability to generate and modify Excel documents dynamically. Yet just because it's feasible doesn't mean it's the right approach. Excel isn't designed to function as a database, and it's disheartening to witness individuals grappling with it as such. Developing scripts that interact with Excel through PowerShell necessitates the use of Microsoft Office Programmability components, which are integrated into .NET when Office is installed. These components, in turn, rely on a Component Object Model (COM) interface that Microsoft hasn't updated in ages.

It's hard to watch administrators crafting scripts that involve extensive Excel-related code, resulting in a time-consuming, exasperating, and unproductive experience. We strongly advise against pursuing this approach. However, the need to store data will inevitably arise. In such cases, a more suitable alternative is available.

## 26.1 Introducing SQL Server!

We're pretty sure you've heard of Microsoft SQL Server. If you have one in your environment, see if you can get a small database set up on it for your use. You won't be loading it with work, and it won't cost a dime. Or, if nothing else, install the free SQL Server Express (the 2022 edition can be found at http://mng.bz/K9Pn, but you can use whatever version you like as far as this chapter is concerned). We recommend downloading the one with Advanced Services (although the name is slightly different from version to version), which includes Reporting Services. We also recommend downloading SQL Server Management Studio (SSMS); frankly, it's easier for you to Google "SQL Server Management Studio download" than to give you a URL because Microsoft moves that around a good bit.

**NOTE** We don't want this chapter to get bogged down in teaching you about SQL Server or how to manage it. If you need some place to start, take a look at *Learn SQL Server Administration in a Month of Lunches* (Manning, 2014; http://mng.bz/9QP8). Manning also has a live video "book" titled *SQL in Motion* by Ben Brumm (2017, www.manning.com/livevideo/sql-in-motion). You can also check out *Learn dbatools in a Month of Lunches* (Manning, 2022, http://mng.bz/VRJ5).

Here are some of the advantages of using SQL Server (or, honestly, any relational database management system—if you prefer one over SQL Server, most of what's in this chapter will still work fine for you):

- Databases simplify adding, deleting, updating, and querying data, making these tasks *very* easy.
- SQL Server Reporting Services (SSRS) can produce beautiful reports, which you design in a friendly, drag-and-drop designer environment. The non–Express Reporting Services can run and deliver those reports on a schedule for you.
- PowerShell works *excellently* with SQL Server (and other databases).

You'll need to master a few pieces of terminology and a couple of concepts:

- Of course, you connect to a server, but you also connect to a specific database. There's a particular database called *master* that you connect to when you want to create a new database for yourself.
- The connection is made by specifying a *connection string*, essentially a database's contact location. It also includes authentication information.
- A database consists of *tables*, each of which is roughly analogous to an Excel sheet. Therefore, you can think of a database as an Excel workbook.
- A table consists of *rows* and *columns*, like an Excel sheet. Database geeks sometimes refer to these as *entities* and *domains* as well.

## 26.2   *Setting up everything*

Frankly, the one-time server and database setup takes longer to explain and perform than using the dang thing. First, as already stated, we assume you've installed SQL Server Express. We're using 2016, and we performed a Basic install (which doesn't prompt for anything else). Subsequent editions won't be much different to install, and you can accept all the defaults if there are any setup prompts. If you're using an SQL Server on your network somewhere, have the administrator give you the *server name* and, if there is one, the *instance name*.

**NOTE** Whatever user account you used to install SQL Server Express will usually be set up as Administrator of the SQL Server Express instance. This is true whether you're in a domain environment or not.

Second, you need a database. If you're using an SQL Server on your network, the administrator must create a database (2 GB to 3 GB is acceptable; advise them that the Simple

Recovery model is okay for now). They'll need to give you the database name and let you know whether you can connect using your Windows log-on credentials or if there's a separate username and password for you to use.

If you installed SQL Server Express locally and used all the default settings, then you've installed an instance named SQLEXPRESS. Run the PowerShell script in listing 26.1 to create a new database named Scripting. Use your Windows log-on credentials to connect; the new database will be the default minimum size (usually about 2 GB). Note that this isn't suitable for a production environment because there are several database options you'd typically set, and you'd want to arrange for backups; read *Learn SQL Server Administration in a Month of Lunches* (http://mng.bz/9QP8) if you'd like to explore those tasks.

**Listing 26.1  Set up a new database on SQL Server Express instance**

Configures the connection object

Defines the connection string

Creates the connection object

Defines a SQL query

Creates a SQL Command object

```
$conn_string =
"Server=localhost\SQLEXPRESS;Database=master;Trusted_Connection=True;"
$conn = New-Object System.Data.SqlClient.SqlConnection
$conn.ConnectionString = $conn_string
$conn.Open()
$sql = @"
CREATE DATABASE Scripting;
"@
$cmd = New-Object System.Data.SqlClient.SqlCommand
$cmd.CommandText = $sql
$cmd.Connection = $conn
$cmd.ExecuteNonQuery()
$conn.close()
```

Executes the command

Closes the database connection

Configures the command to use the connection

Configures the command to use the query

Third, there's no third thing. You'll need a connection string, but you should already have everything you need. Ours is this:

```
Server=localhost\SQLEXPRESS;Database=master;Trusted_Connection=True;
```

As you can see, we used that in the code to create a new database; when we're ready to use that database, we'll change `master` to `Scripting` in the connection string. That same connection string works for any database where you can use your Windows log-on credentials to connect. If, instead, you need to specify a username and password, it will look like

```
Server=localhost\SQLEXPRESS;Database=master;un=xxxxx;pw=yyyyyy;
```

where xxxxx and yyyyy are your SQL Server username and password, respectively.

**TIP**   We use ConnectionStrings.com to come up with our connection strings. It's an invaluable reference. Why remember that stuff when you can look it up?

## 26.3   *Using your database: Creating a table*

You first need to decide what you'll put in the database. This isn't a one-time decision; just as with Excel, you can add and remove sheets (tables) and modify the columns used in each table at any time. Let's start with the command in listing 26.2. Like most commands we write, this produces objects as output, so it's a perfect starting point (and yes, we've used this particular command before).

**TIP**   For development and testing purposes, you'll save this script as its script module. You'll add additional commands to this .psm1 file as you go, keeping everything nicely grouped together.

**Listing 26.2   Start with a command that produces objects as output**

```
function Get-DiskInfo {
    [CmdletBinding()]
    Param(
        [Parameter(Mandatory=$True,
                   ValueFromPipeline=$True)]
        [string[]]$ComputerName
    )
    BEGIN {
        Set-StrictMode -Version 2.0
    }
    PROCESS {
        ForEach ($comp in $ComputerName) {
            $params = @{'ComputerName' = $comp
                        'ClassName' = 'Win32_LogicalDisk'}
            $disks = Get-CimInstance @params
            ForEach ($disk in $disks) {
                $props = @{'ComputerName' = $comp
                           'Size' = $disk.size
    'Drive' = $disk.deviceid
                           'FreeSpace' = $disk.freespace
                           'DriveType' = $disk.drivetype}
                New-Object -TypeName PSObject -Property $props
            } #foreach disk
        } #foreach computer
    } #PROCESS
    END {}
}
```

Examining the command, it produces the following:

- *Computer name*—A string
- *Disk size*—A large integer
- *Drive type*—A small (single-digit) integer
- *Disk free space*—A large integer
- *Drive ID*—A string

Therefore, you need to create a table that can contain this information. In addition, you'll add a field to track the date that each row is added to the table. That way, you can periodically inventory drive information and construct a trend line of free space. (We'd use SSRS to produce that trend report; it's beyond the scope of this book to get into report production, but PowerShell.org offers a free e-book on the subject if you'd like to investigate further on your own.) Listing 26.3 shows what we're adding to our .psm1 file (the downloadable version of this listing at http://mng.bz/rjgE is the entire thing; we're saving some space in the book by only showing the additional code here). Most of the code should start looking familiar because we used it earlier.

> **Listing 26.3   Adding code for table creation**

```
function New-DiskInfoSQLTable {
    [CmdletBinding()]
    param()
    $conn = New-Object System.Data.SqlClient.SqlConnection
    $conn.ConnectionString = $DiskInfoSqlConnection
    $conn.Open()
    $sql = @"
        IF NOT EXISTS (SELECT * FROM sysobjects WHERE name='diskinfo' AND
xtype='U')
            CREATE TABLE diskinfo (
                ComputerName VARCHAR(64),
                DiskSize BIGINT,
                DriveType TINYINT,
                FreeSpace BIGINT,
                DriveID CHAR(2),
DateAdded DATETIME2
            )
"@
    $cmd = New-Object System.Data.SqlClient.SqlCommand
    $cmd.Connection = $conn
    $cmd.CommandText = $sql
    $cmd.ExecuteNonQuery() | Out-Null
    $conn.Close()
}
$DiskInfoSqlConnection =
"Server=localhost\SQLEXPRESS;Database=Scripting;Trusted_Connection=True;"
Export-ModuleMember -Function Get-DiskInfo
Export-ModuleMember -Variable DiskInfoSqlConnection
```

We want to point out that we've added a module-level variable outside any function to contain the database connection string. That makes it easier to reuse that information in numerous functions. You explicitly export that variable, along with the first function, so that all will be added to the global scope of the shell whenever the module is loaded. Similarly, if the module is unloaded, they'll all be neatly removed from the global scope. Why don't you export the new table-creation function? There's no reason for anyone outside this module to run that, so by not exporting it, you make it private to this module.

The new command does what we think is a neat trick: it first checks to see whether the table exists. If it doesn't, the command creates the table. This way, you can repeatedly call the new command, and it'll always make sure the table exists.

This is probably a good time to go over the broad process this code uses because you'll see it again two more times:

1 Create a new `System.Data.SqlClient.SqlConnection` object. This represents the connection to SQL Server. Set its `ConnectionString` property to your connection string, and then call its `Open()` method. If the connection string isn't right, this is where you'll generate an error. You also fill in a call to the `Close()` method at the end of the command.

2 Build the query in a here-string, mainly to format it nicely. You use double quotes for the here-string because SQL Server uses single quotes as its string delimiter. Double quotes make it easy to use single quotes inside the here-string and insert variables and subexpressions. Having the query in a variable makes it easy to output it using `Write-Verbose`, so you can double-check the query syntax easily if there's an error.

3 Create a new `System.Data.SqlClient.SqlCommand`, and set its `Connection` property to the opened `Connection` object. Set its `CommandText` property to your query, and ask it to `ExecuteNonQuery()`. That method is used when you know your query won't return any results; it *will* return -1 for a successful query, so you pipe that to `Out-Null` to suppress it.

You'll use these same two objects in the same way in the upcoming commands.

**NOTE**  If you aren't using SQL Server, .NET includes the equivalent `System.Data.OleDbClient` namespace along with `OleDbConnection` and `OleDb-Command` classes for connecting to other databases.

You may be wondering how we came up with all the data types for the CREATE TABLE statement. Simple—we looked them up. Googling "SQL Server data types" took us to http://mng.bz/j1l9, which was pretty useful. In reality, we find ourselves lazily using just a few data types:

- `VARCHAR()`—This lets you specify a maximum field length and takes up less space if you use less than the maximum. `VARCHAR(MAX)` enables you to store any amount of text.
- `CHAR()`—Creates fixed-length text columns.
- `TINYINT`—Holds integers from 0 to 255.
- `BIGINT`—Holds pretty much any size integer.
- `DATETIME2`—Holds date/time values.

You may also have use for `FLOAT` or `INT`, and you can read all about them in the SQL documentation.

## 26.4 Saving data to SQL Server

Now, you're ready to make a third command, shown in the listing 26.4, which will accept the output of the disk inventory command and export that information into your SQL Server table. Once again, the downloadable version of this includes the *entire* script module for your convenience.

**Listing 26.4  Adding a command to export data to SQL Server**

```
function Export-DiskInfoToSQL {
    [CmdletBinding()]
    param(
        [Parameter(Mandatory=$True,
                   ValueFromPipeline=$True)]
        [object[]]$DiskInfo
    )
    BEGIN {
        New-DiskInfoSQLTable
        $conn = New-Object System.Data.SqlClient.SqlConnection
        $conn.ConnectionString = $DiskInfoSqlConnection
        $conn.Open()
        $cmd = New-Object System.Data.SqlClient.SqlCommand
        $cmd.Connection = $conn
    }
    PROCESS {
        ForEach ($object in $DiskInfo) {
            if ($object.size -eq $null) {
                $size = 0
            } else {
                $size = $object.size
            }
            if ($object.freespace -eq $null) {
                $freespace = 0
            } else {
                $freespace = $object.freespace
            }
            $sql = @"
                INSERT INTO DiskInfo (ComputerName,
                    DiskSize,DriveType,FreeSpace,DriveID,DateAdded)
                VALUES('$($object.ComputerName)',
                    $size,
                    $($object.DriveType),
                    $freespace,
                    '$($object.Drive)',
                    '$(Get-Date)')
"@
            $cmd.CommandText = $sql
            Write-Verbose "EXECUTING QUERY `n $sql"
            $cmd.ExecuteNonQuery() | Out-Null
        } #ForEach
    } #PROCESS
    END {
        $conn.Close()
    }
}
```

**NOTE** Notice how we're checking to see whether `Size` and `FreeSpace` are `Null`? That can happen with disks like optical drives. We set those values to `0` in those cases so that we have a valid value to add to the database.

There's a big caveat that we need to point out. The new command's `-DiskInfo` parameter does accept pipeline input—but you'll notice that it accepts *anything* because its data type is `System.Object`. Therefore, it's entirely possible to pipe the parameter a service object, a process object, or something else it won't know how to deal with. You can't do much about that. Yes, you could modify the `Get-DiskInfo` function to add a custom type name, but that won't allow you to specify that type name as the only allowable input to `Export-DiskInfoToSQL`; PowerShell unfortunately doesn't work that way. If you wanted to tightly couple these two commands and ensure that `Export-DiskInfoToSQL` could only accept the objects produced by `Get-DiskInfo`, you'd need to create your own class. PowerShell v5 and later can do that, but it's a more complex topic that's out of the scope of this book. (*The PowerShell Scripting & Toolmaking Book* gets into it, and it can be updated because it's online only [https://leanpub.com/powershell-scripting-toolmaking]. The situation with classes in PowerShell is highly fluid and ever-changing at this time.) For now, you must accept that you must be careful about using `Export-DiskInfoToSQL`. Let's take a look at our code in the following listing.

---

**Listing 26.5   Adding member checks for input objects**

```
function Export-DiskInfoToSQL {
    [CmdletBinding()]
    param(
        [Parameter(Mandatory=$True,
                   ValueFromPipeline=$True)]
        [object[]]$DiskInfo
    )
    BEGIN {
        New-DiskInfoSQLTable
        $conn = New-Object System.Data.SqlClient.SqlConnection
        $conn.ConnectionString = $DiskInfoSqlConnection
        $conn.Open()
        $cmd = New-Object System.Data.SqlClient.SqlCommand
        $cmd.Connection = $conn
        $checks = 0
    }
    PROCESS {
        if ($checks -eq 0) {                       ◁── Checks the
            $checks++                                  first input
            $props = $DiskInfo[0] |                     object
                    Get-Member -MemberType Properties |
                    Select-Object -Expand name
            if ($props -contains 'ComputerName' -and
                $props -contains 'Drive' -and
                $props -contains 'DriveType' -and
                $props -contains 'FreeSpace' -and
```

```
                $props -contains 'Size') {
                    Write-Verbose "Input object passes check"
                } else {
                    Write-Error "Illegal input object"
                    Break
                }
        }
        ForEach ($object in $DiskInfo) {
            if ($object.size -eq $null) {
                $size = 0
            } else {
                $size = $object.size
            }
            if ($object.freespace -eq $null) {
                $freespace = 0
            } else {
                $freespace = $object.freespace
            }
            $sql = @"
                INSERT INTO DiskInfo (ComputerName,
                    DiskSize,DriveType,FreeSpace,DriveID,DateAdded)
                VALUES('$($object.ComputerName)',
                        $size,
                        $($object.DriveType),
                        $freespace,
                        '$($object.Drive)',
                        '$(Get-Date)')
"@
            $cmd.CommandText = $sql
            Write-Verbose "EXECUTING QUERY `n $sql"
            $cmd.ExecuteNonQuery() | Out-Null
        } #ForEach
    } #PROCESS
    END {
        $conn.Close()
    }
}
```

### Avoiding SQL injection

In listing 26.5, we left intact something that's a no-no for most public-facing applications: dynamically constructing a query by inserting variable contents into a string. In production-style applications, this opens you to an attack called *SQL injection*. We're fairly safe from it because we're the only ones using this database, but it's something you need to be aware of and read up on if you start to accept data provided by other people.

What you *could* do, and what the listing does, is create some checks on the input to the command. We decided to ensure the objects we fed had the expected properties. This will slightly slow things down as we make the check, so we only check the first object fed to us and assume all the others are just like it.

Go ahead and put some data into the database:

```
get-diskinfo $env:ComputerName | Export-DiskInfoToSQL
```

## 26.5 Querying data from SQL Server

Although we don't think there's an immediate real-world use for this—we would intend to load data into SQL Server and leave it there for SSRS to create reports from—we want to show you an example of querying data. The following listing is the final chunk of code to add to your module. Again, we suggest using the downloadable version if you want to try this because it has all the code in one place.

**Listing 26.6 Adding a command to retrieve data from SQL Server**

```
function Import-DiskInfoFromSQL {
    [CmdletBinding()]
    Param()
        $conn = New-Object System.Data.SqlClient.SqlConnection
        $conn.ConnectionString = $DiskInfoSqlConnection
        $conn.Open()
        $cmd = New-Object System.Data.SqlClient.SqlCommand
        $cmd.Connection = $conn
        $sql = @"
            SELECT ComputerName,DiskSize,DriveType,FreeSpace,
            DriveID,DateAdded
            FROM DiskInfo
            ORDER BY DateAdded ASC
"@
        $cmd.CommandText = $sql
        $reader = $cmd.ExecuteReader()           ◁─┐ Loops through the
        # spin through the results                 │ results and creates
        while ($reader.read()) {                 ◁─┘ a custom object
            $props = @{'ComputerName' = $reader['ComputerName']
                       'Size' = $reader['DiskSize']
                       'DriveType' = $reader['DriveType']
                       'FreeSpace' = $reader['FreeSpace']
                       'Drive' = $reader['DriveId']
                       'DateAdded' = $reader['DateAdded']}
            New-Object -TypeName PSObject -Property $props
        }
        $conn.Close()
}
```

Notice again that you follow the toolmaking patterns we've taught throughout this book—you produce a command, which uses parameters for its input (and, in this case, a module-level variable), produces objects as output, and so on. The only thing we've omitted in this book, purely for space considerations, is the comment-based help we'd typically always include.

We also want to acknowledge that not everyone would code this command as we did. Some folks prefer to use a `DataTable` object versus a `DataReader`, and we admit that a `DataTable` can be faster for this precise scenario. We took this approach because it's more educational and procedural. It reads the result set one line at a time and constructs output objects one at a time, reinforcing the pattern presented throughout this book.

Finally, you'll notice a discrepancy if you've been paying close attention. The original `Get-DiskInfo` outputs an object having `Size` and `Drive` properties, and `Import-DiskInfoFromSQL` mirrors those output property names. But the table in SQL Server uses DiskSize and DriveID as column names. Why the mismatch? We did this so that we could emphasize that the table structure doesn't need to match the object structure *exactly*. In this case, the `Import` and `Export` functions translate the property names into what the table uses. This is a useful technique when you don't have control over the object or table structure and need to switch things up as you store and retrieve data.

To complete the circle, let's pull the information we just added:

```
PS C:\> Import-DiskInfoFromSQL
DateAdded    : 9/23/2023 5:24:01 PM
Drive        : C:
FreeSpace    : 27722903552
ComputerName : WIN11
DriveType    : 3
Size         : 206266429440
DateAdded    : 9/23/2023 5:24:01 PM
Drive        : D:
FreeSpace    : 16025034752
ComputerName : WIN11
DriveType    : 3
Size: 26843541504
```

## Summary

We hope this chapter has demonstrated how relatively straightforward it is to use SQL Server as a database rather than something database-esque like Excel. You followed proper toolmaking practices and created a set of commands that work with disk-inventory information. You enabled automated reporting through SSRS if you decided to sit down and design the reports there. By using a scheduled task to run the inventory and SSRS to create periodic reports automatically, you could completely automate data collection and data reporting processes, taking yourself out of the loop and freeing up your time to work on other tasks. The SQL team at Microsoft also has a fantastic SQL server module, and don't forget about DBATools.

# *Never the end* 27

Welcome to the end! Or is it? Of course not—you're just beginning—but you've made it to the point where you can start to be an effective toolmaker. Now it's time to begin thinking about what comes next.

## 27.1 *Welcome to toolmaking*

At this point, we're hoping you've seen the light about this *toolmaking* word. It isn't just about scripting. It's about making small units of work that follow PowerShell's rules, so that they can connect. It's about making *controllers* that put those tools into a specific situation and context, giving those tools a purpose for that moment in time—but leaving the tools themselves free to have another purpose at another time. Hopefully, you've also seen the value in examining how PowerShell does things natively and in duplicating its approaches in your work.

The best compliment we get when we teach this material—whether in a class, at a conference, or in a book like this—is something like, "Well, thanks a lot—now I have to go and rewrite *all* of my scripts!" We love that because it shows that we've taught someone effectively and done a good job of making them realize how valuable this approach is. Of course, this doesn't mean they must rewrite their existing work. If you have something that works, let it be. But if the occasion arises where you need to fix a bug or add a feature, then begin to incorporate the changes inspired by this book.

Of course, we can only take you so far in one book. You're going to need to go further, and you'll need to do that soon. Like, as soon as you finish reading this chapter—until you start doing this stuff for real, your brain won't completely lock on to the concepts and the techniques. You're already forgetting stuff from chapter 2—so it's crucial to start putting things to work right now.

## 27.2 *Taking your next step*

Our best advice is to *stop learning* for a minute and *start doing*. You have plenty of facts and techniques to tackle your first tool and controller. As soon as you do, you'll realize you forgot a few things—and that's great news! No, really—you'll realize that you forgot something, flip to the right chapter, and refresh yourself. This relearning strengthens the bonds between the neurons in your brain responsible for remembering this material, making it easier to recall the information the next time. But you won't realize you've forgotten, and you won't take the steps to relearn until you dive in and *start doing*.

With that in mind, we have a few recommendations for your next step:

- *Don't try to tackle the biggest problem on your plate.* Look for something small that you may already have a pretty good idea of how to conquer. That way, you can focus on the new approaches and techniques you've learned. As you gain confidence, you can build more complex tools and controllers.

- *Don't give in to expediency.* The approaches and techniques we've shared don't add much time to your coding, but they do add a bit. You're going to have to take time to do parameter design, for example, and code for accepting pipeline input. The investment is worth it because you'll quickly begin to do those things almost by reflex. The alternative—"I'll bang it out for now and go back and fix it later"—is a bad idea. You may not have time later to do it right, and then you'll be stuck with something that is, well, wrong.

- *Get stuck.* For better or for worse, human brains seem to learn better when they're conquering a problem than when they're being passively fed information. With that in mind, dive into something, get stuck, and unstick yourself. Forums like those at ServerFault.com and PowerShell.org are valuable resources—state your problem, describe what you've tried, and provide some details (like error messages) about what didn't work. *Don't* ask people to write your script for you—be clear that you only need a nudge in the right direction.

- *Share.* Every time you figure out a problem, blog about it. The act of recalling the problem and the solution is what strengthens neural connections in your brain. Writing down what you did—even if it's for an internal company blog that nobody but you and your team will read—helps you learn. If you're able to blog publicly, you'll help someone. Remember, many people are smarter than you, but due to the birth rate, new people are always struggling with the same thing you just solved. Help them out.

- *Do the math.* Anytime you're automating something, begin by figuring out how much time your organization spends doing it manually per year. If you can, calculate that in hours, perhaps by looking at your help desk ticketing solution for a report. Get an average salary for the people who spend time solving that problem manually. Multiply that salary by 1.14 (a rough way of calculating a fully loaded salary, at least in most of North America), and then divide by 2,000 (the average number of working hours in a year). The result is a fully loaded hourly rate for that person, which you can multiply by the number of hours spent performing a task manually. The end result is the amount of money your organization spends on that problem. It becomes easy to calculate a return on investment when you know how much was being spent, how long it took to automate the problem, and how much time it needs to be paid now that the problem is automated.

- *Don't "script by Google."* When starting a new project, your first step should not be to open a browser and search for an existing script. Even if you find something, how do you know it works? Will it work in your environment? Do you have the PowerShell chops to determine whether it's good PowerShell? Plus, you'll most likely spend much time revising hardcoded variables and the like. That's a waste of time. You'd be better off beginning with PowerShell's help system and going through the process yourself. Yeah, it might take longer, but you'll learn, and at the end, you'll have a tool that you know works in your environment. It's fine to search for examples of how to use a particular cmdlet or parameter, but you'll never succeed with copy-and-paste scripting.

This is all about becoming a more professional toolmaker.

## 27.3   *What's in your future?*

So, what's in the long term? What are some of the things you should be exploring in the PowerShell universe? Keep in mind that it's a rapidly changing space and requires constant attention if you want to keep up. Here are some areas to think about:

- PowerShell Core is an open source project at https://GitHub.com/powershell that will run on macOS, a variety of Linux distributions, and, of course, Windows. Explore it.
- Open source projects such as PlatyPS, Pester, and the PowerShell Script Analyzer (PSScriptAnalyzer) are great tools—look into them, and start learning to use them in your everyday toolmaking. Even better, get involved by posting problems and maybe even contributing code.
- Community events such as PowerShell Saturdays, the annual PowerShell + DevOps Global Summit (powershellsummit.org), and regional PowerShell Conferences (e.g., PowerShell Conference Europe and PowerShell Conference Asia) are all worth your time—as are the dozens of local PowerShell user groups scattered throughout the world.
- Finally, always be on the lookout for new sources of learning material. Manning has several books and new things coming out all the time that may help. We're also responsible for a lot of content on Pluralsight (www.pluralsight.com). If nothing else, follow James on X (formerly Twitter) @PSJames. PowerShell (plus toolmaking) is a big, exciting universe with a lot to explore. Set aside a little time each week to catch up with the latest and explore something new. And, of course, keep toolmaking in your organization!

## *Summary*

The concluding chapter of our book, titled "Never the end," served as a motivational call to action as you embark on your journey of toolmaking with PowerShell. It emphasized that reaching the end of the chapter is not the end of the learning process but rather the beginning of an exciting new phase.

We encouraged you to reflect on the significance of toolmaking in PowerShell, highlighting its role in creating reusable units of work that adhere to PowerShell's principles. We stressed the importance of practical application and urged you to start implementing what you've learned immediately to solidify your understanding.

Additionally, we provided practical advice for your next steps, including starting small, embracing the learning process, seeking assistance from forums, sharing knowledge, calculating return on investment, and avoiding reliance on copy-and-paste scripting. We offered insights into future areas of exploration within the PowerShell universe, such as PowerShell Core, open-source projects, community events, and additional learning resources.

Overall, this chapter served as a reminder that the journey of learning and toolmaking with PowerShell is ongoing and encouraged you to continue exploring, growing, and contributing to the vibrant PowerShell community.

# index